The Master Musicians

New Series Edited by Eric Blom

MOZART

UNIFORM WITH THIS VOLUME

Wolfgango amadeo Mozart

The Master Musicians

MOZART

by

ERIC BLOM

Illustrated

London J. M. Dent and Sons Ltd.
New York E. P. Dutton and Co. Inc.

Made in Great Britain
at The Temple Press Letchworth
for
J. M. Dent & Sons Ltd.
Aldine House Bedford St. London
First Published 1935
Reprinted (with corrections) 1937

TRUE genius without heart is a thing of naught—for not great understanding alone, not imagination, nor both together make genius—Love! Love! that is the soul of genius.

GOTTFRIED VON JACQUIN
(in Mozart's autograph album)

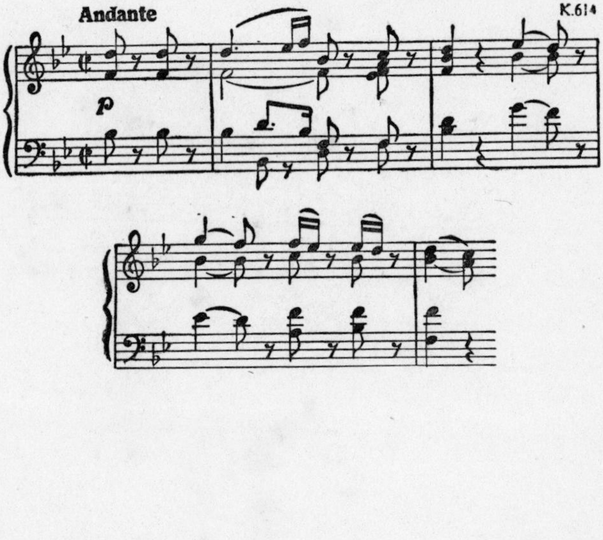

PREFACE

A FOREWORD to a book is usually a veiled apology or an explanation. This is both. While I feel it hard to discover an excuse for writing the story of Mozart's life for the hundredth time, I ought perhaps to explain that a series such as this demands some kind of biographical treatment on a more or less extended scale, and that for various reasons the book originally contributed to the first edition of the 'Master Musicians' was found to be no longer adequate. Whether the present volume is so remains to be judged by others, and it is doubtless too much to hope that in another quarter of a century or so it will not in its own turn have grown out of date.

In order to guard against that as far as possible, however, I have availed myself of the Mozart literature that embodies the latest research, especially Hermann Abert's monumental revised edition of Jahn's biography, which sums up pretty well all that had been previously written by responsible authors. Only one or two minor facts discovered by later authorities required some modification of Abert's narrative, which my own follows in conjunction with the Mozart correspondence in Schiedermair's complete edition. The translations of all extracts from the letters are my own, and I have endeavoured to reproduce, as far as that is possible in another language, their eighteenth-century style, their characteristic phraseology, and, up to a point, even their erratic spelling and punctuation.

If no new biographical facts of importance are to be discovered in the life of Mozart, it is always possible to attempt a personal interpretation of those which have long been known to all the world. Without going out of my way to set up new theories, I have ventured here and there to make a suggestion that may lead the reader to an unsuspected conclusion or to an expression of dissent—it does not very much matter which. In the last six chapters, on Mozart's music, where opinions predominate over facts, I did not deliberately aim at originality of outlook; but such as they are, the views expressed are my own, even where they happen to show a suspicious resemblance to those of other people. If I have managed to say something once or twice that has not been said before, it was not for the mere sake of disagreeing, but by the sheer good fortune that cannot fail to strike even the dullest lover of Mozart's work occasionally.

Perhaps I have done enough apologizing and explaining. In any case, the chief aim of these few words was to make a few acknowledgments, not only to the chief authors consulted, such as those mentioned above, Wyzewa and Saint-Foix, Robert Haas and others enumerated in the Bibliography (Appendix D), but most of all to the outstanding English Mozart scholar, Mr. C. B. Oldman, who was good enough to look over my proofs, and to Dr. Alfred Einstein, who very kindly gave me the benefit of his labours on a new edition of Köchel's catalogue, on which my own list of Mozart's works (Appendix B) is based.

E. B.

October 1935.

PS. (1937)—I am further indebted to Dr. Einstein for a few corrections and one or two new discoveries, which have gone to improve the second edition.

CONTENTS

LIST OF ILLUSTRATIONS

CHAPTER I

AT SALZBURG

NEVER was a stage better set for the appearance of a great artist than Salzburg was in the middle of the eighteenth century for the birth of Wolfgang Amadeus Mozart. A little town that was a gem of tasteful artifice, set incongruously amid a mountainous but not austerely mountainous landscape —could anything have been more apt to a genius who understood nature only through art and whose art was an unconscious glorification of artificiality?

Providence might easily have sent his mother, in a fit of apprehensive home-sickness, to her native village of St. Gilgen to give birth to this child. Providence, as it happened, did not make that mistake, which musical history would have found it hard to forgive, if indeed such a trespass had not wiped out that particular chapter of musical history from the first. For really, it is unthinkable that the child could ever have grown into the Mozart we know had not Salzburg seen him into the world. It is as though the town had here embodied its soul.

The town, not the country round it. There Mozart is not at home at all. Approach the Salzkammergut through Bavaria or through the Tyrol—it is all much the same—you cannot possibly imagine him to have lived anywhere in that neighbourhood. He must have taken the mountains for granted at a distance, and we simply cannot see him going for walks even in the plains round his birthplace, that board-flat country on which round hills are set at a venture like so many sand-castles at the seaside.

But the seaside—that is even farther off anything we connect with Mozart. We know that he crossed the Channel as a boy, but we cannot fancy him reacting to the experience otherwise than by being either asleep or distressingly sick. There is nothing in nature, nothing at all, with which we can fill our thoughts of him. Perhaps he was once amused at the Austrian haystacks, mounted on poles, which, as we approach Salzburg in the morning mist, look like performing bears of preternatural shagginess striking fantastic attitudes. He might well have been: they are the most artificial feature of the landscape.

His town is the most gracious product of human craft. The Salzach tumbles through it in a disarray of little hasty waves as though it felt embarrassingly out of place. And so it is. Nothing else is natural. The path up to the Kapuzinerberg, with its Stations of the Cross, has almost as little business out of doors as a series of chapels in any of Salzburg's churches; through the Mönchsberg on the other side one of the prince-bishops drove a tunnel whose rock-hewn portals are as stagy as those leading to the fire and water caves in *The Magic Flute*; the ornate horse-ponds arrest the exuberances of equine nature rigidly in stone; the fountains animate their jets of water in symmetrical patterns. It is all very precious and vain and lovely. It is human not as mankind out in the country is human, but as that of such a city cannot help being: cultivated in a half-courtly, half-provincial sort of way, fickle and a little false, gay and convivial, pious in various degrees of sincerity, kindly when kindness is easy, gossiping and respectable for fear of gossip. In Mozart's time, one feels, the Salzburgers were quizzically indulgent and philosophically resigned to the dubious goings-on of those who ruled them spiritually and temporally, humbly unquestioning as to their superior rights to indulgence and not jealous enough of worldly advantage to warp their own fundamental soundness and honesty in too many little imitation profligacies. They could humour their betters.

Into this pretty, easy-going, theatrically ecclesiastical but endearing and enchanting place, then, was Wolfgang Amadeus Mozart born on 27th January 1756. His mother recovered with difficulty from the confinement. That was exceptional: as a rule it was her offspring who did not recover. She had seven children in all, but only two survived: Wolfgang and his elder sister, Maria Anna, or Marianne, called Nannerl with an affectionate Salzburg-dialect familiarity.

The boy's Christian names sound important, as though the child this time were meant to live and cut a figure. But those which he has made immortal, one coming from a minor local saint, the other commending the infant to the especial regard of God, were not the only ones bestowed on him, as will be seen from the following certificate issued at the cathedral, where the poor, puny and precarious morsel of humanity was christened in all haste, lest, conceived in sin though sinless himself, he should be consigned to everlasting fire if he happened to die:

> The baptismal register of the cathedral of Salzburg for the year 1756, p. 2, testifies hereby that Joannes Chrysostomus Wolfgangus Theophilus, legitimately begotten son of the honourable Mr. Leopold Mozart, court musician, and of Maria Anna Pertl,[1] his spouse, born on 27th January 1756 at eight o'clock in the evening, was baptized on 28th January 1756 at ten o'clock in the morning in the presence of the honourable Mr. Johann Theophilus Pergmayr, municipal councillor and merchant, as sponsor, by Town Chaplain Leopold Lamprecht according to the Catholic ritual.

Leopold Mozart was a Bavarian, from Augsburg, and can scarcely have felt like a stranger on stepping over the border into a town that was hardly a pistol shot's distance outside his own country, and Austrian only by accident. His name is to be traced back at Augsburg, in various forms such as

[1] The original document has Pertlin, the feminine form of the name used according to a custom of the time that has led to much confusion among later biographers. The mother's name was not Pertlin any more than it was Mozartin, though it sometimes appears thus in the signature of her letters.

Mozart, Mozert, Motzart, Motzhardt and Motard, to the middle of the seventeenth century. Indeed there were Mozarts in the town since 1551, but the first to be proved an ancestor of Wolfgang Amadeus is one David Mozart (1620–85), who came from the village of Pfersee close by and acquired citizen's rights. He was a master mason, and so were his three sons. The youngest of these, Franz (1649–94), was destined to beget the composer's grandfather, Johann Georg (1679–1736), who became a bookbinder. He had two daughters and six sons, the eldest surviving of the latter, Johann Georg Leopold, born 14th November 1719, being the first of the family to take to music.

But the music for which we can never cease to thank Leopold Mozart is that which we owe to him as father and teacher of Wolfgang. He was not himself a negligible composer, though, and that as a theorist he left the world a treatise on violin playing is not yet forgotten, for there have been violinists, within living memory, who owed their earliest training to this book. His father's ambition was that he should enter the priesthood, and to this end he was sent as a chorister to the monasteries, first of the Holy Cross and afterwards of St. Ulrich. But here music laid hold of him: he learnt all about church music, as much as he could about the rest, and found opportunities to study the organ. In 1737 he entered the university of Salzburg for two years. According to the acts he studied logic, but in all probability law as well. He passed an examination with distinction in 1738, but no mention of his name occurs in the university's rolls the following year. He seems by that time to have decided to make music his career, and in 1740 he entered the service of the president of the cathedral chapter, Count Johann Baptist of Thurn and Taxis, as valet and musician. In spite of the subordinate position which was at that time regarded as his inevitable lot by one who practised music by the good grace of some patron or another, Leopold Mozart appears to have been on excellent terms with his employer, to whom he very soon dedicated a set of six church and chamber sonatas for two violins and bass, engraved by himself. During the next three years he wrote two Passion cantatas and a Latin comedy for the university.

In 1743, at the age of twenty-four, Leopold was offered the post of fourth violinist in the band of the archbishop, Count Sigismund von Schrattenbach. The archbishops of Salzburg did not hold ecclesiastical sway alone; they also had a very powerful secular influence as counts palatine.[1] These dignitaries, who needless to say were invariably scions of noble and wealthy houses, enjoyed their privileges much like other princes of the period, taking advantage of their religious duties to impress morality on the rest of the world with such assiduity that they deemed it to be superfluous to themselves. They were all dissolute more or less, perhaps as much by tradition as by inclination, for the populace had whispered amusedly about the doings at court for so long and so submissively that it would doubtless have been almost shocked if an overlord who was not only pious, but acted upon the principles of piety, had ruled over them for a change. Meanwhile things were accepted as they were, and as they had always been. The Archbishop Wolf Dietrich had built the charming Mirabell Palace for his mistress Salome Alt; at the *Residenz* there was high dining and scarcely less high fasting; at Hellbrunn, three or four miles off, ever since the time of Marcus Sitticus, there had been less ingenuous sports than those afforded by the childishly amusing waterworks in the classical park and the hunting-box castle.

Schrattenbach maintained a band of thirty-three instrumentalists, not counting the field and court trumpeters or the town musicians who, among other duties, had to play from the church towers on certain feast days. Any of these extra musicians might at times be added to the regular orchestra. There was, moreover, a body of some thirty adult singers, both soloists and choristers, as well as one of fifteen choirboys.

[1] Their position, which offered them the best of both worlds, resembled that of the bishops of Durham in England.

Leopold taught the latter the violin, and towards the end of his life the clavier as well.

On 21st November 1747 he married Anna Maria[1] Pertl.[2] She was a little more than a year younger than her husband and a good-looking girl; in fact the Mozarts were at that time called the handsomest couple in the town. In other ways, if they proved satisfactorily matched, it was by contrast rather than affinity of character. Leopold was grave, severe, and not a little sour at times, while his wife had the local traits of gaiety not unmixed, perhaps, with some emotional shallowness, a good heart, excellent qualities as a housekeeper and that kind of shrewd, decent sense which is not spoilt by a relish for coarse talk and indelicate jests. Neither sensitive nor imaginative, she made a capital mother of two children for whom a woman of more vibrant sensibility might only too readily have made the usual excuses for the artistic temperament. This, too, would have irritated Leopold, who was proud of his children but not inclined to stand any nonsense from them. When all is said, the family could hardly have been happier; it certainly could not have been much better assorted or capable of much greater mutual attachment.

They lived in the fine, solid house which is still there for all the world to see, almost unchanged. The wide, handsome front door now faces a mere street that abuts on the Getreidegasse; but in those days the Mozarts looked out upon a square, the Löchelplatz, with one of those fountains that give Salzburg the look and the purling, cooling sounds of an Italian town. No doubt they had to fetch their water there in copper pails of an evening—the medieval scene of Goethe's Gretchen and Lisbeth might have been enacted there in the midst of this rococo town; a small boy might have watched it from the window, feeling without understanding, little dreaming of

[1] The names are more often reversed, as in Wolfgang's birth certificate, but the present order is here adopted to distinguish Mozart's mother from his sister.

[2] Or Bertl.

the poet who would one day say, when it was too late, that Mozart was the composer who could have matched his *Faust* with music. Perhaps Goethe was wrong, as he could be about music if about nothing else. Yet who knows? Such scenes of heartbreak—think of Donna Elvira—were well within Mozart's reach.

The flat-fronted house, with no visible roof, looks Italianate from the outside, but has a Germanic homeliness within. How apt a setting for a master whose manner is Italian, whose soul German. A curious odour strikes the visitor as he enters the whitewashed and roughly paved entrance hall, a smell that makes one think of drains and cats and dinners all in one, without being exactly redolent of any of these things. Somehow one cannot imagine eighteenth-century people who had no use or no time for country walks to have been healthy there. The Mozarts, indeed, were inclined to be frail, and it is not difficult to imagine that this house must have had a store of illnesses ready when Leopold brought his bride to it in 1747—for they lived there from the beginning of their wedded life. No wonder that so many babies died and that in 1780 Nannerl was with difficulty saved from falling into pulmonary tuberculosis. However, that was the usual way of things in those days. Nature was left to her own drastic and wasteful methods. The lower Hagenauer house on the Löchelplatz,[1] as it was called after its landlord, was of course not out-of-the-way unhealthy. Indeed, as middle-class houses went, it was well set up.

On ascending the bare stone stairs to the third floor, we realize that the Mozarts' lodging itself was cosy in a severe German way. It is not self-contained: the rooms open straight on to the stone-flagged landing, and on carrying dinner into the living-room in front the people above stairs might have been met at any time, eager, no doubt, to report in this small nest of tittle-tattle what the Mozartin had been cooking on

[1] Now No. 9 Getreidegasse.

a laboriously kindled fire in her neat kitchen, with its marble slabs, which overlooked the courtyard at the back. So did the chamber behind the best room, in which the children were born. From there, through a narrow arch between two deep walls, may be seen a strip of the court with its arcaded galleries leading to the next building, over which peeps one of the elegant twin towers of the Collegiate Church in the market square behind. There are two more rooms: one in front, smaller than the living-room, and another giving on to the courtyard, accessible only through the middle bedchamber.[1] Plain as this lodging is, it shows the love of artistic ornamentation so characteristic of Salzburg in its fine moulded ceilings and wrought-iron locks and hinges on the doors.

It was here, then, that Leopold began to teach his children music as soon as they could walk and talk, indeed sooner, if as a mere audience they may be regarded as pupils. Nannerl, who was four and a half years older than Wolfgang,[2] was no less quick to learn than her brother, for all that she did not possess his creative gift. She played the clavier with striking virtuosity at the age of eleven. Later she showed great accomplishment in improvisation and in playing from figured bass. The lessons given her by her father naturally impressed Wolfgang from his earliest infancy, and at the age of three he began to pick out on the clavier combinations of notes which pleased him especially—thirds, we are told, which with their inversions, sixths, are his harmonic staple and, it is true, that of the time altogether. In his fourth year he was able to learn small pieces from memory and to play them faultlessly; in his fifth he began to devise little minuets and other pieces of his own

[1] The house was acquired by the International Foundation of the Mozarteum in 1917 and the third floor turned into a museum containing many interesting Mozartian relics. More recently the second floor was added with an exhibition of stage models showing old and modern settings of operas by Mozart.

[2] Maria Anna (Marianne) Walburga Ignatia Mozart was born on 30th July 1751.

ROOM IN WHICH MOZART WAS BORN

'Oragna figata fà,
Marina gamina fà,'

sang the little boy, kissed the tip of his father's nose, promised to keep him in a glass case when he was old, and settled down to sleep in perfect contentment.

Contentment with what, one wonders. One hears of piteously little in this young life that could have given pleasure to the average small boy. His father must have been out much, performing his duties at the frivolous ecclesiastical court, and then perchance his young son may have been taken to snatch a little sunshine, of which there cannot have been abundance in the Löchelplatz. Or he may not. We can only guess; we do not know. Whatever change he had, it can hardly have been anything ordinary children would have enjoyed. But then, Wolfgang Amadeus Mozart was no ordinary child.

CHAPTER II

THE WONDERCHILD

WHAT Bach did for his second wife, Anna Magdalena, Leopold Mozart did for his children. He put together manuscript music-books from which he taught them to play the clavier. Hermann Abert[1] gives an exhaustive description of the book compiled for Wolfgang, which until a few years ago had remained unknown in private possession. It contains no less than 135 pieces, divided into twenty-five suites arranged according to keys. Unfortunately Leopold gave particulars of composers in only nineteen instances, but they are nevertheless of immense interest, and Abert succeeded in identifying a few more of the earliest compositions which we now know must have influenced Mozart. Among the composers are Telemann, Hasse and Carl Philipp Emanuel Bach. Abert points out the interesting fact that this collection shows a greater acquaintance of the youthful Mozart with the North German school than had hitherto been suspected in so Italianate a master. It should be borne in mind, however, that Leopold's choice was not necessarily dictated by a preference of the North Germans to the Italians, but by the need to confine himself to composers who wrote for the clavier, which the Italians on the whole neglected. In any case Germanic influences, generally and quite naturally exaggerated by German writers on Mozart, are conspicuous in his work by their strikingly exceptional appearances rather than by a steadily permeating presence.

At the age of six Wolfgang had learnt so much that there was no holding Leopold's pride in any longer. After all, the

[1] In his revised edition of Jahn's biography, vol. i, pp. 32 ff.

younger the gifted child, the greater the miracle: and so his incredible gifts had to be shown the world as soon as might be. Besides, Nannerl was getting on for eleven: it was quite time she too was exhibited before her own precocity began to look too normal. Thus in January 1762 the children were dragged off to Munich. Leopold for the first time obtained leave from the archbishop, as he was to do with such frequency during the next few years that this may well be the reason why, good musician and conscientious servant though he was, he never advanced to the post of musical director at the *Residenz*. In this very year it passed from Johann Ernst Eberlin to Joseph Franz Lolli, Leopold being overlooked and obtaining merely a vice musical directorship the following year. He knew, no doubt, that more was not to be expected if he absented himself too frequently, knew too that he was making a sacrifice for Wolfgang—by no means the only one.

Of the visit to the Bavarian capital we only know that it lasted three weeks and that the children played to the Elector Maximilian Joseph. He must have been duly astonished. But Munich never took more than passing notice of Mozart all his life. Leopold came back to Salzburg with his two bewildered little freaks, who had not seen a court before, for they do not appear ever to have been taken to the archbishop at so early a stage. Perhaps he did not believe in local miracles.

For a while the Mozarts lay low, crouching to leap the better next time. For by September Leopold was ready to tackle Vienna and the empress. He left with the two young victims of their own genius on 18th September, and this time they made an impression such as he had scarcely dared to hope for. The Bishop of Passau first delayed them for five days, anxious to hear Wolfgang and kind enough to bestow a ducat on him. Then, accompanied by Canon Count Herberstein, they proceeded to Linz, where Count Schlick induced them to give a concert under his patronage. Next, at the monastery of Ips, Wolfgang lured the monks from their dinner by his organ playing, and on their arrival in Vienna he saved his father the toll by making friends, in his confiding, childish way, with the customs official.

The Austrian capital, not yet at the height of musical glory which was to reach its climax in the next century, nevertheless vied with Paris and London for the honour of being the world's chief musical centre. No Italian city was quite so alive even with Italian musical culture, of which Vienna was the central seat. No Italian operas achieved fame without sooner or later coming to Vienna, and many of them were actually produced there. Naturally enough there was also a German element. Gassmann had just been invited to set up as a composer of ballets, Wagenseil produced serious instrumental music, and Reutter, as chapel master at St. Stephen's Cathedral, turned out his famous showy masses. Reutter's former pupil, Haydn, now aged thirty, was no longer anything but a visitor to the capital, and his services were confined to the house of the Esterházy for a long time to come. Still, he existed and was making his great name. Gluck was still writing French comic operas for the court, for performance at Schönbrunn or at Laxenburg.

That court was musical. Maria Theresa sang well and had appeared in an opera by Fux at the age of seven. Francis I was fond of music too, and the archduchesses, including Marie Antoinette, sang in that very year of the Mozarts' visit in a private performance of a setting of Metastasio's *Il trionfo di Clelia*.[1] The empress heard of the remarkable children, probably from Count Herberstein or Count Schlick, or possibly from young Count Palffy, who had been astonished by them during the visit to Linz. The nobility also seem to have been prepared for the wonders to come. At all events Leopold received a command to reveal them at Schönbrunn on 13th October. They stayed at the splendid yet domesticated palace for three hours in the afternoon. The emperor called Wolfgang a little conjurer and made him play various tricks on the keyboard; Marie Antoinette, who was only two months

[1] Probably Hasse's setting, produced at Dresden that year.

older than Wolfgang, helped him up, so the story goes, when he slipped on the polished floor, and received an offer of marriage in return; the empress, into whose lap he jumped, kissed him. He asked to see Wagenseil, one of whose concertos he played and whom he allowed to turn over the pages. Nannerl was less of a success only in so far as she was less of a sensation. Leopold received a honorarium and the children various presents, including the court dresses, pink and silver for the girl, lilac and gold for the boy, in which they were afterwards painted.[1]

Now the Viennese aristocracy began to take notice. The family were called for to go here, there and everywhere by carriage. They were well rewarded for showing off their tricks. The ladies were enchanted with the self-possessed little artist and innocent little boy. But suddenly he went down with scarlet fever, and though the attentions did not cease, they became markedly less personal. An invitation to some nobles at Pressburg came as a welcome change after Wolfgang's recovery, and on 11th December a journey in terrible weather and over atrocious roads was made to the Hungarian border. Back in Vienna, the children played at a feast given by Countess Kinsky in honour of Field-Marshal Daun. Early in January they returned home. Their mother's ears must have ached from all the excited talk poured into them.

Before long it was her heart that was made to ache again. She was rooted to her home, but Leopold had tasted success and wanted more. Level-headed as he was, and careful about his children's welfare, he could not resist trying a grand tour. After a short spell at home, during which Wolfgang perfected himself on the violin, which he was found one day to be able to play without any tuition whatever, the four of them were off on 9th June 1763.

At Wasserburg, on the way to Munich, the diligence broke down, and they had to wait a day; but as Wolfgang for the

[1] The portraits, by an unknown and indifferent artist, are in the Mozart house.

MOZART AT THE AGE OF SIX, IN THE GALA DRESS
GIVEN HIM BY MARIA THERESA

Portrait by an unknown Salzburg Painter

first time came across a pedal organ there, time was not wasted. Leopold showed him the instrument, and of course he could play at once, standing on the pedals which he could not reach when seated on the bench. The Elector of Bavaria was at Nymphenburg, where Wolfgang played both the clavier and the violin, producing a concerto on the latter and improvising the cadenzas.

At Augsburg, Leopold's native town, they stayed a fortnight. There were relatives to be visited, though they put up at the inn of the 'Three Moors,' and three concerts were given. On 6th July they departed for Ludwigsburg, the luxurious country residence of Duke Carl Eugen of Württemberg, who, however, did not consent to hear them. Leopold, always ready to suspect jealousy and intrigue, especially on the part of Italian musicians, who indeed were not as a tribe above using questionable means to maintain their supremacy in foreign countries, had no doubt that Niccolò Jommelli, the duke's musical director, was responsible for the rebuff. That Jommelli had himself listened to Wolfgang with astonishment and interest carried no weight with Leopold, who thought that the Italian master was merely dissembling. There is no reason, however, to suspect Jommelli, who was a serious composer of noble music and an honourable man, not to mention that he was perfectly secure in his fame, happily unaware that he would be unfairly forgotten by later generations. He had no reason for wishing to stand in the way of a small boy whose genius, spirit and fire he, like a true Italian, thought to be almost incredible in a child of Germanic race. It is quite possible that the duke maintained a musical establishment merely because it was expected of him, but that he was not interested in itinerant musicians, whether recommended by his *Capellmeister* or not. He may also have been busy with more important or agreeable matters, as such people often were at their summer residences.

Other triumphs soon compensated for this one failure. The Elector Palatine Carl Theodor, who spent his summer at the palace of Schwetzingen, received the family graciously and arranged a concert for them that lasted four hours. The orchestra was that of Mannheim, 'without contradiction the best in Germany,' says Leopold in a letter to his landlord Hagenauer, a band in connection with which the historically important school of early German symphonists had arisen, and which Mozart was to meet again later, to make his first acquaintance with the clarinet as an orchestral instrument in its midst. Just as in the Stuttgart band at Ludwigsburg the Mozarts had met the famous violinist Nardini, a pupil of Tartini's, so here they first came across the flute player J. B. Wendling, who was to become a friend later on.

Passing through Heidelberg, Wolfgang played the organ at the church of the Holy Ghost and amazed the hearers to such an extent that the dean had a description of the event inscribed on the instrument. At Mainz the elector was ill and could not hear them, but they gave two concerts at the 'King of Rome' and made two hundred florins. At Frankfort a concert held on 18th August was so successful that three more were given. Among the audience was Goethe, aged fourteen. The poet never forgot the impression made on him by 'the little man with wig and sword,' as he told Eckermann, his Boswell, a great many years later. Marianne and Wolfgang were now celebrities, and no mistake. They had to behave accordingly; Leopold saw to that. He loved music, but he loved honour more, and honour was not to be had in such large quantities as his rapidly growing appetite for fame demanded except by satisfying not merely the good taste of the few, but the curiosity and love of sensation of the many. The announcement of the last Frankfort concert, to be given on 30th August, shows what was expected of that little freak Wolfgang. He would not only play a concerto on the violin and accompany symphonies on the clavier, but cover up the keyboard with a cloth and play as well as if he saw the keys. Moreover, he would tell the intervals of all notes played singly or in chords on the clavier or any imaginable instrument, such as bells, glasses, clocks, etc. And finally he would play, on the organ as well as on the clavier, for as long as the public would care to listen, and extemporize in all keys, even the most difficult, that people would choose to name.

On they went, to Coblenz, Bonn, Cologne, Aix-la-Chapelle; but they played only at the first and the last. At Aix it was before Princess Amalia of Prussia, the sister of Frederick the Great, who was taking the waters. She was a genuine music lover, and, falling in love with little Wolfgang, tried to persuade his father to visit Berlin; but the astute Leopold saw no profit in such a modification of his plans. As he wrote to Hagenauer:

She has no money, and her whole equipage and retinue as much resemble the suite of a doctor as one drop of water does another. If the kisses she gave to my children, and Master Wolfgang in particular, were as many new-coined *louis d'or*, we should be fortunate enough; howbeit, neither mine host nor the postmaster are to be contented with kisses.

Thus they continued to Brussels. Leopold wrote on 17th October showing some interest in the Flemish and Dutch painters whose pictures he had seen, and speaking of the fairly assiduous religious observances he had noticed, which showed, to his mind, that they were in Maria Theresa's territory. That part of the Netherlands, indeed, was under Austrian rule, Prince Charles of Lorraine, brother of the Emperor Francis I, being governor-general. He was in no great hurry to hear the Mozart children. Leopold complained on 4th November:

We have now been nearly three weeks in Brussels . . . and nothing has happened. Indeed, it looks as though all were in vain, for his highness the prince does nothing but hunt, gobble and swill, and we may in the end discover that he has no money. . . . I own, we have received sundry valuable presents here, but do not wish to convert them into cash. . . . What with snuff-boxes and leather cases and such-like gewgaws, we shall soon be able to open a stall.

At last they succeeded in giving a grand concert, which the prince condescended to suspend his more urgent pleasures to attend, and on 15th November they left for Paris, where they arrived on the 18th. The Bavarian ambassador von Eyck, whose wife was a daughter of the Salzburg chamberlain Count Arco, invited them to stay at the Hôtel Beauvais in the Rue Saint-Antoine.[1]

The Mozarts, even the fairly worldly Leopold, must have opened their eyes wide when first they set them on the French capital, which was then less regularly beautiful than it is to-day, but no doubt far more fascinating, varied and picturesque. Indeed the district of the Marais in which they stayed, much less changed than any other part of Paris, still shows the kind of place the city as a whole must have been before the Revolution and before the artificial face-lifting which its beauty has been undergoing ever since that upheaval.

The house to which they were invited had formerly belonged to Madame de Beauvais, lady-in-waiting to Anne of Austria, who, with Henrietta Maria of England, Turenne and Mazarin, had watched the entry into Paris of her son, Louis XIV, and the Infanta Maria Theresa, on 26th August 1660, from the balcony. Narrow and irregular streets, ill-paved and ill-lighted, but with houses that matched stateliness with comfort, the lovely backwater of the Place des Vosges close by, and drawn straight through it all the Rue Saint-Antoine with its marketing and merchandise, its beggars and loafers, with cartloads streaming endlessly towards the Bastille and away from it—any one who knows the district may still imagine it all very nearly as the Mozarts saw it.

They had various letters of recommendation from and to nobles and diplomats, but found that the cold shoulder was turned on them everywhere. Only Friedrich Melchior Grimm, who had been settled in Paris for fifteen years, become almost wholly frenchified, contributed to the *Encyclopédie* of Diderot and d'Alembert, and learnt the art of advancement by wire-

[1] To-day the house is 68 Rue François-Miron.

pulling and log-rolling to perfection, was found willing enough to help his fellow-countryman. (He was born at Ratisbon.) Perhaps he felt that by being the first to introduce the wonderchildren to a people that has ever been quick to pounce on a new interest and quick to relinquish it for one newer still, he would earn some temporary credit. At least he seems to have been clever enough to see that there was matter for credit. Be that as it may, the Mozarts were asked to appear at court.

On Christmas Eve they were at Versailles, invited to stay a fortnight. The arrangements for their appearance before the royal family, elaborately made by the courtiers charged with the *menus plaisirs,* who had to justify their decorative existence, went forward, as Leopold said, 'even more than those at other courts, by the snail's post.' But by degrees things happened—exciting things for the good provincials. They paid a visit to the quarters of Madame de Pompadour, whom Leopold describes as if she were the chief sight of France; the children were smiled upon and hugged by the king's three musical daughters, Madame Adélaïde, Madame Henriette and Madame Victoire, pleasant, friendly creatures who played the violin, the *viola da gamba* and the clavier; Wolfgang was made to stand on a chair to be examined by the Pompadour, who would not let him kiss her, whereupon, as his sister remembered later—and one hopes correctly—he audibly made unfavourable comparisons with his own empress, who did allow herself to be kissed; then, on New Year's Day, the four of them were graciously allowed to attend the royal dinner, not, of course, to eat at the table, but at any rate to stand behind the chairs of the king and queen. The latter, Marie Leczinska, spoke in German to Wolfgang and passed him various dainty morsels from the table, as to a lapdog. They felt honoured, it appears, to stand about with the lackeys. At any rate they were near the royal fire and had not to shiver with the fur-clad court ladies farther down the table in the icy gallery of that sumptuous and comfortless palace, where the dishes had to be chafed on their endless journey up from the kitchens and where it was no unknown occurrence for the wine to freeze on the board.

The nobility now began to take notice of the little royal favourites. They were invited to play at various aristocratic houses, including that of Prince Conti, where, as Ollivier's picture in the Louvre shows, Wolfgang played to a brilliant assembly. The British and Russian ambassadors, the Duke of Bedford and Prince Galitsin, took a great fancy to them, and Madame de Clermont, who lived in the Hôtel Beauvais, procured them an invitation to appear twice at the house of a M. Félix in the Rue Saint-Honoré, where there was a small private theatre. It was only through powerful influences that permission was to be had to give these two concerts, on 10th March and 9th April 1764, all rights of performance being vested by patent in the Opéra, the Théâtre Italien and the *Concert spirituel.* Marianne performed the most difficult keyboard music that could be found. Wolfgang did everything: played the clavier, the violin, the organ, accompanied at sight, transposing, amplifying thorough-bass and even inventing new accompaniments at various repetitions of the same air or piece without any indication of the bass. What is more, he improvised astonishingly, according to Grimm and Suard, from whom one gathers the usual impression of all the great masters in their youth—that they must have played far more mature music extempore than they ever wrote down at the same period.

The unanimity of such reports, which always compare more than favourably with one's own criticism of such contemporary music by their heroes as may have been preserved in manuscript or print, is so persistent that one feels bound to seek for an explanation of these wonders of improvisation other than the witness's enthusiasm, exaggerated though that is sure to be by reminiscent sentiment and pride. It is very probable, all things considered, that when the performer was surrounded by an admiring crowd, a more than normal heat of inspiration may have infused itself into his invention, a heat that could not fail to cool down considerably in the merely mechanical and delaying act of committing the notions to paper.

Wolfgang did write down some music during these Paris days, and Leopold had four Sonatas for clavier with violin accompaniment (K. 6–9) engraved, the first two being dedicated to one of the kindly princesses, Madame Victoire, the other pair to the Comtesse de Tessé. Grimm undertook the writing of the dedications, but the countess, who was lady-in-waiting to the dauphine, surprisingly declined the first version of this document as being too flattering. It must have been fulsome indeed if a lady of the French court could not bear it, and it was replaced, much to Leopold's regret, by a more moderately polite epistle.

Wolfgang underwent various influences in Paris, especially that of two German musicians who had settled in the French capital as clavier players and composers: Johann Schobert, a Silesian, who was in the service of Prince Conti, and Johann Gottfried Eckhardt, born, like Leopold, at Augsburg. Schobert seems to have behaved far from well: he was ambitious and jealous. But there is no doubt that the susceptible young genius came under the sway of his music, an influence far more powerful than that of the French operas, some of which he may have heard at the theatres and separate pieces from which he must have come across all over Paris, from the street-corner to the drawing-room. Italian opera held the field, for the *guerre des bouffons* of a decade or so ago had been decided in its favour. Such composers as Galuppi, Jommelli, Pergolesi, Piccinni, Sarti and Traetta were fashionable. French comic opera, too, with less verve and spirit, but more grace and gentleness, was popular, and the Mozarts might well have heard pieces by Monsigny and Philidor, or by the Franco-Italian Duni. What is more immediately significant is that Wolfgang may have been present at a performance of the ballad opera, *Les Amours de Bastien et Bastienne,* which the charming and virtuous actress, Madame Favart, had put together for herself from Rousseau's little opera, *Le Devin du Village,* which might also have been revived during their stay in Paris, either this time or on their return in 1766. It is pleasant to think that the boy may have known the prototypes of a little opera of his own that musically made an immense improvement on both.

CHAPTER III

ENGLAND AND HOLLAND

LEOPOLD had not been sure about venturing so far as England when the family left Salzburg; but in Paris every one urged him to try London. They took coach to Calais on 10th April 1764, stayed there more expensively than Leopold liked, dined with the Procureur du Roy et de l'Admirauté, and arrived in London, after an unpleasant crossing in a specially hired boat—the packet boat being full—on 22nd April. The address was given to Hagenauer as follows in Leopold's letter of 25th April:

à Monsieur
Monsieur Mozart at Mr. Couzin
Hare cutter in cecil court
St Martinslane
att
London.

As early as the 27th they obtained permission to present themselves at court. George III and Queen Charlotte both had a great liking for music, and the Mozarts' reception at St. James's was so friendly and unceremonious that it warmed their hearts. Leopold is full of enthusiasm, for all that their reward was 'only twenty-four guineas,' which were handed them immediately on their departure. A few days later they met the royal carriage in St. James's Park, and although they 'all wore different clothes,' they received the most affable greeting from the king and queen. On 19th May they were invited again, to play to a small gathering from six until ten in the evening. The king made Wolfgang play pieces by Handel, Wagenseil and others at sight, the boy went from the clavier to the organ, accompanied the queen in an aria, then played with a flautist, and finally improvised a new melody and harmony on the bass of a Handel air.

Handel had been dead five years, but he dominated music in London still. Half a dozen at least of his oratorios were to be heard during the Mozarts' stay in London, and everywhere Wolfgang met with his music, which made impressions on him that he never forgot. Not that a Handelian influence became at all conspicuous in his music at any time, except in fleeting glimpses, but it would have been strange if the solidity of Handel's noble workmanship had not made its mark on his receptive young mind. He must have affectionately recalled his early acquaintance with the musical circle of Handel's declining years later on, when Baron van Swieten engaged him to provide additional accompaniments to four of the master's oratorios.

There were more immediate influences at work on him in London. Here again, as in Paris, two German musicians taught him most. The less important of the two was Carl Friedrich Abel, a former pupil of Bach's in Leipzig, a famous *viola da gamba* player and a composer of some reputation. Then there was Bach's own youngest son, Johann Christian, aged twenty-nine, who had lived in Milan and transferred himself to England in 1762, to remain in London until his death. He had turned Roman catholic in Italy and composed a good deal of church music; but he brought several Italian operas to London with him; in fact he was wholly italianized, and finding no musical outlet for his faith in a protestant country he became more and more secularized as a composer. With his great father he had nothing in common as an artist. His music does not sound like Bach; it sounds much more like Mozart. The truth is that he influenced Mozart to a great extent.

Apart from J. C. Bach and Abel, not to mention Handel again, Wolfgang must have heard some English music, by Arne and Boyce, for example, as well as Italian operas and pasticcios at the King's Theatre in the Haymarket, if his strict and solicitous father did not consider it a place unfit for a little boy of eight to visit. However that may be, they made the acquaintance of the two famous male sopranos Manzuoli and Tenducci, and the former, from pure friendship and astonishment at Wolfgang's gifts, undertook to teach him singing. The boy had a poor little voice, but picked up that branch of his art, like every other, as though he had always known all about it.

The season was not favourable to a public concert. The nobility and gentry were out of town. Still, Leopold was clever enough to realize that many of them would pour into London for the king's birthday on 4th June. He accordingly arranged a performance on the 5th. It was a success. The grandees turned up in masses, and Leopold had 'the shock of taking a hundred guineas in the space of three hours.' There were counter-shocks, it is to be feared, for he found that the expenses were heavy: five guineas for the hall, without lights or music stands, half a guinea for each clavier (the children played a double concerto), five or six guineas for each of the singers, three for the leader—and then the orchestra, at half a guinea a head. However, he found in the end that most of the musicians would take nothing. Who would charge children a fee for the privilege of playing with them? And such children!

Having made a profit, Leopold was not averse to doing a little advertising. He let Wolfgang play at a charity concert at Ranelagh for the benefit of the new maternity hospital on 29th June, 'a way to earn the love of this very special nation.' A planned visit to Tunbridge Wells, where many fashionable people were taking the waters, fell through, but a private performance at Lord Thanet's was doubtless profitable. From this Leopold returned with an inflammation of the throat that worried him terribly. Poor little chicks, what would they do if anything happened to him in a strange country? Friends were kind, the mother very capable—but still . . . He writes apprehensively to his landlord friend, preparing him for the worst. His handwriting alone will show good Hagenauer how ill he is; clysters, purges, blood-letting have been tried; he cannot eat, scarcely think. A day or two later he is well enough to be taken into the country—the idyllic riverside village of Chelsea. On 9th August it still depends on the will of God whether he will recover or not. But on 13th September he is sufficiently restored to endeavour to convert the son of a Dutch Jew, who has abandoned his faith and not yet embraced a new one, to catholicism.

During their father's illness the children were not allowed to touch an instrument for some time. Wolfgang therefore amused himself by writing two Symphonies (K. 16 and 19[1]), urging his sister to remind him now and again to give plenty of interesting work to the horns for the exceptionally good London players. Here, then, is Mozart at the age of eight, a fully fledged composer. An instrumental composer, too—this genius of whom it has so often been said that all his music sings, and whose vocal writing would entice musically minded people with the voices of rooks, crows and ravens to sing mellifluously. He was a symphonist before he became a conjurer with song. It is possible that his first vocal work[2] was not produced until the end of the visit to England, when, in July 1765, he presented the so-called madrigal, 'God is our refuge' (K. 20), to the British Museum. It would be curious indeed if this Austrian boy of German descent with an Italian veneer and some quickly acquired French manners had first sung to us in English. In any case, he began his career in the very way in which he was to gain immortality. For Mozart among all great musicians is the most universal, the least locally rooted.

[1] But not, as Jahn-Abert have it, K. 17, which is spurious. So too is K. 18, which is included in the complete Mozart edition, but is now known to be by Abel.

[2] The tenor aria, 'Va dal furor portata' (K. 21), may have come first, but Köchel gave this work a later number.

Towards the end of September 1764 Leopold was well again, and the family returned to town. They played at court once more on 25th October, the fourth anniversary of the accession of George III. There is a great deal for royalty to do on such occasions; that they had time to think of making the Mozarts take part in the celebrations shows in what esteem the Salzburg family—and music—were held by them. It was high time something were done in return. Leopold therefore had six Sonatas for clavier with violin or flute[1] (K. 10–15) engraved at his own expense and dedicated to the queen, who returned fifty guineas for the compliment. The dedication is dated 18th January 1765, and on 20th March the Sonatas were on sale.

On 21st February the Mozarts gave another concert on their own account, with the usual artistic success, but with small profit. The king was ill, politics were inauspicious and other entertainments interfered. The notorious Mrs. Cornelys was just beginning her subscription concerts under the direction of Abel and J. C. Bach, Samuel Arnold brought out his first opera, *The Maid of the Mill,* Dibdin appeared in it, Bach produced his *Adriano in Siria* and Burney brought out his adaptation of Rousseau's *Devin du Village* under the title of *The Cunning Man.* Several times the Mozarts' reappearance was announced, but it did not take place until 13th May, when reduced prices combined with a hint that the wonder-children were about to leave England produced a revival of interest. A novelty at this concert was Wolfgang's playing on Shudi's new harpsichord with two manuals and a set of

[1] Those who still persist in thinking of the piano part in a sonata as an accompaniment will receive a wholesome shock on discovering that in the eighteenth century the opposite if equally erroneous view prevailed: the clavier was generally regarded as the principal instrument, and it played the outstanding part. Alternative flute parts were the rule in London, where the German flute was much cultivated. Arrangements for it of the popular music of the day flooded the market.

pedals. But fickle London had had its sensation, and its busy life held other things. It was time to make an end of this long and on the whole prosperous visit. Before the family's departure, however, Leopold undertook to let his son be privately examined by any one who chose to do so, first at the lodgings in Frith (then Thrift) Street, Soho, to which they had moved from St. Martin's Lane, then at one of the rather obscure inns in the neighbourhood. But a severer and at the same time more flattering test yet awaited the boy. The Hon. Daines Barrington subjected him to a thorough scientific examination, a detailed report of which is preserved in the *Philosophical Transactions* for the year 1770 [1] and which not only confirms all the rumours of Wolfgang's incredible capabilities, but makes them appear the more marvellous because the report is free from exaggerations.

In actual composition, however, as Abert shows,[2] Wolfgang still had very much to learn. A manuscript book [3] of the time contains forty-three small pieces which are far from mature and sometimes positively faulty. There can thus be no doubt that the sonatas and symphonies of this period were extensively revised by Leopold, and some possibly by J. C. Bach. It does not, surely, detract from the miracle of the genius of a child approaching his ninth birthday to admit that he must have been helped in committing his ideas tidily to paper. What matters is that he did have ideas, and as to his skill, Barrington's testimony, if no other, is beyond suspicion. To reconcile the wonders he performed at the keyboard with the comparative helplessness of the work which we know him to have written down unaided we need only remember once again that there is a great difference between the immediately if transitorily creative process of improvisation and the slowed-

[1] Vol. xl. Also in Barrington's *Miscellanies on Various Subjects* (London, 1781).

[2] Jahn-Abert, i. 66.

[3] Published in 1908 by Breitkopf & Härtel, edited by Dr. G. Schünemann.

down and mechanical act of setting down such inspirations on paper; and we need not regard the interference of Leopold, or J. C. Bach, or anyone else, in the act of composing with the aid of the pen as anything more than the effort of a finished technician to give shape to what a child of genius was plainly striving after but could not force his hand to fix in black and white.

London, huge but friendly, dirty and haphazard, yet gay and sympathetic, was left at last on 24th July. Nannerl's diary shows, in the spidery writing of a child and the spelling of a little foreigner doing her best to wrestle with an erratic language, some of the places they saw in London:

> London bridge, St. Paul kirch, Soudwark, Monument, foundling hospital, enchange, Lincolnsin fiels garten Tempel bar, Soumerset hauss.[1]

Then, 'zu Canterbury, die haupt kirch': they spent a day there and saw the cathedral, evidently. Thence they went to the country seat of Sir Horace Mann, 'very beautiful,' according to Nannerl, where they saw a horse-race and remained as guests until the end of the month.

Leopold had meant to return home by way of Milan and Venice. A grand tour without Italy, forsooth, was unthinkable. But it was not to be. The Dutch ambassador had let him know that the Princess Caroline of Nassau-Weilburg was anxious to hear the children at The Hague. The invitation was not to be refused—'you cannot deny a pregnant woman anything,' Leopold said—much as the archbishop was by that time fretting to have his servant back and sending out impatient summonses. They left Dover for Calais on 1st August, visited Dunkirk, and got as far as Lille, where Wolfgang

[1] Leopold reported to Hagenauer: 'I shall describe the Tower (i.e. the fortress) to you by word of mouth and tell you that the roaring of the lions there frightened our Master Wolfgang exceedingly.'

fell ill with catarrh and Leopold with fits of dizziness. A month had to be wasted there.

On the way to Holland the boy tried the new organ at a church in Ghent. At Antwerp he played in the cathedral. On 11th September 1765 The Hague was reached at last. How tired and battered these brave travellers must have been —and the 'Ville de Paris,' an inn much frequented by artists, was far from comfortable. But the Prince of Orange, William V, and his sister, Princess Caroline, received them very graciously at the Stadtholder's court. A public concert was arranged for 30th September, but Wolfgang must have played alone, as on the 12th it was Nannerl's turn to be taken ill—so ill that on 21st October she was given extreme unction. Patience, patience! We think of mere flying visits; but how the weeks must have dragged in these strange towns when one or another was not well; how often the Mozarts must have felt the archbishop's nagging reminders of home to be sweetly reasonable after all; what a blessed shelter the cool whitewashed walls at the back of the Löchelplatz must have seemed from afar. Now what could Salzburg do? Leopold, frantic with anxiety, had masses read there for his daughter's recovery.

Wolfgang had the kind of success to which he was used by this time. He played with an orchestra of resident musicians, he extemporized, he undertook to read anything at sight that might be put before him. At home—such a home as could be found for a time—he practised and composed while Nannerl lay in the next room, alternately raving and meekly discussing with her parents the blessedness of leaving a world of whose wickedness she as yet knew only by hearsay.

The princess sent the court physician, Professor Thomas Schwencke, who saved Nannerl. She had scarcely recovered when Wolfgang was seized with a fever. So time crept on wearily until January 1766, when he was well enough again to write a soprano aria, 'Conservati fedele' (K. 23), with string accompaniment, for the princess. The words were from the *Artaserse* of Metastasio, the eighteenth century's universal librettist and—hard to credit in a librettist—a poet to boot. A second concert took place on the 22nd, and towards the end of the month they all went to Amsterdam for four weeks. On 29th January and 26th February they gave concerts there, a Symphony in B flat major (K. 22), which Wolfgang had finished at The Hague, being performed for the first time. The story goes that a special dispensation was necessary to allow the children to perform in Lent. To make known such wonderful specimens of humanity was an act in praise of God, they said, and all was well.

From quiet, middle-class Amsterdam, where trade prospered on a metropolitan scale and its traffic went on vastly but mutely on the silent canals, the family returned to The Hague, with its courtly, fashionable life and its more cosmopolitan setting. The Prince of Orange came of age on 8th March, and on the 11th the little Mozarts again played at court, to provide not the least of the fireworks let off for the occasion. Wolfgang wrote six more Sonatas for clavier with violin (K. 26–31), which were engraved and dedicated to the Princess of Nassau-Weilburg; he also wrote variations for clavier on an air which the local conductor, Christian Ernst Graaf, had written for the festivities (K. 24) and another set on the national song, *Wilhelmus van Nassouwe* (K. 25), which, we have seen, Wolfgang had known from his earliest childhood in some form or another and had already varied in his own babyish way. For the celebration itself he wrote, clearly with Leopold's help, a kind of quodlibet or potpourri on popular airs, beginning with a quotation from Handel and closing with a fugue, a work he called a *Galimathias musicum* (K. 32). It was a comic piece frankly calculated to be entertaining, and much of it is in the vein of Leopold's descriptive pieces illustrating peasants' weddings, hunts, sleigh-parties, village bands and so forth. The subject of the fugue, as might be expected, is the *Wilhelmus* song.

Some time in the middle of March came a visit to Haarlem, where Wolfgang played the famous organ. After another lengthy stay at The Hague, during which Leopold's treatise on the violin was published in Dutch to his immense gratification, they gave a last concert at Amsterdam on 16th April, followed by one at Utrecht. Then, by way of Mechlin and Brussels, they returned to Paris, where some of their belongings had been sent straight from Calais. 10th May 1766 saw them once more in the French capital, where Grimm had procured a lodging for them. Both Marianne and Wolfgang were considered to have made great progress, and they were several times asked to appear at Versailles again.[1] It was at this time that Mozart composed his first piece of catholic church music, a *Kyrie* in F major (K. 33), based on a French song and dated 12th June.

Paris was left on 9th July. An invitation from the Prince de Condé brought them to Dijon. Four weeks were spent at Lyons. Switzerland came next: three weeks at Geneva, five days at Lausanne, a week in Berne and a fortnight at Zürich, where they were the guests of the painter and poet Solomon Gessner and gave a concert with the Musical Society. After a very brief call at Winterthur and Schaffhausen, they re-entered Germany, being eagerly awaited by Prince Joseph Wenzeslaus von Fürstenberg at Donaueschingen, with whom they spent twelve days and played nine times from five o'clock until nine in the evening. At Biberach Wolfgang met another boy prodigy two years older than himself, Sixtus Bachmann, and they engaged in a friendly contest on the organ. Ulm, Günzburg, Dillingen and Augsburg were the stages that brought them nearer Munich, where they arrived on 8th November and appeared before the elector during dinner the following day.

Towards the end of November 1766 they were back home at Salzburg, after an absence of three and a half years. Wolfgang

[1] Concerning the violin Concerto supposed to have been written for Madame Adélaïde and dedicated to her on 26th May, a work recently edited and published by Marius Casadesus, see footnote on p. 343.

was now nearly eleven; the Hagenauers and other good Salzburgers no doubt exclaimed, with the usual innocent astonishment of grown-ups at nature's persistence in her old habits, how little Wolfgangerl had grown. The change that had wrought itself upon Nannerl while they were not looking was more amazing still. Indeed, she was quite a young lady. These familiar voices must have been pleasant, like the bells of the Collegiate Church behind, the clanging of buckets and clacking of the servant-wenches at the fountain in front, like the colour-washed rococo houses in the better streets, the eternal smell of beer and dinner issuing from the inns that stuck their wrought and gaudy signs across the Getreidegasse.

Thus ended the grand tour—grand even without Italy.

CHAPTER IV

AUSTRIAN YEARS OF FORMATION

THE Archbishop Sigismund's first act on hearing Leopold Mozart's account of the family's travels was to show that he suspected the proud father of exaggerating. Wolfgang's powers as performer were easy enough to test, though even then difficult to believe in, but there was no reason for not taking the young prodigy's compositions to be very largely, if not wholly, Leopold's. They were, the archbishop may have thought, not nearly bad enough to be the work of a child.[1] No doubt the suspicions were not unjustified, for it is not to be supposed that a father who was himself a composer could have borne to withhold all advice from a marvellously gifted but inexperienced son for the mere sake of discovering how far his skill would go unaided.

At any rate Leopold realized well enough how much Wolfgang still had to learn, for after the grand tour he made him undergo a regular course in strict counterpoint, as an exercise book of the period still testifies in which the father entered specimen problems for the different species and the son added his own efforts, not without a great many corrections and occasional playfulnesses, such as his marking of the parts as 'Sign. d' Alto, marchese Tenore, duca Basso.' The theoretical work used was old Fux's *Gradus ad Parnassum* in Mizler's modernized German translation.

During his confinement at the *Residenz* Wolfgang was made

[1] Points of view change strangely as time goes on: in the eyes of an enlightened posterity these early works do not look good enough to be the independent efforts of one of the great masters.

to write music for a kind of dramatic oratorio, on the model of the old mystery plays, apparently, entitled *Die Schuldigkeit des ersten und fürnehmsten Gebotes* (*The Obligation of the First and Foremost Commandment*) (K. 35), by Father Jacobus Antonius Wimmer. He composed only the first part, the second and third being given to Michael Haydn, who had been at the Salzburg court as musical director and concert master since 1762, and Anton Cajetan Adlgasser, the archbishop's chamber composer and organist. Thus Wolfgang made his appearance in good company as composer to the archiepiscopal court. The play must have been a curious piece of medieval ingenuousness, with 'a lukewarm and afterwards zealous Christian' as its protagonist, attended, in the manner of *Everyman,* by personifications of the Christian Spirit, the Worldly Spirit, Divine Compassion and Divine Justice. The performance took place on 12th March 1767, and it was repeated on 2nd April.

The music, written in a childish, untidy hand, showed astonishing sureness of workmanship, if little originality of invention. The oratorios of Leopold Mozart and of the late Salzburg *Capellmeister,* Eberlin, served as its models, with Johann Christian Bach offering some suggestions in the way of a more modern treatment than the baroque oratorio was supposed to admit. These influences are to be discerned also in a Passion cantata entitled *Grabmusik* (K. 42), although the woodcut stiffness of its text pointed much farther back, to the old sacred concertos and dialogues of Schütz, Hammerschmidt and others. This piece was performed during Lent.

Almost immediately Wolfgang received another commission for a dramatic work, this time from the university, where it was the custom to give annual performances of Latin plays in which the students appeared in the handsome theatre built for the purpose as long ago as 1661. The subjects were either Biblical or mythological, the author was one of the professors, and local composers were asked to provide music. Eberlin, Adlgasser, Michael Haydn and Leopold himself had been among the more recent contributors, and now Wolfgang was asked to compose *Apollo et Hyacinthus seu Hyacinthi Metamorphosis* (K. 38), a musical intermezzo to the tragedy of *Clementia Croesi* by Father Rufinus Widl. On the printed libretto the composer was pompously described as *auctor operis musici nobilis dominus Wolfgangus Mozart, undecennis, filius nobilis ac strenui domini Leopoldi Mozart, Capellae Magistri.* The stilted Latin libretto was feebly adapted to the desired morality, if not the taste, of the scholars. The music, astonishing for the work of a boy, was less interesting and alive than that of the oratorio and the cantata. Wolfgang's Latin was perhaps nothing to make songs about, and altogether this commission does not seem to have attracted him greatly.

On the other hand he attracted the audience, for after the performance, on 13th May, he played the clavier for them until late into the night. He was improving steadily and began to feel the need of more music to play, especially with the orchestra. Thus, between April and July, he produced his first four pianoforte Concertos (K. 37 and 39–41), and he seems to have been so much in a hurry that they turned out to be not strictly his. These four works are in fact known now to be arrangements of sonata movements by other composers, and as those definitely ascertained all belonged to a group of Germans active in Paris,[1] it seems clear that the Mozart family must have brought back sonatas of that school from their journey. Wolfgang left the original keyboard parts unchanged, but added light accompaniments to them and inserted orchestral *tutti,* not without some significant symphonic elaborations that

[1] Thanks to the researches of Wyzewa and Saint-Foix all but two of the originals are now definitely known. K. 37, movement i, K. 39, i and iii, K. 41, ii and iii are by Raupach; K. 37, iii, K. 40, i, K. 41, i by Honauer; K. 39, ii is by Schobert and K. 40, ii by Eckhardt. K. 37, ii is also by Schobert according to the same authorities, but cannot be found among that composer's extant works. It may possibly be Mozart's own. According to Alfred Einstein K. 40, iii comes from Carl Philipp Emanuel Bach.

look like anticipations of his later practice. Curiously enough Johann Christian Bach is absent from these works, but Wolfgang had already in London arranged three of his sonatas as concertos with string orchestra (K. 107, 1765). Two Symphonies, both in F major (K. 43 and 76), came shortly after the brief Salzburg period of 1767.

Brief indeed. Once again the Mozarts' home was broken up. On 11th September they all left for Vienna, where the marriage of the Archduchess Maria Josepha to King Ferdinand of Naples was to take place shortly. It was not like Leopold to miss such an opportunity to let his children shine at festivities that promised to be of exceptional splendour. Unhappily all that Wolfgang and Nannerl got from the young princess was the smallpox, of which she died on 15th October. The court went into deep mourning and suspended all entertainments. The Mozarts fled to Olmütz (Olomouc) in Moravia, where Count Leopold Anton von Podstatsky, dean of the cathedral, and a canon of Salzburg, where he knew them, gave them shelter and had the children nursed with every possible care. Both were desperately ill: Wolfgang was blind for nine days and had to take great care of his eyes for some time after. Not until 23rd December were they able to start on their return journey to the capital, interrupted by a fortnight's visit to Brünn (Brno), where Count Franz Anton von Schrattenbach, a brother of the Archbishop of Salzburg, invited them to stay and showed them much kindness.

They were back in Vienna on 10th January 1768. Maria Theresa sent for them on the 19th. They were received without ceremony in the imperial family circle, the empress-mother talking affably to the young musicians' mother of such things as they had in common, her son, Joseph II, discussed music and other topics with Leopold and Wolfgang while, it is said, he made Nannerl blush a great many times by his condescending freedom of speech. But Joseph was by no means inclined to lavish money on music, and his widowed mother, especially in her more recent bereavement, shunned operas and concerts as unbecoming frivolities. There was no chance to play at court, and apart from a handsome and valueless medal, the Mozarts departed without remuneration. The nobility followed the court in its apathy as far as official example went, and diverted itself mainly with balls and masquerades. Only Prince Galitsin, the Russian ambassador, gave a 'grand academy' in honour of the young Salzburg artists.

They soon found that they were no longer young enough to make a sensation, though. Their feats were taken more and more for granted by the public; at the same time they began to alarm the professional musicians, who, for their own peace of mind, were anxious to disbelieve in the solidity of Wolfgang's gifts. Here was no longer a wonderchild who would be superseded and forgotten in a year or two, but an upstart who looked like growing into a formidable rival before long. They must look to their laurels and overhaul their armoury of intrigue. Leopold tells us how it was done:

> I find that all clavier players and composers in Vienna set themselves against our progress, Wagenseil alone excepted, who, however, being confined to the house by illness, cannot help us or contribute much to our advantage. The chief maxim of these people is to avoid carefully every opportunity to see us and to recognize Wolfgangerl's knowledge. And why? So that whenever they are asked, as they so often are, whether they have heard this boy and what they think of him, they may ever reply that they have not heard him and that there cannot possibly be any truth in it.

There was good reason for jealousy. Before long the lukewarm emperor took sufficient fire to suggest to the manager of the opera, Affligio, that an opera by the young composer would be sure to prove interesting, especially if he himself conducted it from the clavier. Leopold, getting wind of this, was not slow to depict the certain success of such a venture to the opera singers in the most enticing colours. At the same time he had a poor opinion of the artists who appeared in such serious works as Hasse's *Partenope* and Gluck's *Alceste,* both of which the Mozarts had heard in Vienna. Nor, to be sure, did he care much for Gluck's reforms, and it is not likely that his young son, whose tastes he still influenced, understood them any better. At any rate they preferred to plan an *opera buffa,* a species for which excellent interpreters were available.

Marco Coltellini, a Florentine who had come to Vienna as theatre poet in 1758, furnished the book of the comedy of *La finta semplice* (*The Pretended Simpleton*) (K. 51), which according to the traditions that attached to this kind of thing he deliberately trimmed to all the current conventions, although he was an operatic reformer on the literary side second only to Calzabigi, Gluck's librettist.[1]

If the Mozarts failed to appreciate Gluck, it could hardly surprise them to find that he in turn mistrusted them. At any rate he appears to have looked coldly upon the prospect of hearing a new opera of a kind he no longer regarded as vital. The experienced and somewhat worldly artist of fifty-four was not impressed by the prospective exhibition of a child of twelve as composer and *maestro al cembalo.* For Leopold, of course, nothing less would do than the suspicion that Gluck was the chief mischief-maker among the composers who did their best to thwart his Wolfgangerl. Which was obviously absurd.

However, the fact remains that the production of the opera was frustrated by intrigues. At first it was said that for a mere child to direct a performance would be to inflict an indignity on the artists. The orchestra jibbed. The singers, who had begun by highly approving of their arias, now took it into their heads to object to them. Vienna contradicted itself wildly by saying, now that the setting was worth nothing, as the boy did not know Italian sufficiently well, now that it was not by him at all, but by his father. Then Leopold made more enemies by inducing Hasse and Metastasio to declare,

[1] His *Ifigenia in Tauride,* composed by Traetta in 1758, according to Jahn-Abert (i. 123), actually anticipated some of Calzabigi's and Gluck's new departures.

or by pretending that they had declared—one cannot be sure which—that they had heard as many as thirty operas in Vienna recently which did not come anywhere near that of young Mozart, whom they admired immensely. Next Leopold convinced some sceptics by making Wolfgang set any aria from Metastasio to music in their presence, not realizing that nothing would annoy them more than to be thus proved fools or liars. Finally another opera was put into rehearsal, with the promise that *La finta semplice* should come next, which it never did. Leopold went on persisting, casuistically declaring that he owed it to God to prove to the world the reality of the wonder which had been bestowed on him, and to Salzburg to vindicate the honour of its miraculous young citizen.

Thus their visit dragged on to the end of the year; but nothing happened at the opera, which was farmed out to Affligio, who could therefore do what he liked without interference even from the court. Meanwhile the young composer made himself as busy elsewhere as he could. Dr. Franz Anton Mesmer, who was to become so famous later by his discovery of healing by magnetism, had married a wealthy woman and erected for himself a little theatre in the garden of his country house on the Landstrasse.[1] He admired Wolfgang and was anxious to have a little opera from him for performance there. The libretto was ready and its choice not without a touch of humour, seeing that its subject is the performance of a pretended feat of magic by the mere application of common sense and knowledge of human nature. Was Mesmer indulging in a little joke at his own risk?

Be that as it may, the book was F. W. Weiskern's *Bastien und Bastienne,* a German translation of *Les Amours de Bastien et Bastienne* by Madame Favart and Harny, the French ballad opera which in turn was a parody of Jean-Jacques Rousseau's *Le Devin du village,* produced before the court at Fontainebleau in 1752 and brought to Paris the following year. Weiskern's

[1] It may have been an open-air theatre made of trimmed hedges.

version had already been heard as a German ballad opera in Vienna, partly with the music selected for it by Madame Favart, four years before it came into Mozart's hands. *Bastien und Bastienne* (K. 50) was Wolfgang's first German musical play of the kind, a direct forerunner of *Die Entführung aus dem Serail,* not to say an indirect one of *Die Zauberflöte.* Its music, however, was largely influenced by composers of French comic opera like Monsigny and Philidor, whose pieces Wolfgang must have heard in Paris. The pastoral and extremely simple character the subject required naturally suited the composer of twelve far better than an Italian *opera buffa,* the complex intrigues of which he can scarcely have understood. Thus *Bastien* is, with all its ingenuousness, much more mature and poetical a work than *La finta semplice.*

Two Symphonies, both in D major (K. 45 and 48), were also written during this year in Vienna, the former in January, the latter in December. They were not performed, but Wolfgang at last had a chance to produce some music, though of quite another kind, in public. A Jesuit, Father Ignaz Parhammer, who had been confessor to Francis I, was head of an orphan asylum for which a new chapel was being erected in the Rennweg—the fine country high road near the Belvedere. Parhammer, who knew the Mozarts, asked Wolfgang to compose a festival Mass and the Offertory for the occasion, as well as a trumpet Concerto to be played by one of the boys of the institution. Of these three works, which Wolfgang conducted on 7th December, only the offertory, 'Veni sancte spiritus' (K. 47), is preserved,[1] but about the same time he exercised himself once more in church music by turning out a *Missa brevis* in G major (K. 49).

The court was present at the inauguration of the chapel, much to the satisfaction of Leopold, who felt that at last his ill-used son had been avenged for the disappointment his first

[1] Some authorities, however, regard the Mass in C minor-major (K. 139) as identical with this festival Mass; others reject this suggestion on internal evidence.

Italian opera had cost him. Indeed he deserved this triumph, for the last of the manœuvres at the opera had been the most galling of all: pressed uncomfortably hard to proceed with the production of *La finta semplice,* Affligio had finished by declaring that he would bring it out under protest and see to it that the artists should thoroughly ruin it by a bad performance. After that there was nothing left but to withdraw it with such dignity as an irate father and a tearful son could muster.

Nothing, that is, save a cutting of losses and a return to Salzburg, where the family arrived on 5th January 1769. Here the archbishop, instead of scolding Leopold for his prolonged absence, dropped balm on his wounded pride by ordering a performance of the opera at his court. The singers, who included the wife of Michael Haydn, Maria Magdalena, *née* Lipp, were all in the archbishop's service and, it may be hoped, not any too well versed in such profanities as *opera buffa*; but there was a handsome theatre in the palace, the orchestra was good, and if the performers were not consummate actors, they could certainly sing, so that the Mozarts must have enjoyed the long-deferred performance of this ill-starred work. The archbishop, too, on whose nameday it took place, must have been not a little pleased and astonished at his young dependant's successful imitation of a sophisticated art. No doubt he was flattered by the thought of what a talent he had fostered, and it would seem that flattery went even farther, for apparently the recitative and aria, 'Sol nascente' (K. 70), was sung in the course of the evening as a *licenza*—a piece in praise of a patron frequently included in a musical work with which it had no connection whatever beyond the fact that without him neither the chief work nor the dedicatory piece would have been performed at all, and even the former perhaps never written.

For the rest, the greater part of 1769 passed quietly enough. We do not hear that Wolfgang ever went to school, but unless Leopold found his own good education enough to teach him at home, he must have done so. That he continued his musical studies assiduously is certain. He composed a good deal, beginning in January with a *Missa brevis* in D minor (K. 65). A Mass in C major (K. 66) and an Offertory (K. 72) followed, while instrumental music was enriched by a Symphony in C major (K. 73), two Cassations[1] (K. 63 and 99), a Serenade (K. 100) and three sets of Minuets (K. 103–5), to mention no more.

Orchestral works of this kind are typical of the whole of Mozart's Salzburg period from now on. They represent a lighter, more popular art than that of symphony and chamber music. Whatever they are called, they all come from the older species of the suite which music was now rapidly leaving behind, and the suite, being a string of dance movements, had always been a form more readily accepted by the people at large than anything that developed out of it was accepted later. It was also more essentially open-air music and thus more accessible to the crowd. That character it preserves in

[1] The cassation belongs to the same class as the serenade and the divertimento. Like them, it is a suite in which only one of the old dances, the minuet, is still regularly represented, and which verges towards the sonata form. Its name is a characteristic remnant of an obsolete musicians' jargon: everybody knows the kind of work it stands for and nobody is clear about its exact meaning. In law (court of cassation) it means annulment, from the Latin *cassare, cassatio,* and it may thus originally have been a piece played at the end of a festive evening—a cessation or dismissal (for the verb 'to cashier' also comes from the same source). Wyzewa and Saint-Foix explain it, by way of the French *casser,* as a kind of broken suite, played in the course of an evening with long intervals between the movements. Riemann goes to the Italian *cassa* (drum) and connects this with the opening march movement. Jahn points out that there is an Austrian dialect expression, *gassatim gehen,* which means to roam about at night courting and serenading girls at their windows. C. B. Oldman points out that Constanze Mozart, discussing the classification of her husband's works in a letter to André dated 29th November 1800, speaks of *Gassationen* and adds a marginal note to the effect that this is 'an ugly, incomprehensible provincial expression.'

Mozart's works of this type, in which wind instruments frequently play a predominant part and which are often—especially in the cassations—opened, and sometimes closed, by a march. There was something in the air of Salzburg, half countrified and half urbanized, to which this natural and yet highly stylized art-type was particularly suited, and it is not very surprising to find that he cultivated it assiduously as long as he lived there. It is remarkable that after 1781, the year in which he irrevocably left Salzburg for Vienna, only three compositions of the serenade species are to be found in his catalogue. Less surprising is the fact that church music stopped at the same time, since he held no ecclesiastical appointment in Vienna and began to lean towards freemasonry, which in those days affected people's religious outlook far more in the direction of free thought than it does nowadays.

But these observations anticipate. Much ground is to be covered yet before Mozart even enters any regular service in his native town. Some of that ground, to be trodden next, is the land of Leopold's wildest dreams for his son—Italy.

CHAPTER V

THE GREAT ITALIAN JOURNEY

THE mother and sister were both left at home this time. Leopold and Wolfgang departed alone on 13th December 1769, armed with a letter of introduction from Hasse to the Abbate G. M. Ortes at Bologna. Hasse, who had been much impressed by Wolfgang in Vienna, though, as his rather cautious letter to Ortes shows, he was not entirely free from suspicions about the genuineness of the boy's gifts, was a sponsor whose name was sure to carry weight in Italy, where he enjoyed the greatest fame of all foreign composers of Italian opera. He was over seventy now—as old as Handel had been when Mozart was born—and belonged more to the school of that master and of Alessandro Scarlatti than to the group of younger composers by whom Mozart was to be more or less influenced: Gassmann, Gazzaniga, Guglielmi, Jommelli, Majo, Mysliweček, Paisiello, Piccinni, Sacchini, Sarti, Traetta and others. Hasse had married one of Handel's London prima donnas, Faustina Bordoni, and he became a friend of Bach's when he was *maestro di cappella* at the then wholly italianized court opera of Dresden.

There was no lack of other recommendations, which did much to make the Mozarts' brief sojourns at various stages of the journey agreeable. At Innsbruck, for instance, they were received by Count Spaur, who had a relative at the Salzburg court. Wolfgang gave a concert there with a violinist, a horn player and an organist. At Rovereto Leopold found an old friend who had been brought up by one of the family's Salzburg acquaintances and had learnt the violin from him. Wolfgang gave a concert at the house of Baron Todeschi and played the organ at the principal church to a crowd which mobbed the building so that the young performer could hardly get at the instrument. At Verona his success was even greater. Here he met one of the famous Italian violinist-composers, old Locatelli, gave various proofs of his gifts before a private assembly, including a performance of one of his symphonies, and played the organ at the church of San Tommaso, which proved even more difficult of access than that at Rovereto, for the same reason. A newspaper published a rapturous notice, an Italian poem compared him to Apollo, a Latin distich to Orpheus, one Zaccaria Betti produced a sonnet, and the receiver-general, Pietro Luggiati, had his portrait painted by Cignaroli.

It was much the same at Mantua, except that the attentions this time seemed to come mainly from the ladies. A Signora Bettinelli took Wolfgang under her motherly care; a Signora Sartoretti invited father and son to luncheon, sending Wolfgang the following day a nosegay into whose ribbons a delicately disguised gift of four ducats was sewn, accompanied by a highly flattering poem. On 16th January 1770 an interminable concert was given by the Philharmonic Society, the programme of which, flanked by two of the boy's symphonies, included all manner of tricks and tests calculated to astonish his audience. Again a newspaper praised him extravagantly and a noted scholar declared him to be 'a wonderwork of nature.'

They went to the opera both in Verona and Mantua, hearing *Ruggiero*[1] in the former city and Hasse's *Demetrio* in the latter. Wolfgang wrote a characteristic account of the performance—without a word about the work—to his sister in one of those comically untidy, irresponsible, ill-spelt, childish and some-

[1] No composer mentioned. Jahn-Abert can only counter the conjecture of Wyzewa and Saint-Foix that it may have been Hasse's by pointing out that his setting was not produced until 1771; it is Schiedermair, in a footnote in his edition of the Mozart letters, who suggests Guglielmi's, produced in Venice in 1769.

times naïvely coarse letters which now begin to accompany his biography, and from which it is time to quote a specimen:

I am right heartily glad that you were so much diverted by that sleigh party, and I wish you a thousand opportunities for diversion, that you may spend your life very merrily. But one thing grieves me, that you let Herr von Mölk sigh and suffer so much, and that you did not go sleighing with him, so that he might have upset you: how many handkerchers he must have used this self-same day on your account, with weeping. . . . I have no news besides that Herr gelehrt [1] the poet has died at Leipzig and never wrote another piece of poetry after his death. Just before I began this letter, I indited an *aria* from *Demetrio.*[2] . . .

The *opera* at mantua was pretty, they played the *Demetrio,* the *prima Dona* sings well, but quiet, and if she were not seen to act, but only to sing, one would think, she did not sing, for she cannot open her mouth, but whines everything to herself, which it is true is nothing new for us to hear. *La seconda Dona* is a sight like a *granadier,* and has a strong voice too, and verily sings not badly seeing that she is acting for the first time. . . . *Primo ballerino.* good. *prima Ballerina*: good, and they say she is no dog, but I have not seen her closely, . . .

and so on and on, with a comparison of his own handwriting to an elementary physical function of pigs, not easily repeatable nowadays, but clearly an ordinary embellishment of conversation in eighteenth-century Salzburg, since Wolfgang mentions this kind of thing even to his mother, though not necessarily in relation to pigs.

Another opera by Hasse, more important in view of later events, *La clemenza di Tito,* they heard at Cremona, which they visited on their way to Milan, where they arrived at the end of January, finding very comfortable shelter in the Augustine monastery of San Marco. How glad they were of the warmed beds which one of the monks, especially entrusted with their service, prepared for them nightly; for they had almost perished with cold, especially in marshy Mantua, where, Leopold grumbled, everything he touched was ice.

[1] Gellert. [2] Metastasio's poem. The music is lost.

The Governor-General of Lombardy, Count Carl Joseph von Firmian, younger brother of a former Archbishop of Salzburg, took them under his wing, introducing them to the best society. They also met the venerable Giovanni Battista Sammartini, Gluck's former master, and the latter's future Paris rival, Piccinni, whose *Cesare in Egitto* they heard at the opera. As usual, Wolfgang at once picked up the influences of his new musical surroundings. Features of Hasse's and of Piccinni's style appear in four arias he composed to poems from Metastasio's *Demofoonte* and *Artaserse* (K. 77–9 and 88) at the instigation of Count Firmian, for performance at a musical party to which a very distinguished audience was invited, including the Duke of Modena with his daughter and the Cardinal-Archbishop of Milan. Wolfgang and Leopold also took part in the carnival. They dressed up with the rest of Milan, and Leopold, while delighting in his son's attractive appearance in the disguise, felt that he owed it to his Germanic dignity to write half-humorously to his wife how little he expected to take part in such tomfoolery at his advanced age. (He was fifty!)

Firmian rewarded Wolfgang handsomely enough and was instrumental in procuring him the *scrittura* for the following opera season, i.e. a commission to write an opera for Milan. One of the conditions was that he should have the permission of his patron at Salzburg, which he received in due course. The libretto was to be sent on to him at whatever Italian city he might happen to be; he was to deliver the recitatives by October and return early in November in order to finish the work in consultation with the singers, a general practice of the time to which he adhered throughout his life. It was not a bad practice either, provided that the composer was man and artist enough not to allow himself to be unduly swayed. It is true that more than one Mozartian part[1] written for a

[1] e.g. Constanze in *The Elopement,* with its excessive ornamentation, Fiordiligi in *Così fan tutte,* with its dangerously wide skips, the Queen of Night in *The Magic Flute,* with its abnormally high notes.

particular voice was doomed to be for ever after a stumbling-block for average singers; but it must be remembered that operas in the eighteenth century were never thought of as being written for posterity. They were made for special occasions or to a special order: the current operatic repertory consisted of novelties, not of revivals, which were the exception. Hence the extraordinary productivity of most composers, including A. Scarlatti, Handel and Hasse, where dramatic works were concerned, and also, it is as well to remember, the almost equally extraordinary perfunctoriness of others. Even Rossini's often slapdash workmanship, at a much later period, is still due to this tradition of an incessant appetite for something new; and it was enough for the libretto to be novel, whereas the music might take the line of least resistance.

One of the most astonishing voices, for which even Mozart would hardly have ventured to write special parts, since they would have remained for ever inaccessible to others, was that of Lucrezia Agujari, who, saddled with the misfortune of a bar sinister, was more affectionately than elegantly nicknamed *La Bastardella.* It was at Parma that the Mozarts met her, but not before they had visited Lodi, where on 15th March Wolfgang finished his first string Quartet, in G major (K. 80). Agujari invited them to a meal and gave them an exhibition of her powers which staggered them both, Wolfgang so much that he could not forbear to write down a florid passage that issued from her 'gallant gullet' and sending it to Nannerl. It soars impudently up to C *in altissimo* (a fifth higher than the highest note Mozart ever wrote for a soprano) and descends to only one tone short of three octaves below; but Leopold, who tells his wife that he would believe nothing but his own ears, mentions low G (another fifth below that).

On 24th March they reached Bologna, always one of the gloomier of Italian cities, with an austere university and full of serious scholars and savants, but also, Leopold reported, possessing fine buildings and a musical reputation that was by no means merely theatrical. At the cathedral and at the vast though unfinished San Petronio, church music was cultivated with much dignity, and the town intently upheld its fame as a seat of theoretical teaching. At the head of the musical scholars was the Franciscan Padre Giovanni Battista Martini, aged sixty-four and at the height of his celebrity.

Although Martini had given up concert-going, he was induced to attend an *accademia* given by the Mozarts' latest patron, Field-Marshal Count Pallavicini, two days after their arrival. The great theorist possessed, as Burney recorded, a matchless musical library; he had turned out innumerable distinguished pupils; had published a first volume of a musical history by this time, while a great work on counterpoint was in the making; he was in correspondence with famous musicians and scholars all over Europe; his advice was sought in controversies and in the matter of important musical appointments. With all this, he was utterly free from conceit and by no means above examining Wolfgang's exercises in fugue, with which he declared himself always satisfied.

A very different personality from Martini, and a year older than he, was the famous male soprano Farinelli (Carlo Broschi), whom the Mozarts visited at the country house near Bologna to which he had retired to meditate on his phenomenal successes, especially in England, to sigh regretfully over his past glories as singer and diplomat at the court of Spain, to solace himself with the harpsichord, the *viola d'amore* and a fine collection of pictures. Wolfgang here came into direct contact with the greatest representative of an art—the technically astounding singing by the artificial voice of the *castrato* —which was then beginning to decline, but to which he was still to pay his own tributes up to the time of *Idomeneo* (1781).

There was no settling at Bologna for the moment. On 30th March the travellers reached Florence, which accorded them the kind of reception to which they were accustomed by now. The imperial ambassador, Count Rosenberg, at once announced their arrival to the Grand Duke Leopold of Tuscany, who had already heard the children in Vienna. Wolfgang was asked to play at court on 2nd April. He remained five hours, played with another of the famous violinist-composers, Nardini, and solved a number of technical intricacies submitted to him by a musical courtier, the Marquis de Ligniville, who himself dabbled in composition, if the writing of church music in elaborate canons may be called dabbling. Wolfgang must have been impressed by these works, for he copied some of the canons and wrote a *Kyrie* (K. 89) for five soprano voices in various canonic forms imitating Ligniville's style. He also amused himself with the production of a sketch for another canon, in five voices, and five riddle canons (K. 89A), in which the entries of the various voices were not indicated, but had to be guessed. The direct incentive to these, however, may have come from Martini, who gave Wolfgang the first volume of his *History*, which was ornamented with vignettes showing such contrapuntal ingenuities.

As a reminder of their London days the Mozarts met the singer Manzuoli again. Wolfgang was the more delighted because Manzuoli was negotiating with the Milan opera for an engagement, and was thus likely to sing in the work commissioned by that establishment. A closer connection with England he unexpectedly found at Florence was a sudden tender friendship with young Thomas Linley, a gifted boy of his own age who studied under Nardini and was already a remarkable violinist. He was the son of the composer of the same name and a member of that uncommonly musical family of Bath the eldest of whom, Elizabeth Ann, was to become the wife of Sheridan in 1773. Thomas was afterwards associated with his father in composing and compiling music for Sheridan's *Duenna*, but he was unfortunately drowned at the age of twenty-two. Mozart never forgot a friendship that had been no less ardent than brief. The feeling was mutual, for Thomas presented Wolfgang with a valedictory sonnet written on his behalf in the most adulatory terms by the poetess Maddalena Morelli, who had brought the two boys together.

They both shed tears on parting. Burney says that their names were coupled together in Italy as those of the two most promising young musical geniuses of the age.

The stay at Florence was short: they wished to be in Rome for Holy Week. After a journey in wretched weather, during which they found but the most miserable inns to eat and sleep in, they arrived on Wednesday, 11th April, just in time to hear the famous *Miserere* by Allegri in the Sistine Chapel. The work was supposed to be the exclusive property of the papal choir, and although it was not true that copies of it were never given to other churches, certain conventions of performance were carefully kept a secret, so that Metastasio, on hearing the work in Vienna, after having been deeply impressed by it in Rome, declared that it had fallen flat. But Wolfgang was not to be thus put off: he sat down and wrote out the whole work, which was in four and five parts, with a final nine-part chorus, from memory immediately after the service.

Leopold had twenty letters of introduction to the most fashionable houses: the Chigi, Barberini, Bracciano and other noble families received him and wished Wolfgang to play at their houses. Leopold says they met many English people, including a Mr. Beckfort [*sic*], whom they had come across at Lady Effingham's in London and who may not impossibly have been Alderman William Beckford, Lord Mayor of London and the father of the author of *Vathek,* although he died that same year. With him and several other English people the father and son went sightseeing. Wolfgang composed two more arias from Metastasio's *Demofoonte* (K. 82–3) for soprano, and even Leopold may have felt urged to take to composition again, for the Symphony in D major, dated 27th April and included in the complete Mozart edition as well as in Köchel's catalogue as No. 81, may be by him rather than by Wolfgang, which, though confusing, would at any rate go to show that the boy of fourteen had by this time matched his father's skill, to say the very least.

The next stage of the journey was to be Naples; but they

had heard of some murderous robberies committed on the road from Rome and were by no means anxious to start until they were informed that some of the highwaymen had been captured, which was satisfactory, and the rest dispersed, which was less reassuring. They appear to have felt none too safe even when at last they did depart on 8th May. At any rate they left in the company of four Augustinian monks, whose protection was perhaps more imaginary than real.

Not that Leopold appears to have been credulous. At any rate he fulminates against the appalling superstitions of the Neapolitans, 'a veritable heresy that is looked upon with indifferent eyes.' Altogether he found the populace 'godless' and 'certain people so stupid that they cannot conceive their own stupidity.' It would seem that Ferdinand IV, who had in the meantime married another Austrian archduchess, Maria Carolina, was not exempt from this criticism of Leopold's, who wrote to his wife:

> Whether we have played before the king? Anything but! It stopped short at the mere compliments which the queen made us at every place where she met us. The queen can do nothing, and what kind of *subjectum* the king is will be more fitly told than described here.

They were well received elsewhere, however. The minister, Tanucci, Princess Francavilla, Princess Belmonte, Metastasio's old friend, and the British envoy, William Hamilton, all treated them kindly, and they were more than once seen in the carriages of the grandees at the *corso,* attended by footmen with blazing torches. The first Lady Hamilton, as she was soon to become[1]—the angelic Catherine, not the notorious Emma—was a fine harpsichord player, though Leopold reports with much satisfaction that she trembled at the prospect of playing to Wolfgang, and her husband was a more than tolerable violinist as well as a protector of the arts and sciences.

On 28th May the Mozarts gave a grand concert, and

[1] Hamilton was knighted in 1772.

throughout their stay in Naples they attended various operas at the Teatro de' Fiorentini and the Teatro Nuovo, hearing works by Paisiello and Piccinni among others. At the royal opera house, moreover, the Teatro San Carlo, they attended a gala performance of Jommelli's *Armida abbandonata* on the king's birthday. Jommelli had shortly before returned to Italy from Stuttgart, only to be met with the disappointment of finding his operas criticized as too learned and old-fashioned in Naples. The Mozarts met him there, and he treated them with great kindness, dispelling, it may be hoped, Leopold's former impression that he had once prevented his infant son from being heard by the Duke of Württemberg. Paisiello, too, made himself agreeable; in fact Wolfgang might have obtained a commission for an opera for the San Carlo, had he not already been similarly bound to Milan.

They visited Mount Vesuvius, Pompeii and Herculaneum, went for a sea excursion, saw Nero's baths and Virgil's grave besides all sorts of caves and grottoes. It is clear, too, that they took some interest in the Neapolitan people. 'As regards the impertinence of the rabble, I am not sure that Naples does not outdo London,' Wolfgang writes to his sister; 'for the populace here, the *lazzaroni,* have their own captain or head, who draws twenty-five silver ducats from the king each month for nothing more than to keep the *lazzaroni* in order.'

On 25th June father and son left Naples by an exceptionally fast coach that brought them to Rome the next day, with no greater penalty than a damaged leg for Leopold and such fatigue that Wolfgang went to sleep in a chair as soon as he sat down. On 8th July the Order of the Golden Spur was conferred on the boy by Pope Clement XIV. It carried the title of *cavaliere,* which he used for some time, probably more in order to please his proud father than from any personal gratification, for, unlike Gluck, who held the same distinction and laid stress on this 'knighthood' all his life, Mozart soon came to treat it with the indifference he attached to all worldly advantages.

The second Roman visit was very short. Already on 20th July Bologna was reached again after a ten days' journey via Civita Castellana, Loreto and Sinigaglia. Count Pallavicini offered them a delightful *villeggiatura* at his country house. Padre Martini now became an even closer friend than before, and a new acquaintance was the Bohemian composer Mysliweček, who was so popular in Italy that he was given the nickname of *il divino boemo*. But he was busy with an oratorio for Padua, whereas Martini was always ready to receive the Mozarts and discuss all sorts of musical questions with them. His inexhaustible learning stimulated Wolfgang immensely: he sketched a number of complicated polyphonic exercises and finished a *Miserere* in A minor for three voices and organ continuo (K. 85).

The ancient and honourable musical society of Bologna, the *Accademia filarmonica*, held a solemn service on 13th August at which the mass and vespers were chosen from the compositions of ten distinguished members, who themselves conducted. Burney was present as well as the Mozarts and was delighted to meet them. The *Accademia* then decided that Wolfgang should be elected a member, and although that honour was by statute reserved to composers over the age of twenty, it was agreed to make an exception in the case of this boy of genius, provided that he passed the usual very stiff examination satisfactorily. This took place on 9th October. He solved a task of the most hair-raising difficulty in a surprisingly short time and was unanimously elected. The test piece was the antiphon, *Quaerite primum regnum Dei,* for four voices on a *cantus firmus* (K. 86). Even the Golden Spur of Rome was less of an incentive for him than this Bolognese academic distinction, if only because he had become attached to Martini and was glad to do him credit as a pupil, though one of very short standing.

A roundabout journey by way of Florence, Pisa, Leghorn and Genoa had to be abandoned on account of Leopold's bad foot, the result of the little accident during the journey from Naples to Rome, as Wolfgang wrote to young Linley with much regret. Thus they went straight to Milan, where they arrived on 18th October. It was all that Wolfgang could do to finish the composition of his opera, to a libretto by Vittorio Amadeo Cigna-Santi, based on a tragedy by Racine and entitled *Mitridate, Rè di Ponto* (K. 87). The book came from Turin, where a setting by Quirino Gasparini had already been produced in 1767. Wolfgang's recitatives had been partly written at Bologna, but the arias and concerted numbers were composed in close contact with the singers, who were delighted with the music and perhaps, too, with a boy who was willing enough to bear with their caprices and may, all things considered, have profited not a little by their experience. Such a sop to their vanity could not fail to be useful.

Still, there were the usual annoyances, of course, and Leopold had at times to exercise all his diplomatic talent to get even with the singers, but hoped to eat his way through, as he said, 'like Merry Andrew through a mountain of dirt.' An enemy tried to persuade the prima donna, Antonia Bernasconi, to refuse Wolfgang's arias, but was indignantly repulsed by her. Both she and her master, Lampugnani, were in fact highly satisfied with the music. Then a tenor, Guglielmo d' Ettore, made trouble, and finally the Mozarts were disappointed to find that their old friend Manzuoli did not join the cast after all, but was replaced by another male soprano, Santorini, who did not arrive until less than a month before the production.

The first performance of *Mitridate* took place on 26th December 1770 under Wolfgang's direction. It had a wonderful success. The audience became more and more vociferous with pleasure, applauded nearly every number, demanded one of them a second time, the opera was repeated twenty times, and the copyist received orders for five complete full scores besides any number of copies of separate arias.

On 5th January 1771 the *Accademia filarmonica* of Verona, not to be outdone by that of Bologna, elected the young *maestro* a member. Leopold and Wolfgang now allowed themselves some relaxation. They dined here and there in Milan, paid a visit to Turin, where they saw a 'magnificent opera,' and then went to spend part of the carnival in Venice. There they attended many receptions and operas, gave a concert, and had the private gondolas of various noble families placed at their disposal, much as they had had the carriages at Naples. A visit to Padua followed, where Wolfgang received a commission for the composition of an oratorio on the text of Metastasio's *La Betulia liberata.* With that he carried home another for a second opera, to be produced in Milan during the carnival of 1773, with an increased honorarium. But he also brought away more tangible trophies, including several Symphonies (K. 84, 95, 97 and 110).

After brief visits to Vicenza and Verona, where they enjoyed the usual enthusiastic receptions—unless they were too exhausted and too sated by success to enjoy them any longer—father and son reached their home on 28th March 1771. Leopold's fondest wish had been amply fulfilled: Italy, always reluctant to grant musical genius to foreigners, had taken his son to her effusive heart.

CHAPTER VI

GLORY—SERVITUDE—EMANCIPATION

No sooner was the family reunited than a letter arrived from Count Firmian in Vienna informing Leopold on behalf of Maria Theresa that Wolfgang would be commissioned to compose a serenata for the wedding of the Archduke Ferdinand and Princess Maria Ricciarda Beatrice of Modena, which was to take place at Milan in October 1771. There would have been plenty of time to compose it, but the libretto, by the Abbate Giuseppe Parini, had to be taken from Milan to Vienna for imperial approval, and back again. It was never sent to him at Salzburg; he received it only in Milan, where he and Leopold arrived on 21st August. Even then it was so chopped and changed about that little could be done with it until early in September. Work now progressed with astonishing rapidity, however, and that in spite of disturbances which would have driven another composer frantic. Indeed because of them, it would appear from the postscript to Wolfgang's letter of 24th August to his sister:

> Above us is a violinist, below us another, next to us a singing master who gives lessons, in the last room facing ours an hautboy player. A merry state in which to compose! It gives one plenty of notions.

The name of the serenata was *Ascanio in Alba* (K. 111). It was not the festival opera itself, for that had been commissioned from Metastasio and Hasse, but a shorter pastoral and mythological *festa teatrale* with the usual allegorical allusions to the event for which it was devised. Manzuoli was engaged as male soprano this time and Tibaldi, the tenor, proved as friendly as their old London companion. Rehearsals went without a hitch serious enough to be written home about, and the piece was staged on 17th October, the third day of the festivities, having been preceded on the 16th by Hasse's *Ruggiero.* The boy's piece was more successful than the celebrated old man's: it had to be repeated the next day and was given more frequently than the festival opera. Hasse, however, who was above jealousy, remained perfectly amicable, though he might not have done so had he known that Leopold wrote home vaingloriously that Wolfgang's serenata had so defeated the Hasse opera as to defy description. Maria Theresa, to mark the occasion, gave the boy a diamond-studded gold watch bearing her portrait in enamel.

Providence, too, was kind. Among the many entertainments, which included horse and carriage races, masked processions and the like, was a great public distribution of victuals, with wines flowing from ornamental fountains. Leopold and Wolfgang by sheer chance arrived too late to take the seats reserved for them on one of the temporary scaffoldings, which collapsed as soon as they had been given a place among courtiers on a balcony. More than fifty people were killed.

A Symphony in F major (K. 112) and a Divertimento in E flat major (K. 113) were composed in Milan. Back in Salzburg by the middle of December, Mozart wrote another Symphony, in A major (K. 114), and then settled down to his task for Padua, *La Betulia liberata* (K. 118).

Early in 1772 there was great agitation among the archiepiscopal retinue, though no doubt it was adroitly enough concealed behind a typically Salzburgerish politeness and sly caution. The Archbishop Sigismund had died on 16th December 1771. He had had his faults, God rest his soul, but he had been easy-going. What one heard of his successor, Hieronymus Joseph Franz von Paula, Count of Colloredo, and so far ecclesiastically nothing more exalted than Bishop of Gurk, did not augur too good a time at the *Residenz* for the near future. A more stringent regimen was foreseen, if not for his lordship himself, then at any rate for his dependants.

By some means or other Leopold succeeded in impressing the new ruler at once with the genius of his young son, for whom a commission to compose a festival opera for the installation was procured. Like the work he had just done for Milan, it was not on a large scale, but again in the nature of a serenata or *azione teatrale,* and an old libretto of Metastasio's, *Il sogno di Scipione,* which had been composed by Predieri as long ago as 1735, was raked out for a purpose to which it was none too well suited. It had originally alluded to the birthday of the Empress Elisabeth and to the vicissitudes of war in Italy; but it was used as it stood, although in the new circumstances a good deal of it was sheer nonsense. Even the *licenza* in praise of the hero of the moment was taken over bodily, Wolfgang, in the ardour of composition, forgetting at first to change the name to the Italian equivalent of Hieronymus—Girolamo. The formal installation took place on 29th April 1772, and the performance of *Il sogno di Scipione* (K. 126) probably in the first days of May.

For a youth of sixteen Wolfgang did not at first fare badly with his father's new master—perhaps not even for a genius of sixteen, if one considers that the course of true greatness never did run smooth. He was, 'for the time being,' appointed concert master at court on 9th August, with a salary of 150 florins. What is more, he was given leave to go to Italy a third time in the autumn. Before that, however, he contrived to write a number of works on a large scale. A Symphony (K. 124) is dated 21st February, and three more (K. 128–30) followed in July and August. In March a Litany, 'De Venerabili' (K. 125), appeared, and a *Regina Coeli* (K. 127) came soon after. A Divertimento (K. 131) was written in June and three others (K. 136–8) a little later. Six string Quartets also belong to 1772, though not all of them seem to have been finished before the last Italian journey. One, at any rate, is known to have been composed on the way, at

Bozen, where Wolfgang wrote it to beguile himself during a miserably rainy day spent in what he describes to his sister as a dismal hole—to translate his drastic language fairly decorously. Another work of the kind is mentioned by Leopold in a letter from Milan the following February.

From the letters to Nannerl dated about this time we gather that the future creator of Cherubino was suffering from an attack of the calf-love of which he was to give the world the classic musical expression once and for all later on. There are obscure hints at messages to be given to—well, Nannerl would know [1]—and expressions of gratitude to his sisterly *postillon d'amour* for having done what there was no need to particularize. In one letter, written in Italian, Wolfgang uses the code to which the whole Mozart family would cautiously resort whenever they fancied that discretion was indicated.

Father and son were back in Milan on 4th November 1772, and the latter settled down to the composition of the opera of *Lucio Silla* (K. 135), ordered during his first sojourn there. He had finished only some recitatives beforehand and even these were found to a great extent useless, for the librettist, Giovanni da Gamerra, had in the meantime submitted his work to Metastasio, who had made considerable changes.

The singers being slow to arrive, Wolfgang next composed the overture and the choruses. After some of the minor soloists, the male soprano, Venanzio Rauzzini, arrived from Munich, and not until 4th December did the prima donna, Maria Anna de Amicis, who came from Venice, put in an appearance. As the production of the opera was to take place on the 26th, there was no time to be lost. Wolfgang had his head full of the music, could think of nothing to write to his sister, and feared he might set down a whole aria instead of words in his letter to her. Amicis was not easy to satisfy: she insisted, it seems, on showy passages; but the young

[1] In a letter of 12th December 1772 Leopold points out a daughter of Dr. Sylvester von Barisani, court physician to the archbishop, as having engaged Wolfgang's interest.

composer, with his genius for compromising between the demands of singers and his own artistic conscience, pleased her in every way. Both she and Rauzzini, according to Leopold, sang like angels.

Meanwhile the tenor, Cardoni, was reported to be seriously ill. The management, in frantic anxiety, sent to Turin and Bologna in search of another artist who could fill the title part with dignity, not only musically, but as an actor. But nobody was found, and in the end Bassano Morgnoni, a church singer of Lodi, who had next to no stage experience, had to be engaged. The rehearsals were already in full swing when he arrived on 17th December, and his four arias had still to be composed in great haste. But the work was ready on the appointed day and, in spite of various mishaps, was well received, though not with the same astonishment as *Mitridate* had been exactly two years earlier. The Italian public was becoming accustomed to the wonder, which was moreover somewhat diminished by the fact that the composer was now a young man of nearly seventeen—a mature age in the Italy of a sophisticated period. Still, the work was given more than twenty times.

Rauzzini must have been a remarkable soprano to sing the difficult and high passages that occur in the motet, *Exsultate, jubilate* (K. 165), written for him in a brilliant operatic style in January 1773.[1] But there was really nothing to keep the Mozarts any longer in Milan, except that Leopold was suffering from rheumatism and that he tried, with some promise of success, but in the end vainly, to secure an appointment for Wolfgang at the court of the Grand Duke Leopold of Tuscany in Florence. They left Italy early in March, never to return. On 13th March they were back at Salzburg.

Two dull and disappointing years were now in store for the young genius. After his triumphs abroad he was vexed to find that the new archbishop began to take his gifts calmly

[1] It contains a curious anticipation of a phrase in the Austrian hymn composed by Haydn in 1797.

for granted as no more than was due to him from a servant. The drudgery started with a number of compositions, including a Symphony in D major (K. 181) and the *Concertone* for two violins and orchestra (K. 190), written in May 1773, with the Holy Trinity Mass (K. 167) following in June.

Salzburg had given Colloredo as cool a reception as was compatible with an outward show of respectful submission. The lighthearted and long-suffering people could scarcely help meeting a new ruler, who exacted order and unquestioning servility disdainfully as a matter of course, with a kind of sullen hypocrisy he was more than intelligent enough to see through and unsympathetic enough to counter with an unbending, freezing haughtiness. Fussy old Leopold Mozart and his conceited young spark of a son were no exception. The father held a subordinate post at court, after all, and the boy had better be shown at once that uppishness would not be tolerated by one in whose pay he was. It was not the archbishop's fault that his predecessor had been slack, and he was not aware of being more harsh and distant than most of the great of the earth, particularly those who had just entered upon a splendid career of despotism. All the same, the Salzburgers felt that they had been there first, and the Mozarts, seasoned to the world's admiration, were perhaps hardest of all to inure to discipline.

At any rate, Leopold was not happy about letting his son vegetate at Salzburg. He had his eye on Vienna once again. The empress would remember the share Wolfgang had taken in her son's marriage feasts, and it was as well to take advantage of the situation before she forgot. Leave was sought to go to the capital. Apparently it was granted only because Hieronymus himself was going to be absent, if one may judge from the fact that it was extended when his lordship decided not to return as early as he had originally planned.

No appointment at court was to be had. Maria Theresa was very gracious, but if Leopold did venture to throw out hints, she was too well bred to take them. The emperor was in Poland and does not seem to have received them at all on his return in September. Gassmann, who was musical director to the court, was seriously ill,[1] and rumour had it that Leopold was hanging about to snap up the post for Wolfgang. He denies the charge in one of his letters with an indignation that might look a little suspicious, if one did not reflect that, for all his adulation, he was surely too level-headed to imagine for a moment that such an appointment could come the way of a lad of seventeen, however gifted—and though he was his own son. But that he was hoping for some sort of an opening cannot be questioned. Friends, including the Mesmer and Martinez families, were visited and doubtless carefully sounded by the astute father. Bonno, the court composer, and Noverre, the French ballet master, were also approached. Wolfgang was not allowed to be idle. He composed the Serenade in D major (K. 185) for the Andretter family, as well as six string Quartets (K. 168–73), during the sojourn in Vienna.

It was all in vain, and early in October they were home again. For more than a year nothing happened to raise their hopes, though a few things to keep the interest of posterity. Towards the end of 1773 Wolfgang wrote his first string Quintet, in B flat major (K. 174),[2] which shows his growing interest in the viola as an independent instrument; the piano Concerto in D major (K. 175); three Symphonies (K. 182–4), including a significant work in G minor; and five Divertimenti (K. 166, 186–8, 205).

During 1774 came the bassoon Concerto (K. 191), dated 4th June; a *Missa brevis* in F major (K. 192) and another in D major (K. 194); four more Symphonies (K. 199–202) and a Serenade (K. 203). What he was chiefly busy with, however, was a new comic opera, *La finta giardiniera* (*The Pretended*

[1] He died on 22nd January 1774.

[2] The Quintet in the same key appearing as No. 46 in the earlier editions of Köchel's catalogue is an arrangement of the later Serenade (K. 361).

Garden-Girl) (K. 196). It was commissioned by Munich for the carnival of 1775, and as the Elector of Bavaria, Maximilian Joseph, himself desired that Mozart should compose it and be present at its performance, the archbishop could not very well refuse to give him leave again so soon, much as he must have wished to do so. Like many patrons, he seems to have disliked the idea that an artist employed by him, and not striking him as a person of much importance, should reap glory elsewhere.

The librettist of *La finta giardiniera* is not known. Raniero da Calzabigi has been suggested—suspected would be the better word—but it is not very likely that the poet who wrote *Orfeo, Alceste* and *Paride ed Elena* for Gluck could have been responsible for a farrago that surpasses even the average Italian *opera buffa* libretto of the eighteenth century in absurdity, with its noble heroine disguised as a gardening wench, most of the other personages pretending very unconvincingly that they are somebody else, and the hero and heroine becoming raving lunatics in the last act, only to recover their sanity when it is time for all to end well. If Calzabigi did concoct this book, one can only suppose either that Gluck exercised an irresistible influence on him or that he lent himself to a piece of deliberate and shameless pot-boiling for the Munich carnival.

Leopold and Wolfgang left for the Bavarian capital on 6th December. The excessively cold journey in a draughty coach no doubt accounted for the boy's developing one of his violent toothaches soon afterwards, which obliged him to stay indoors for a few days. As the production of *La finta giardiniera* was fixed for 29th December, much of the music must on this occasion have been ready before the composer got into touch with the singers. However, it was twice postponed and took place on 13th January 1775. The performance, for which Nannerl had followed her father and brother, was a brilliant success. The theatre was packed to bursting, as Wolfgang wrote to his mother the next day, and there was a 'frightful din of clapping and cries of *viva maestro* after each aria.' Soon after the first performance the Mozarts' lord and master visited the elector, but left again before the opera was repeated. According to Leopold's probably not unbiased report he had only a shake of the head and a shrug of the shoulder for the congratulations he received from the whole of the Bavarian court on having such a genius in his service. The second performance was given on 3rd February in the presence of the elector palatine, who had come from Mannheim, and the third not until 3rd March, for Munich was a comparatively small town and the repertory had to be constantly varied to secure a full theatre each night.

Between the performances of the opera Munich heard some of Wolfgang's church music on Sundays: the B flat major Litany was given with another of Leopold's composition, and the two short Masses were also done. These works so delighted Maximilian Joseph that shortly before the family's departure he commissioned an offertory from Wolfgang, who produced the 'Misericordias Domini' (K. 222). He also wrote six clavier Sonatas (K. 279–84) for a musical nobleman, Thaddeus von Dürnitz, though all of them may not have been finished during the stay in Munich. At any rate he did not receive his honorarium then—or in fact at any time.

There is no doubt that Wolfgang would have liked, failing an appointment in Vienna, to attach himself to the Bavarian court, and if Leopold was anxious to dismiss rumours to that effect as washerwomen's gossip, it was merely because he was prudent enough not to spoil his son's chances at home before he was sure of others abroad. He was wise, for nothing happened to indicate that the elector entertained any idea of engaging Wolfgang, who was not even asked to write another opera for the next carnival. Thus servitude in Salzburg had to be endured and the best made of it.

That best was assiduous composition. First of all he was ordered to turn out another opera for his own patron, a dramatic festival play entitled *Il Rè pastore* (K. 208) and intended to celebrate the visit of the Archduke Maximilian to the Salzburg court on 23rd April. A libretto of Metastasio's was once more dragged from the shelves for the purpose. Next he wrote five of his violin Concertos (K. 207, 211, 216, 218, 219), the earliest music of his which has maintained itself permanently in the world's concert repertory.

The year 1776 was outwardly uneventful, but may have seen some unhappy development of that mysterious emotional crisis through which Wolfgang, now a young man of twenty, seems to have gone. But even such hints as his letters contained before are now absent, for the good reason that, being kept at home, he had no occasion to write to his sister, but could confide in her on the spot.

Meanwhile he turned out some of that rococo church music which, with its florid, half-secular exuberance, fits so well into the Salzburg ecclesiastical setting. The most important works of the kind were the Offertory, 'Venite, populi,' for double choir, strings and organ (K. 260), and two Masses in C major with full orchestra and organ (K. 257, 262). By this time most of his Sonatas for organ and strings, which are simply ornamental and unusually elaborate voluntaries, had been supplied for the use of a courtly church.

In January he wrote the *Serenata notturna* for double orchestra (K. 239), in February the Concerto for three pianos (K. 242) for the Countess Lodron and her two daughters, with one part much easier than the others throughout for a player (the young ladies were both his pupils) who was evidently less advanced. The Offertory followed in March. Two Divertimenti (K. 247, 251) are dated June and July respectively. But the most memorable event of the year was the marriage of a daughter of Sigmund Haffner, burgomaster of Salzburg, on 22nd July, for which the young master, as a friend of the Haffner family, composed a March (K. 249) and the Serenade in D major (K. 250) which is the first of his purely orchestral works that has remained universally known. In January 1777 he gave the world his first truly characteristic and significant piano Concerto, the splendid work in E flat major (K. 271), with its highly original slow movement where the tricks of the Italian operatic recitative are subtly adapted to an instrumental form.

But the archbishop did not encourage composition, except for the church, for which Mozart again produced several works (K. 273, 275–7) early in 1777. Beyond four Divertimenti (K. 270, 287–9), probably intended for dinner parties at court, the catalogue contains little or nothing that can be assigned to the first eight months or so of that year, during which Mozart remained more or less resignedly at Salzburg. Much of the music of this period is too formal to suggest that it was the outcome of a personal creative urge. A notable exception, however, is the concert aria, 'Ah, lo previdi' (K. 272), written for the soprano Josepha Dušek of Prague when she paid a visit to Salzburg in the summer. But no new symphony had appeared for the last three years; no new opera was even contemplated. His patron grew more and more ungracious and unappreciative, more and more tyrannical in his insistence on regulations. The artist strained at a leash that was becoming intolerable.

At last the Mozarts tried to obtain leave to undertake another tour. Their master refused point-blank. That they should once more go gadding about the world instead of performing their duties was not to be countenanced. Leopold sent a formal petition, whereupon they were both dismissed and told that they might seek their fortune where they liked. However, Leopold was reinstated in the interests of peace and quietness; but he had to stay where he was.

Perhaps Wolfgang was secretly relieved at this turn of events. He was of age now and none too anxious to be taken about in leading-strings by a well-meaning but surely rather oppressively devoted father. What, was he really to see life at last? Or was that too good to be true? It was: he had not reckoned with the fact that if his father could not accompany him, his mother could. And she did. Not the best thing that could happen in Leopold's view, no doubt; but at least the next best. Having bethought him of this solution, he breathed again. Wolferl was a good boy, but too volatile, too ready to trust people who gave him fair words, and—who knew?—far too ready to lose his head or even his heart. His mother might be inclined to let herself be twisted round his little finger; still, she could keep an eye on him. So Leopold resigned himself to staying at home, to be looked after by his daughter, whom indeed he would need, for he was fifty-eight now. And Anna Maria, only a year younger than he, bravely resolved to be dragged across the high roads of Europe, which were dusty when they were not muddy, heaven knew how far from two of the three people for whom she was accustomed to do everything. She must have gone with a heavy heart, lightened only by the thought that the most important one, the one for whom the greatest sacrifices must be made, would be there to keep her company—and he could be good company. With mixed feelings mother and son left on 23rd September 1777, bound for Munich first of all.

CHAPTER VII

FROM MUNICH TO MANNHEIM

IN the Bavarian capital another effort was made to secure Wolfgang some sort of an appointment. Various people were visited and friends made. Invitations to dinner came from many houses. Anna Maria declared that she would not be sorry to live in Munich, but would like to divide herself not to miss Salzburg and the two she had left behind, for whom she was full of care. In her letters home, which are more illiterate than those of the rest of the family and quite as coarse as Wolfgang's on occasion, she especially recommends Leopold to look after his health, not to let a single grey hair grow through worry, while Nannerl is to look after him, the dog Bimperl, the pet birds and what not. After a momentary complaint about her own discomforts, she eagerly sends greetings to all and sundry:

I swet so that the Watter runns down over my Face from shere Pains with Packing, may the deuce take travell, I feel as tho I would push my Feet in my mouth with Weeriness. i hope you and nanerl may find yourselfs well. I send my hartiest *Compliment* to my dear Sallerl and *Monsieur* Bullinger, to nanerl I send a message, not to give bimperl too much to eat, so that he may not grow too fatt, to thresel my greetings, *adio* I Kiss you both a *Milion* times Maria Anna Mozart. Minichen, 11th evening around 8 oclock 1777.[1]

---

[1] I try to reproduce Anna Maria's erratic spelling. A specimen in the original, written from Augsburg on 14th October, follows for comparison:

'Wir sind den 11ten Mitags um 12 Uhr von Münichen [*sic,* this time] abgereist, und abdns um 9 Uhr glicklich in augspurg

Among all the nobility Wolfgang met in Munich he hoped to find ten persons who would each offer him a ducat monthly to keep him in the town; but, as Leopold wisely pointed out, it was difficult to see where all these charming people would come from and what sort of an arrangement they would make between them to share his son's services. The devil's own work, he thought it would be. If it can be done at once, accept it—that was his advice; if not, waste no time and money, but go and try one of the German courts where it is no longer so much the fashion to keep Italian musicians—Mannheim, Trier, Mainz, Würzburg.

Early in October the Bavarian court went off hunting, so that not even a temporary occupation was to be expected there, and nothing came of the fair promises of the nobles. Wolfgang and his mother left on 11th October, having a few days earlier heard, with much enjoyment, a German version of Piccinni's *La pescatrice.* A good translation, Wolfgang writes, but they have no original German pieces as yet and want him to compose a serious opera to a German libretto. But no such book is to hand, though he has 'an inexpressible desire to write an opera once again.'

At Augsburg, Leopold's birthplace, they visited the relatives, but again stayed at an inn. The family of Wolfgang's uncle, Franz Aloys Mozart, gave them a hearty welcome, and he was soon on terms of an unembarrassed, childishly silly friendship with his young cousin, Maria Anna Thekla, a pretty, merry chit of a girl with whom he diverted himself

angelanget, und haven also diese Reise in 9 stunden mit einem Rosslehner gemacht, welcher noch darzue eine stunde gefuethert hat. . . .

'Und von mir auch alles erdenckliches an alle guette freinde und freindinen.'

She is always, friendly soul, sending 'all that is thinkable' (wrongly constructed) to everybody she has the least interest in, even the servant-girl. Bimperl (a bitch, but always called 'he') is rarely forgotten by any of the family.

affectionately but quite unsentimentally. The goings-on between them seem to have been nothing more than a combination of youthfully idiotic repartee, frank flirtation and rough horseplay.

No doubt Wolfgang was much bored by being dragged about to see people who had known his father and were therefore supposed to be interested in him, but for whom he, of course, could kindle no spark of interest. After a visit to some pompous city magnate or other which his father had wished him to pay he writes home an amusing description of the stiff reception he was given and of how his uncle was kept waiting in the anteroom like a lackey while he was made to play the clavier. Furious at first, he decided to become more and more polite in the exact measure that his host and family let condescension thaw into courtesy; for 'thus one fares best,' he wisely remarks.

He was accustoming himself to the ways of the world. His letters show that he had by this time fully developed a talent for sizing up and describing people. He had been to see the pianoforte maker Johann Andreas Stein, and after examining his instruments and sending his father an account full of intelligent appreciation, he gives a brief sketch of another visit of which a passage is worth reproducing for the penetrating and vivid observation it discloses. Intending to give Stein a surprise, he had presented himself incognito; but he betrayed himself by his playing, and the manufacturer was delighted beyond measure.

Oh, he cried, and embraced me. He crossed himself, made faces, and in brief was very well contented. . . . Afterwards he took me to a coffee-house, where, as I entered, I thought I must fall back again, for stench and smoke of tobacco. But with God's help I had to endure it for an hour and did not show any displeasure, for all that I could not help believing myself in Turkey. He then made a great to-do of a certain Graf, *Compositeur* (but of nothing but flute concertos). He said, that is something very particular, and whatever exaggerations he could think of. My head, hands and whole body perspired with dread. This Graf . . . is a fine nobleman indeed. He wore a dressing-gown in which I should be ashamed to be seen in the street. He sets all his words on stilts, and will open his mouth sooner than he but knows what he wishes to say;—sometimes it shuts again without having had anything to do. After many compliments he produced a concerto for two flutes. . . . It does not fall well on the ear, not naturally. . . . There is not the least sorcery about it. When it was over, I praised him a good deal; for he deserves it. The poor man must have taken enough pains and studied enough. At last they brought a clavichord out of the closet (by Herr Stein, his work), quite good, but full of muck and dust. Herr Graf, who is musical director here, stood there as though he were especially adept at journeying through the realm of sound, and now found that one may be more especial still without hurting the ear, in a word, they were all in an astonishment.

As for Stein, much as Wolfgang admired his instruments for their power of sustaining and damping, he was both amused and perturbed by the daughter Maria Anna (Nanette),[1] with whom her father was absurdly infatuated. True, she was only eight years of age and had already done wonders at the keyboard; but Wolfgang saw shrewdly how she was being spoiled:

Whoever sees and hears her play and is not compelled to laugh, must be a stone [Stein], like her father. She is seated right up towards the treble, anything rather than in the middle, bless you, so that there should be plenty of opportunity to antic about and make grimaces.

He played the organ in one of the churches and at the monasteries of St. Ulrich and the Holy Cross. At the latter he performed one of his amazing feats, improvising a fugue on a theme given to him, using it both forwards and backwards,

[1] Later the wife of the pianoforte maker Andreas Streicher in Vienna and an excellent friend of Beethoven's, who often sought her help in all sorts of domestic difficulties, from the treatment of servants to the use of emetics.

and combining it extempore with another invented by him on the spur of the moment; all of which he reports to his father and sister with that naïve pleasure in his gifts that is a maximum of conceit with a minimum of offensiveness.

At a small concert given by members of the evangelical denomination he played a sonata and took a violin part in one of his symphonies, which earned him the comment of the ever-watchful Leopold that he would not himself have been dragged to this 'beggarly academy.'

A public 'academy' given on 22nd October had a fair success, though Wolfgang thought the Augsburg orchestra deplorable. A symphony of his was in the programme, together with the Concerto for three pianos and the dear little B flat major Concerto (K. 238). He also extemporized a fugue and a sonata—nothing less—and the audience was beside itself. Stein again gave way to the family failing of making faces and grimaces, Demmler, the organist, not only laughed constantly, as was his habit when anything delighted him, but had to resort to a stronger demonstration of cursing and swearing, while Count Wolfegg, the chief promoter of the concert, ran up and down the room declaring that he had never heard the like in all his life.

Augsburg was left on 26th October, and Wolfgang, who had thought little of the musicians there and less of the rather niggardly grandees, would not have been sorry had it not been for the parting with his cousin—the jolly *Bäsle*—with whom he had evidently enjoyed a great deal of innocent but by no means squeamish fun, as his subsequent letters to her show. There is a frank schoolboy smuttiness about them that used to be anxiously suppressed by the hero-worshipping biographers of the nineteenth century with a dishonest prudery that is on the whole far unhealthier than their Rabelaisian dirt, which is almost wholly free from pruriency. It is merely the relic of a time that had no sanitation, either technically or metaphorically. A time, however, that was artistically more fastidious than our own.

At Hohenaltheim a few days were spent in order to find out whether Prince Kraft Ernst von Oettingen-Wallerstein, who had a country residence there, and where Mozart met the musical director, Antonio Rosetti, and the pianist Ignaz von Beecké, both of whom were well-known composers, had any sort of employment to offer. But nothing happened, his highness not being in the mood for music, and so Mannheim was reached on 30th October 1777.

The Elector Palatine Carl Theodor, before whom the Mozarts had appeared at Schwetzingen in 1763, was a typical German ruler of the eighteenth century—he was as French as possible. French culture had been his chief study at the universities of Leyden and Liége, and he was in correspondence with Voltaire. If his court did not quite succeed in equalling the magnificence of Versailles, it aped its profligacy with a fair amount of success, in a somewhat coarsened imitation. But while there was a good deal of corruption, there was also an enlightened state of artistic cultivation, sustained by a library, various art and scientific collections, a court theatre and above all a singularly fine and unusually complete orchestra. It was here that Mozart, for the first time in Germany, found clarinets permanently established.

For a few years past some efforts had been made to do justice to German art. The French actors had been disbanded in 1770, and five years later the elector became leader of a society for the promotion of the German language and its literature. Klopstock had shown some interest in the movement and both Lessing and Wieland had been asked to join it, though without success. An approach towards German opera was made by translations of French and Italian pieces, and what little original work existed was not discouraged. Thus Wolfgang heard the German opera, *Günther von Schwarzburg,* by old Ignaz Holzbauer, one of the earlier members of the Mannheim school of symphonists which had influenced Haydn, and still holding the post of *Capellmeister.* Anton Schweitzer's *Alceste* was another German work with which he made acquaintance. The libretto was by the great Wieland himself. Mozart, however, did not let this prevent him from regarding this as a poor work, while he much admired Holzbauer's opera, in spite of a bad libretto and its frankly Italianate music. So much, in his young eyes, for Gluck's reforms.

Mozart met Schweitzer early in December, when he came to Mannheim to conduct the production of a second opera written with Wieland, *Rosemunde,* which was frustrated by the death of the Elector Maximilian of Bavaria on the 30th. Wieland himself had also come from Weimar to superintend the performance, and Wolfgang had the satisfaction of meeting the great man. But he was not unduly impressed, to judge by his description of the poet to his father, which is too significant of the future great musical delineator of character not to be quoted:

> He appears to me a little forced in his speech; a rather childish voice, an everlasting ogling through his glasses, a certain learned rudeness, and yet at times a stupid condescension. I am not surprised, however, that he should so comport himself here (even if he does not do so at Weimar or elsewhere), for people here regard him as though he had descended from heaven. They are downright embarrassed before him, they say nothing, they keep quiet, they pay attention to every word he says;—the pity is only that people have often to wait so long, for he has an impediment of the tongue, which causes him to speak very softly and not to be able to say six words without stopping short. Apart from all this he has, as we all know, an excellent mind. The face is heartily ugly, full of pock-marks, and with a somewhat long nose; the stature, I should say, approximately, a little taller than Papa.

Wieland, on the other hand, declared it to have been his true good fortune to have met Wolfgang. Most of the musicians in Mannheim, with the exception of the Abbé Vogler, a sort of eighteenth-century Liszt, and Winter, who were jealous of his superior talent, seem to have felt the same. Holzbauer was delighted with him, and both he and his mother were made welcome by the family of Christian Cannabich, another of the Mannheim symphonists, who was twenty years younger than Holzbauer and acted as conductor under him. With Cannabich's daughter Rosa, an engaging girl of thirteen, the young composer formed one of his quick, confident, easy-going friendships. He was fond enough of her in a playful way, and sufficiently impressed with her gifts as a keyboard player to give her the benefit of his views of musical taste and to include in one of his clavier sonatas (C major, K. 309) a slow movement which he declared to be an exact portrait of her—the only instrumental character-picture of his of which we know.

An excellent friend, too, was the ageing tenor Anton Raaff, who, after a great career in Germany, Austria, Italy and Portugal, was allowed, for the sake of his uncommon art and taste, to exhibit the remaining shreds of a glorious voice and the awkwardnesses of his rudimentary acting on the stage of Carl Theodor's fine new court opera-house. Mozart criticized him mercilessly to his father, but respected and liked him as a man of honour and a sincere friend.

The flute player Johann Baptist Wendling[1] he began by liking even more, perhaps for the very reason that he respected him less, for he was humanly—according to Leopold all-too-humanly—indulgent to people who amused him and were kind to him. And the Wendlings made him and his mother comfortable with a Bohemian heartiness. They interested the artist in him, too. The head of the family was a distinguished member of what was one of the finest orchestras in Europe, his wife, Dorothea,[2] one of the best singers at the opera, and

[1] Mozart scored the accompaniment to a flute concerto by Wendling. He also made an oboe arrangement for Friedrich Ramm, probably of the flute Concerto (K. 314).

[2] An aria from Metastasio's *Didone,* 'Ah! non lasciarmi,' was sketched for her. It was completed (K. 486A) in 1786. For her sister-in-law, Elisabeth Wendling, Mozart wrote two French songs, 'Oiseaux, si tous les ans' and 'Dans un bois solitaire' (K. 307–8).

the daughter, Auguste, played the pianoforte 'right prettily.' The fact that she had been one of the elector's numerous mistresses did not at first weigh greatly with the Mozarts, partly because the family were all so kind and partly because the girl was now discarded by his serenity and seriously ailing. Later on, however, Anna Maria became anxious about the influence the frankly irreligious Wendling might exercise upon her precious and, as she felt, easily led son, particularly if he and the oboist Ramm, rather a loose fish, should act as his companions on the way to Paris. This plan was abandoned, and as there was no question that the mother should herself undertake this arduous journey in the depths of winter, it was decided to remain in Mannheim until the spring and pick up a living by some means or other.

Some small opportunities in the way of lessons presented themselves. The court councillor Serrarius offered to take mother and son into his house against lessons given by the latter to his daughter, and Anna Maria received her midday meal at the house of Christian Danner, whose son was taught composition by Wolfgang, who himself ate at the Wendlings'. A Dutchman named De Jean or Dechamps, who played the flute, also had lessons of some sort, and it is probably for him that the two Concertos and Andante for flute and orchestra (K. 313–15) and the Quartets for flute and strings (K. 285 and 298) were written, although it is possible that some of them at least were commissioned a little later by the Duc de Guines in Paris.

A concert was given at court and a more important engagement came Wolfgang's way in January 1778. He had by that time been introduced by Cannabich to Fridolin Weber, a minor singer, copyist and prompter at the opera, who tried to support a large family on a pittance. The two eldest daughters, Josefa and Aloysia, were sopranos of uncommon gifts, though the elder, who was nineteen, seems to have attracted Wolfgang's attention mainly as a good cook. But with the younger, who was barely sixteen, he was smitten at once, and if his reports to Leopold were true, she was indeed a remarkable singer already. Of the third daughter, Constanze, a sloe-eyed, sharp-nosed girl of not much over fourteen, he appears to have taken no notice at all. She is mentioned with two other children only in passing.

Aloysia could not only sustain her tone beautifully and produce the loveliest *legato,* but was capable of executing with ease the most difficult passages Wolfgang had written for Amicis. He now composed for her the aria 'Non so dònde viene' from Metastasio's *Olimpiade* (K. 249). As a singer she proved to be his ideal. As a person too, it seemed to him. At any rate he had plainly fallen in love with her before long. True, he never says so even in his most enthusiastic letters to Leopold, nor does his mother in her most anxious ones. In fact he explicitly states that he would not think of taking a wife before he was sure to be able to support her, though he had no intention of ever marrying for money. But he so commiserated with the Weber family for their poverty and so eagerly insisted on their honesty that the worldly-wise Leopold rapidly fell from suspicion into panic.

It came about in this way: the Princess of Weilburg, who had been so delighted with the Mozart children in Holland a dozen years ago, desired to see and hear Wolfgang again at Kirchheim, and he went there accompanied by Weber and Aloysia, who was to sing his music. They were away a week or so, and on his return the impressionable young man was wholly captivated by the talented minx. He made extravagant plans to help the Webers and with hot-headed generosity declared himself ready to sacrifice his own prospects in order to accompany them to Italy, where he felt sure that Aloysia would make her fortune at once, with her gifts supported by his own fame, which he believed would last for ever in that fickle country.

Leopold was aghast. He sent thunderbolt after thunderbolt from Salzburg, each more cunningly turned than the last. He reproached both his wife and his son with having been disingenuous. He, kept helpless at home, had been left without news of their appallingly frivolous intentions. Had he deserved this? Had he not always earned their confidence by thinking only of his son's good? He could understand errors; he could forgive them; but why was he not told, so that in his fatherly wisdom he could give advice? He told them how Nannerl had wept, how he himself could not sleep, how ill all this had made him, how he could scarcely hold his pen. He had had no new clothes made for himself for ages, and he and his daughter lived in the most frugal fashion in order that their son and brother might make his way in the world. And to what end, forsooth? That he should throw himself away on a pack of starvelings, utter strangers and, he doubted not, shiftless and inferior people who fully deserved their misfortune. It was too much! Never, never would he consent! Wolfgang must leave Mannheim, where clearly nothing was to be gained from the elector in any case. Off with him at once, to Paris!

Wolfgang, to judge from the dignified tone of his replies, felt these exaggerations to be slightly ridiculous. But he knew his father and capitulated, too sensible not to perceive that in the main the old man was right, though he might have refrained from bringing into play every argument calculated to reduce an affectionate and dutiful son to agonies of compunction. Mannheim, where indeed no adequate appointment had materialized, was quitted, though not without a firm determination and a promise to Aloysia to return as soon as the expected fortune had been made in France. On 14th March 1778, accompanied after all by his mother, who had been given a fright sufficient to dissuade her from following her inclination to return to her dear ones at Salzburg, off he did go to Paris.

CHAPTER VIII

TRIALS AND TRAGEDY IN PARIS

The journey to Paris lasted nine days. 'We thought that we could not endure it,' the love-sick Wolfgang wrote home. 'I have not been so *ennui*ed all my born days.' It was to be worse than that before long, though. To compete with all the musicians in the French capital as a grown-up artist from whom much was expected was a very different thing from the conquests he had made as an infant prodigy who had easily become the talk of the town. Now something else absorbed the Parisians' artistic interest and love of sensation. The feud between the partisans of Gluck and the adherents of Piccinni was at its height, the former standing for progress, naturalness and the sacrifice of convention to truth, the latter for tradition, artifice and a different law for music from that which obtained for life. Both parties were right in a measure and both, with true French logic, had determined to ignore the opposite view for the sake of keeping a strictly delimited argument flawless. There was not much hope for a musician who was wholly disinclined to take sides.

Young Mozart, very well aware of having something of his own to offer, did not intend either to profit from the struggle or to interfere with it. Besides he had been warned by his father to remain independent. Leopold had advised him to avoid composers as much as possible, since he might expect little but jealousy from them, and to keep clear, if he could, even from such men as Gluck, Piccinni and Grétry. 'De la politesse, et pas d'autre chose!' he had written in the language of the country about to be conquered by his son. His old suspicions of Gluck were evidently not allayed, and it was like him to suspect everybody else, probably quite as unfoundedly. His caution is amusing: 'With persons of high rank you may always be quite natural, but with all others act the Englishman,' he characteristically commands.

At the same time Leopold had an unbounded and irrational confidence in Grimm, with whom he got into correspondence, and who, not meaning to put himself out unduly over a young genius whom it might quite possibly do him credit to patronize, did not hesitate to advise a visit to Paris. Neither Leopold nor Wolfgang doubted that this step was well worth taking. The fond father could not see how any one could possibly resist so dazzling a talent; his son's self-confidence was heightened by the flattery which Mannheim had just offered him in a variety of forms.

But he now plunged into a Paris agitated by what was in the main merely an excuse to revive the old *guerre des bouffons* of a quarter of a century ago. Over an artistic-nationalist question once again the intellectuals of the whole city engaged in an acrimonious and therefore enjoyable warfare of pamphlets, epigrams and high words, poison-spattering pens being now and again exchanged for more deadly weapons. It was all very engrossing, and nobody had much time, in the midst of all these musical controversies, for music itself. Unfortunately for Mozart, music was all he had to offer.

Music without literary trimmings and a spice of scandal was not very acceptable. He went from pillar to post in order to make and renew acquaintances among the nobility and gentry, quite unprofitably. Marie Antoinette, now Queen of France, could perhaps not be expected to remember the offer of marriage he had once made her as an infant at Schönbrunn; but it was disheartening to find that not so much as a letter of recommendation to her was to be obtained from Vienna. Of his visits to the great houses Mozart was soon tired, and he had but discouraged words to give his father in reply to an exhortation to make himself known there:

On foot it is too far everywhere—or too muddy, for the filth in Paris is not to be described. To go about in a carriage, one has the honour of riding away 4 or 5 livres daily, and in vain. For people will make fine compliments, and that is all. They appoint me for such and such a day; I play, and then it is: O *c'est un prodige, c'est inconcevable, c'est étonnant,* and with that good-bye.

At the house of the Duc de Chabot he underwent a series of humiliations. The duchess first let him wait a long time in an icy room, then asked him to play with numbed fingers on a miserable instrument, and, when he did so, sat down with a company of gentlemen and began to exercise herself in drawing without listening to a note of his music. For the sake of Grimm, whose letters procured him such doubtful advantages, he endured as much as he could; but before long he gave up visiting, with the result that he failed to secure as many pupils as he needed to make a living.

In one noble house, however, he was well received. It was that of the Duc de Guines, who had been French ambassador in London and was an enthusiastic lover of music. Wolfgang himself says that he played the flute incomparably, an instrument the young composer disliked only less than the harp, on which the duke's daughter happened to be proficient. It is perhaps for this reason—to kill two birds with one stone—that he wrote them a double Concerto (K. 299) for the two instruments in combination, and not a separate work for each, as his mother erroneously said in a letter. He was also engaged to give the young lady, who had an astonishing musical memory and knew two hundred pieces by heart, lessons in composition at a very handsome salary. Technically she proved quite an intelligent pupil; the only drawback was that she was incapable of producing any ideas of her own. Concerning which, duly reported to Leopold, the latter observed:

You have given the duke's Mad^elle^ her fourth lesson, and you ask that she should already set down her own ideas—do you think everybody has your genius?—It will come! She has a good memory. *Eh bien!* Let her steal—or politely put, adapt; that will do to begin with, until courage comes.

Before long this 'heartily stupid and heartily lazy' pupil was engaged to be married, which put an end to these burdensome lessons. An end also to an income that proved less brilliant than it had promised, the duke doing his best to fob off the indignant Wolfgang with a mere three *louis d'or.*

Mozart followed his father's injunction to see other composers as little as possible. There was no danger of his meeting Gluck, who was in Vienna, and Grétry he seems to have successfuly avoided. Piccinni he came across where he could not help doing so, at the *Concert spirituel,* where

he is perfectly polite to me, and I to him, if we meet thus by accident; apart from that I make no acquaintance, either with him or with other composers—I know my business—and they too—and that is enough.

The only other eminent figure of whom we hear is Gossec; but he was apparently quite safe—'my very good friend and a very dry man.' With the Mannheim musicians, especially Raaff, Wendling and Ramm, no diplomatic caution was, of course, required, and the moral scruples concerning the last two were forgotten by the indulgent Wolfgang now that the practical objections to his travelling to Paris with them no longer counted. As for honest Raaff, he won the youth's heart more than ever by an old-mannishly sentimental sympathy with his love for Aloysia.

The Mozarts lived at first in the house of some German acquaintances, but moved afterwards to the Rue du Gros Chenet off the Rue de Cléry, thus described by Anna Maria:

Look but first of all for the *Rue Monmartter,* and then for the *Rue Clery* in this *Rue Clery* it is the first street on the left hand, going in from the *Rue Monmarter,* it is a handsome street, and mostly inhabitted by Gentlefolk, very Clean, not too far from the *pulvar* [boulevard], with a healthy air, the people in the house good and honest not grasping the which is rare in Paris.

This occurs in a letter dated 12th June. Both she and Wolfgang are well, God be thanked, though she has been

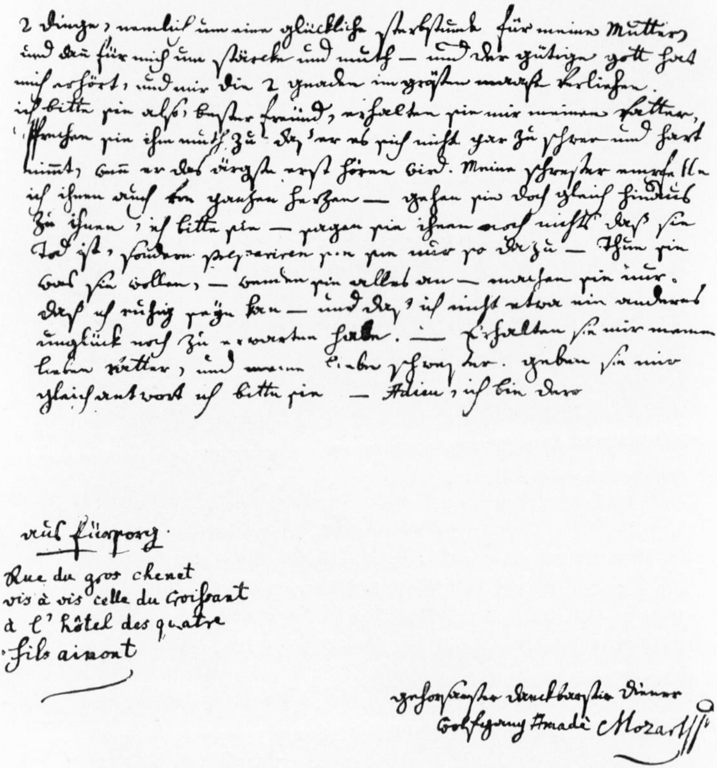

2 dinge, nemlich um eine glückliche sterbstunde für meine Mutter, und dan für mich um stärcke und muth – und der gütige gott hat mich erhört, und mir die 2 gnaden im grösten maaße verliehen. ich bitte sie also, bester freünd, erhalten sie mir meinen vatter, sprechen sie ihm muth zu, daß er es sich nicht gar zu schwer und hart nimmt, wenn er das ärgste erst hören wird. Meine schwester empfehle ich ihnen auch von ganzen herzen – gehen sie doch gleich hinaus zu ihnen, ich bitte sie – sagen sie ihnen noch nichts daß sie tod ist, sondern präpariren sie sie nur so dazu – thun sie was sie wollen, – wenden sie alles an – machen sie nur, daß ich ruhig seyn kan – und daß ich nicht etwa ein anderes unglück noch zu erwarten habe. – Erhalten sie mir meinen lieben vatter, und meine liebe schwester. geben sie mir gleich antwort ich bitte sie – Adieu, ich bin dero

Rue du gros chenet
vis à vis celle du Croissant
à l'hôtel des quatre
fils aimont

gehorsamster dankbarster diener
Wolfgang Amadè Mozart

LETTER WRITTEN ON THE DEATH OF HIS MOTHER

bled the day before. They have the loveliest summer weather, and she has been taken by a friend to the Luxembourg garden and picture gallery. Indeed there is much to wonder at, she says in conclusion.

We speak allmost daily of our Salzburg friends and wish them with us, many would Gape with eyes and mouth to see what is to be seen here. adio keep well both I Kiss you many 1000 times and remain your faithfull wife Mozartin i must close for my arm, and my eyes ake.

Poor Anna Maria. This gave them but the gentlest premonition of the shock to come. In less than a month she was dead. Having been unwell for three weeks in May, she improved, but became more seriously ill very soon after that last letter she wrote home. For a fortnight Wolfgang nursed her with such help as he could obtain from a musician named Heina and the people in the house. The doctor sent by Grimm was helpless, perhaps incompetent: he could not save her. What she died of nobody knows. Wolfgang himself had no idea. It was as though it had to be, he says, unable to explain it otherwise.

With great presence of mind, considering the shock he received in a strange place, whence his Mannheim friends had already departed and where he had no intimates, he wrote the same night (3rd July) to his father and sister, telling them that his mother was gravely ill, and in another letter, to the family's friend Bullinger, he disclosed the true facts, asking him to go and prepare Leopold and Nannerl gently for the worst. Only by the next post did he write full details of what he most pathetically describes as a happy end—so far from home.

The tactful way in which he handled this distressing situation does him the greatest credit. It is true that one has a slightly uncomfortable feeling, reading his letters of this period, indeed the very letter of the fatal day, that he came through this ordeal rather too buoyantly. But apart from the fact that he must have wished to make his position appear as little alarming as possible, some allowance must be made for the natural resilience of youth and the comparative callousness to all other emotions of one who is in love. Most of all is it necessary to remember that here was a great artist growing to full maturity, an artist whose whole life contains no hint that any personal feeling ever quite penetrated through an all-absorbing passion for the creations of his fancy. In his biography his wife plays a purely domestic part, his children are mere shadows, and even his feeling for Aloysia, if we detach the known facts strictly from the sentimental embroideries of nearly all those who have ever written about Mozart's life, begins to look curiously insignificant. He did not *love* her; he was merely *in love* with her.

To revert to the earlier Paris days, Mozart must have heard a good deal of opera, including Piccinni's *Roland* and one or two works by Gluck he had not known before. We also know for certain that he was present at a curious entertainment on 27th April 1778, an opera dealing with musical history, *Les Trois Ages de l'Opéra,* by Grétry, in which Lulli, Rameau and Gluck were impersonated on the stage and scenes in the manner of the Italian *opera buffa* occurred. What was given of original work in this last category can hardly have been new to Mozart; on the other hand it is clear from some features in his works for the stage immediately following the Paris visit that he studied the French *opéra comique* then in vogue, by such composers as Duni, Monsigny and Philidor as well as Grétry and some of the minor writers. How many works he actually heard is not known, but the majority of them were published and easily obtainable by one so curious of current fashions and so unafraid of his susceptibility to their influence. That he had opportunities to look at all kinds of music is certain. The ambassador from the palatinate, Count von Sickingen, delighted in asking him to his house and going through a variety of scores with him at the clavier, to be, as Wolfgang says, 'praised, admired, reviewed, reasoned about and criticized.'

He had an introduction to Jean Le Gros, the conductor of the *Concert spirituel,* which venerable institution gave its performances at the Tuileries. Le Gros asked him first of all to add to a *Miserere* by Holzbauer, work which he duly carried out, but of which nothing remains. In the end it was found too long and was not performed in its entirety. He next wrote a *Sinfonia concertante* (K. App. 9) for flute, oboe, horn and bassoon, to be played by Wendling, Ramm, Punto and Ritter. By some intrigue or other the score was mislaid by a well-planned inadvertence instead of being copied, and when the day of performance came much surprise was affected about such an 'oversight'; but whoever had intended to prevent the performance had succeeded only too well, to the fury of the four soloists and the contemptuous, amused vexation of Wolfgang.

The offer to fill the organist's appointment at Versailles next came his way in May, but was turned down by him, on Grimm's advice and against Leopold's, on account of its relative unimportance and the not too generous pay.

His desire to write an opera he had by no means lost, and a renewal of his friendship with Noverre, who had two years before returned to Paris as ballet master to the *Académie Royale de Musique* (the Opéra), and who was an ardent Gluckist, fired him to try his hand at a French work in the style of that master. Two subjects were considered, an *Alexandre et Roxane* and a French version of Metastasio's *Demofoonte,* one act of the former being actually supplied by the librettist early in April. But in spite of Noverre's enthusiasm these enterprises hung fire, partly because Mozart detested the French language as a musical medium as much as he despised French singing, and partly because there was no getting over his temperamental indifference to the artistic ideals of Gluck.

Meanwhile he wrote something for Noverre on a much smaller scale, but something that concerned the ballet master much more immediately: music for the ballet *Les Petits Riens* (K. App. 10), a kind of pantomime given on 11th June after

Piccinni's *Le finte gemelle.* Noverre's name alone was given in the programme, which perhaps accounts for the fact that the piece disappeared from the catalogue of Mozart's works until the score was discovered in 1872 in the library of the Opéra. The first six numbers were not by Mozart, 'nothing but old miserable French airs,' he said. Noverre made the most of his friendship—for himself: Wolfgang received nothing for his music. There is no evidence, however, that he had wished to ask anything.

The most important work written during this sojourn in Paris, whose name it still bears, was the Symphony in D major (K. 297), performed at the *Concert spirituel* on Corpus Christi Day. It had a great success, perhaps because the composer had been careful to begin it with the famous strong and unanimous attack, the *premier coup d'archet,* of which the Parisians made so much ado and about which he is so caustic in his letter of 12th June:

> Whether it will please, I do not know!—and to tell the truth, I care very little; moreover, who will be displeased? I will guarantee that it will please the *few* intelligent French people present; as for the stupid ones—I see no great misfortune in its not pleasing them. —Still, I have hopes that the asses too may see something in it to delight them; for, to be sure, I have not omitted the *premier coup d'archet*!—and that is enough in all conscience. These oxen here make such a to-do about that! What the devil! I can see no difference—they merely begin together—much as they do elsewhere. It makes me laugh.

Le Gros, who had been full of apologies about the incident of the *Sinfonia concertante,* ventured to suggest that the slow movement of the symphony was too long and contained too many modulations. Curiously enough Wolfgang agreed and willingly wrote another middle movement, with which the work was repeated on 15th August. In spite of asses and oxen, in spite even of a lamentable rehearsal that had promised the worst, it had a resounding success both times. Le Gros promptly asked for another symphony, which according to

Mozart was duly supplied; but the only extant work that might answer to its description is an Overture in B flat major (K. App. 8), as it is now called. A plan to write a French oratorio came to nothing. A set of six violin Sonatas (K. 301–6), begun at Mannheim, was finished in Paris, where the piano Sonata in A minor (K. 310) was also composed, not to mention some others[1] of which he writes to his sister on 20th July. An aria, 'Popoli di Tessaglia,' from Calzabigi's libretto for Gluck's *Alceste* (K. 316), also dates from the Paris days, as do in all probability the Little Fantasy (K. 395) and the Variations for pianoforte on 'Lison dormait' (K. 264), 'Ah! vous dirai-je, maman' (K. 265) and 'La belle Françoise' (K. 353). The first of these three songs is from Dezède's comic opera, *Julie,* which Mozart may have heard. He also produced Variations on a March from Grétry's *Les Mariages Samnites* (K. 352) and on the song 'Je suis Lindor' (K. 354) in *Le Barbier de Séville,* the music of which Beaumarchais had himself provided.

After the death of his mother Wolfgang was taken into the house which Grimm shared with his companion, Madame d'Épinay, where he was given a pretty room with an agreeable view and left as contented as circumstances would allow. He was sadly in need of such shelter, and even though he was given food and lodging, he was so hard pressed for money that he had to borrow repeatedly from Grimm.

Paris, in short, was not to be much longer endured. A yearning to see Aloysia again was becoming unbearable. What was to be done? Suddenly the astounding news came from Leopold that another opening at Salzburg, very well worth considering this time, was to be expected. Adlgasser, the organist, had been visited by a stroke at his instrument, to the horror of the congregation, and died. Lolli, the *Capellmeister,* was also dead. The court did not know what to do. Hints were thrown out to Leopold that his son would not be ill received if he applied for the organist's post, and when the

[1] Most probably K. 330–2.

astute father diplomatically suggested that Wolfgang would not look at such a chance unless it promised a much better salary than poor Adlgasser had received, it transpired that the younger Mozart was actually wanted, so much, indeed, that the elder's appointment as *Capellmeister* was made dependent on his acceptance. Wolfgang, in dismay at the prospect of putting himself in the archbishop's power a second time, wrote home enumerating all the disadvantages: a whole catalogue of woes—a small town, no opera, a tyrant for a master, a court full of intrigues and backbiting, a pack of dissolute and uneducated musicians, and so on. Leopold in turn pointed out all the allurements he could think of, from the prospect of being at home near himself and Nannerl to a very fair possibility—which he knew would be the most enticing bait—of an appointment being secured for Aloysia, as the archbishop needed another treble singer next to Michael Haydn's wife (the 'Haydin' they always call her) and the Italian male soprano, Ceccarelli. Leave would be given Wolfgang to go anywhere he liked to produce an opera, he would be paid a thousand florins, and so forth.

It is hard to believe, but he accepted. Leopold had played his trump card well: no son so affectionate and dutiful as Wolfgang could possibly frustrate the advancement of a father who had indeed done much to deserve a return for all his devotion and all his sacrifices. Wolfgang, still remembering the letters he had received at Mannheim, doubtless had visions of new reminders of these benefits, justified enough if not too scrupulously given, and he could not face them a second time. Besides, his father's relenting where Aloysia was concerned must have touched him, and he had no mind to ask for more trouble in that direction. Quite plainly, he was caught.

Paris he prepared to leave without regret. One pleasure awaited him before his departure, however. In August Johann Christian Bach came from London to write a French opera and brought Tenducci with him. With his former master and the famous singer Mozart was invited for a few days to Saint-Germain by Marshal de Noailles. But nothing of any permanence was to be hoped for, and on 26th September 1778 he left Paris, not after all in such a hurry to go as Grimm proved to be to get rid of him at last, in a frame of mind compounded of kindness and self-interest that prompted him not to let the young man sink further into debt. Wolfgang still had to collect some fees, wanted to write six trios, to correct the proofs of the violin sonatas on the spot and to sell some of his finished compositions. But he was packed off by the well-meaning but none too patient friend.

Grimm had induced him to take a slow coach to Strasburg, where, after breaking the tedious journey at Nancy, he did not arrive until the middle of October, the poorer in patience for what he had saved in cash. He gave a private concert to some connoisseurs on the 17th and was lucky enough to make three *louis d'or.* 'The best part of it all,' he says, 'consisted of bravos and bravissimos.' This encouraged him to give a public concert at the theatre; but the Strasburgers disgraced themselves by leaving the place almost empty, which prompted him to write home that, upon his honour, 'nothing is sadder than to see a great T-shaped table set for eighty people, with only three persons eating.' Nevertheless, he shamed the absentees by playing magnificently for the few who had come and giving them more than he had promised. He played on Silbermann's fine organs at two of the churches and, being detained by floods, gave yet another concert, which brought him in a whole *louis d'or.*

He at last continued his journey by way of Mannheim, an unnecessary deviation which greatly agitated Leopold, who feared lest he might after all remain stuck there. Such anxiety was uncalled-for, Carl Theodor having by that time succeeded to Maximilian Joseph as Elector of Bavaria and transferred his court to Munich, including the Weber family and all the other musicians who did not prefer to remain where they were. But there were enough attractions left at Mannheim for Mozart to stay from 6th November until well into December—and, incidentally, to show how musical interests could appease the lover in him. There was some talk of his being appointed conductor of the German opera at the newly established National Theatre. At any rate he let himself be flattered by his Mannheim friends into declaring that the archbishop and the rest of Salzburg might go whistling for him if he were not offered a very handsome salary for submitting once more to slavery. He was much attracted by a form of melodrama, with spoken dialogue accompanied by music, introduced to him by the *Ariadne auf Naxos* and *Medea* of the Bohemian composer Georg Benda, and he went so far as to begin the composition of a *Semiramis* after this fashion, though he also contemplated a new opera, *Cora.*

All this drove Leopold frantic. He had clearly committed Wolfgang to Salzburg by this time; he was in debt and did not know how to clear himself unless both he and his son earned good money. In his exasperation he no longer argued: he commanded peremptorily, tempering his categorical orders with mere vague promises of another Italian tour and of looking with an indulgent eye upon Aloysia, as well he might, so long as she was a convenient decoy. As usual, his son obeyed, though he must have surrendered to 'slavery' in the worst possible frame of mind. He left Mannheim on 9th December, spent some days with the Prelate of the Realm at Kaisersheim, and arrived in Munich on Christmas Day.

He was to see Aloysia again at last, and he had asked the *Bäsle* to come from Augsburg with a mysterious hint at an important part she might be called upon to play. He may have wanted her as bridesmaid, and some biographers have been anxious to make out that she herself hoped to be 'best girl.' The Webers were sought out at once. Aloysia had made great progress and the aria 'Popoli di Tessaglia' was presented to her with a dedication written at the top of the manuscript. No doubt she sang it superbly—and knew she did. Had she not been taken to Munich and offered a salary greatly in excess of her father's? It was clear that her head had been turned, and it is far from impossible that Carl Theodor had begun to take an interest in her that was by no means wholly artistic. Her parents were just the kind of people to turn a blind eye to gallantries that might mean worldly advantage. In any case she had become a person of importance, and she let young Mozart see it. Mozart indeed! She foresaw very different chances. Her reception of him seems to have been not unfriendly, but so detached that he could not help feeling all his illusions crashing about him with a sickening suddenness of enlightenment. They say that he turned to the clavier with a laugh and sang: 'I gladly leave the maid [or whatever the word was] who will not have me,' but that his heart was broken. No doubt he thought it was, which for the moment was just as bad. But if the little tale of his defiant song is not true, the fact that it could ever have been invented is significant enough. Even in such a crisis he could turn to music—to composition in a small way. Judging from impressions which become sharper and sharper the more one studies him, it is impossible to believe that he really loved Aloysia, indeed that he ever unreservedly loved anyone.

CHAPTER IX

THE LAST OF SALZBURG

In the company of his young cousin Wolfgang reached home at last in the middle of January 1779. It may have been as well that they arrived together: the meeting of the bereaved family all alone might have been too poignant for the young artist, who was given to affectionate demonstrativeness, but cannot have been tolerant of unrestrained outbursts, one cannot help judging, if there is anything at all in trying to understand a musician's disposition from his work. To Leopold and Nannerl the full force of their loss can have come home only now that the absence of wife and mother no longer fitted in with the foreseen course of events; Wolfgang, on the other hand, was by this time less acutely conscious of the tragedy, had indeed experienced another since—and almost got over that too, one guesses.

The Mozarts had moved to the other side of the river, into the low, steep-roofed house that is still to be seen on what is now the Dollfussplatz, but was then called Hannibalplatz and later Makartplatz. Here Wolfgang was received with such festivity as roast capons, his favourite dish, could muster to relieve the family's sadness. Thresel, the cook, had done her best, and no doubt they all made as brave cheer as they could, father and son doing their utmost to hide a feeling of disappointment in each other which recent events and the correspondence arising from them cannot have failed to engender. Their affection remained, but they could not wholly trust each other any more. Had not the son indulged in fantastic plans of his own with all too marked an independence? Had not the father lured him back to servitude by means that were surely not quite clean-principled?

Between the archbishop and his new court and cathedral organist there was to be mistrust pure and simple, unmixed with affection, as it began to become clear quite soon. The exalted patron could not forget that this all too independent young man of twenty-three, who had coolly given notice two years before, had had to be invited to rejoin the court almost by a favour, which was not likely to lower his self-conceit. It was not admirable, but it was humanly understandable that, once secured, he should have been treated in as off-hand a manner as possible, and it was no less human that he should feel resentfully that he had been caught in a trap. And as his father had been asked to set the snare, it was not unnatural that the atmosphere at home should be surcharged at times.

Two unsatisfactory and not very fruitful years were now to come. Mozart was fairly prolific, but little of lasting importance appeared. Only two Masses, both in C major (K. 317, 337) were completed during this period, and it is significant that first this *Kyrie* and then that (K. 322–3, 341) was left in the air, though undoubtedly they were intended to form part of masses. The two Symphonies of April and July 1779 (K. 318–19) show no great creative gusto; they are, however, the last before the series of enduring works in that form begins, for the next, the delicious Symphony in C major (K. 338), completed on 29th August 1780, decidedly foreshadows greater things to come, not to mention that the comic figure of Osmin in the next opera but one already peeps out of it.

Two Sonatas for organ, one with stringed instruments (K. 328) and the other with a fuller orchestra (K. 329), were obviously imposed tasks. They are both in C major, apparently the official key during these two years. But we also meet with two works in one of Mozart's most lucky keys —E flat major—in the course of 1779, and these stand out by enduring qualities, particularly the *Sinfonia concertante* for violin, viola and orchestra (K. 364), a beautiful, dark-coloured work in which a passion not at all suited to an archiepiscopal court, and perhaps disclosing active revolt against it, seems to smoulder under a perfectly decorous style and exquisite proportions. The second work in E flat is the Concerto for two pianos (K. 365), Mozart's only composition for this combination and a very endearing if not a positively great one, with an affecting slow movement and a rondo displaying the liveliest resourcefulness. From among a small amount of entertainment music the Serenade in D major (K. 320), another in B flat major (K. 361) and a Divertimento for strings and horns (K. 334) stand out.

One of Mozart's grievances against Salzburg was that it had no opera. He was never happy for long if he had not something to write for the theatre. Apart from the stage at court, the town had a theatre, but no permanent company. Such actors and opera singers as visited it from time to time cannot have been remarkable, though they must have been good enough to fill Mozart with an irresistible longing to set to work on a new opera. All he could get hold of, however, was a German operetta by one Schachtner, on which he set to work at the end of 1779. He did not compose the final number or the overture, however, and what has been preserved of it lacks a title, that of *Zaide* (K. 344) being merely the name of one of the characters, given to the fragment later by the publisher André.[1]

In 1780 the company of Emanuel Schikaneder visited Salzburg with a mixed repertory which, to whatever depths it may have descended, was topped by German translations of Shakespeare.[2] One of the plays was *Thamos, König in Aegypten* by a nobleman, Tobias von Gebler, whom the Mozarts had already met in Vienna in 1773 and from whose drama Wolfgang had then set two choruses to music. Schika-

[1] Dr. Alfred Einstein has discovered the libretto of an operetta, *Das Serail,* with music by Joseph von Friebert, on which *Zaide* is based.

[2] Mozart not only knew a certain amount of Shakespeare, but was quite ready to criticize it as a man of the theatre. 'If in *Hamlet* the ghost's speech were not so long, it would make a better effect,' he wrote to his father on 29th November 1780.

neder now asked him to compose the rest of the incidental music (K. 345), whereupon he revised one of the old choruses, rewrote the other and added whatever was required, including a new chorus that was not in the play at all and the words of which may have been supplied by Schachtner or Schikaneder.

But these stage works fell into insignificance when in the course of 1780 Mozart was asked by the Bavarian court to write a serious Italian opera for the next Munich carnival. However much it may have gone against the grain with the archbishop to let his organist give another court an entertainment such as his own could not produce, he had to keep his promise to let him accept such commissions, nor could he offend the Elector Carl Theodor by a refusal to lend him the young genius whom the humdrum Salzburg service could not succeed in obscuring. He was well remembered by the Munich musicians who had met him at the end of their Mannheim days, and indeed both Dorothea and Elisabeth Wendling as well as Raaff were to be in the cast of the new work.

The choice fell on *Idomeneo, Rè di Creta* (K. 366), and it was very convenient that the Italian version of the old *Idoménée* composed by Campra and produced in Paris in 1712 was entrusted to the Salzburg court chaplain, Giambattista Varesco. As Mozart knew three at least of the Munich singers and at the same time had the librettist under his eyes, he was able to work more comfortably and confidently than he had hitherto been able to do at any opera.

He began his score in October 1780 and early in November went to Munich to study those singers whom he had not known before. Perhaps his friends, too, required some new care by this time, for Raaff, cast for the title part, was now sixty-six, and the Wendling ladies, engaged to sing Ilia and Electra, were no chickens. Two others of the male singers also proved to be of a mellow age. For compensation the male soprano, Vincenzo dal Prato, had never been on a stage before. It is not known how much of the music was ready before Mozart reached Munich, but I am prepared to judge from internal evidence that it must have been most of the first and second acts, with the possible exception of some of the men's arias, and very little of the solo music in the third act, which is noticeably less human, less profound, less true to character; it tends to degenerate into the kind of thing a composer was then expected to turn out for singers described as *virtuosi di camera,* as five out of six of the *Idomeneo* cast were. But composers in the eighteenth century wrote frankly and as a matter of course for the circumstances of the moment, not for posterity—and Mozart had no idea that he was to be a classic. Great artists never had, in fact; they became classics in spite of work done in accordance with the requirements of their time.

The Wendlings were satisfied with their arias, as well they might be, for Ilia sings the most beautifully and gently expressive music in the opera and Electra the most dramatically effective. One of them, indeed, Wolfgang said, was 'arci-contentissima.' None of the singers seems to have made difficulties over the occasional merging of an aria into the next number by a transition that is musically an astonishing device but leaves the singer without a chance of applause, a sign that Mozart was growing sufficiently authoritative an artist to have his way when he wanted it for good reasons of his own. 'Old honest Panzacchi' cannot but have been pleased with his arias for Arbaces, which are as elaborate as violin concertos, and Valesi, the other old stager, who sang the high priest, had a striking part though a short one. The only troublesome people were 'my *molto amato Castrato dal Prato,*' who sang 'like perhaps the best of the urchins who let themselves be heard in order to be admitted to the chapel,' and, curiously enough, friend Raaff, who wanted an aria in place of the quartet in the third act and was persuaded only in the course of the rehearsals of the outstanding beauty of that concerted number. He also protested at first against the omission of a cavatina between the two agitated choruses at the end of the second act, which Mozart thus explained to his father:

> Here it will be better to put a mere recitative, below which the instruments may work with a will—for in this scene, which (thanks to the action and the grouping, lately discussed with *le grand*[1]) will be the finest in the whole opera, there will be such noise and confusion on the stage, that an aria would cut a poor figure in this place—and moreover, there is a thunderstorm—and that will hardly leave off because of an aria by Herr Raaff.

As late as 20th December the amiable but somewhat petulant and spoilt veteran was still recalcitrant:

> Listen, this Raaff is the best, most honest man in the world, but —the good old slovenly ways are so ingrained in him, that one would fain sweat blood over it all.

And some of the tenor's music had to be artfully bolstered up in the orchestra to cheat the hearer into accepting his vocal senilities as so many virtues.

Only a composer with a genius for accommodation as well as for inexhaustible invention could have made a success under such conditions, and the wonder is not that *Idomeneo* should contain a certain amount of lifelessly artificial material, especially in the third act,[2] but that much the greater part of it is so rich both in lyrical beauty and dramatic truth. Meanwhile Leopold warned his son not to forget a popular element that must needs be inserted into an opera if it is to be a success. But Wolfgang, elated by the raptures which the rehearsals produced in his friends, from Cannabich, the conductor, down to the humblest musicians in the orchestra and up to Count Seeau, the intendant, reassured him by the confident assertion that his music would appeal to all just as he chose

[1] Le Grand was the producer.

[2] The duet between Idomeneus and the priest, for instance, the weakest number in the whole opera, sounds as though Mendelssohn had written it in an attempt at reproducing Mozart's style: it is neither good Mozart nor even good Mendelssohn.

to write it, except 'the long-eared ones.' Some people had said that the second act could not possibly turn out to be more novel[1] and expressive than the first, but they found themselves 'pleasurably deceived.' Finally the elector himself expressed his astonishment that 'such great things were tucked away in so small a head.'

The opera was going to be very long. It was therefore decided not to give a separate ballet, but to include a divertissement in the work itself. Thus Mozart had no sooner finished than he was obliged to set to work again to provide the ballet music for *Idomeneo* (K. 367). In spite of the death of Maria Theresa on 29th November and the formal mourning it imposed on the Bavarian court, *Idomeneo* was produced on 29th January 1781, two days after Mozart's twenty-fifth birthday, on which the dress rehearsal had taken place. Leopold and Nannerl had arrived from Salzburg in time to hear this as well as the performance, and they would have come earlier had the father not thought it prudent to wait until the archbishop had left for a visit to Vienna, in case leave of absence should be spitefully refused him. Posterity cannot grudge them the pleasure they must have taken in Wolfgang's first fully matured work for the stage, although it has been deprived of the full account of the production which would doubtless have been found in a letter had Wolfgang had occasion to write home about the event. Such are the vagaries of musical history. We hear all about the catarrh which attacked the composer in Munich and about Leopold's recommendation of the usual family panacea,[2] 'a heaped knife's point of black powder,' but not a word about the first

[1] Muted horns and trumpets were introduced into the opera. Wolfgang asked Leopold to send him the mutes from Salzburg, to be copied in Munich, where they were unknown.

[2] His letter of 4th December 1780 contains pages of the most primitive recipes and amazing quackeries, and after saying 'here you have half an appotheckary's shop,' he refers to himself as *Clarissimus Dominus Doctor Leopoldus Mozartus.*

performance of *Idomeneo* apart from a newspaper notice that mentions the designs by the 'theatre architect,' Lorenzo Quaglio, but not so much as the composer's name.

A few other works were composed during the visit to Munich, including very probably the *Kyrie* in D minor (K. 341) and certainly the Quartet for oboe and strings in F major (K. 370), written for Ramm, who was among those who had migrated from Mannheim to Munich. Before they returned to Salzburg the Mozarts made the most of the carnival, and Wolfgang enjoyed himself riotously, not only because he had been so hard at work on his opera, but also because he thought to himself: 'Where will you be next? At Salzburg! Therefore refresh yourself!'

They had hardly settled in at home when an order came from the archbishop, who was still in Vienna with a retinue of courtiers and musicians, for Wolfgang to present himself there without delay. He left on 12th March, perhaps in a rebellious frame of mind induced in him by this first sign of 'slavery' after the freedom and the triumph he had just enjoyed, but with no notion that between Salzburg and Vienna a choice of his future lay imminent.

He was to be made to smart for enjoying the temporary release Hieronymus had not been able to refuse him. He was debarred from performing at the houses of the nobles by being compelled to lodge with the archbishop as a member of his suite. It was not the fashion to make distinctions in favour of a servant who happened to be in charge of music instead of food or clothing. But though indignities inflicted on their musicians were by no means uncommon among eighteenth-century princes and princelings, they rankled in the spirited young man who had tasted the glories and independence which people of distinction were beginning to accord to genius outside the tradition-ridden courts. Almost at once he wrote a half-amused, half-embittered account to his father:

At 12 o'clock midday—a little too early for me, I regret to say—we go to the table—there eat the 2 MM. body-and-soul chamber-servants, M. the Comptroller, M. Zetti [the chamber purveyor], the pastrycook, 2 MM. cooks, Ceccarelli, Brunetti and—my littleness.—*NB.* The 2 MM. body-servants sit at the head, and I have at least the honour to sit above the cooks. . . . His lordship the archbishop has the goodness to glory in his people—to rob them of their chances to earn money—and not to pay them for it. . . . I shall now only wait to see whether I shall receive nothing; if nothing, I shall go to the archbishop and tell him straight out—if he does not wish me to earn anything, he had better pay me, so that I need not live on my own money.

Leopold took alarm at these signs of a storm and warned him to be careful; but his self-esteem grew more and more sensitive to slights, particularly when he found that great people like Countess Thun and Count Cobenzl were glad to ask him to dinner. He smouldered for a little while, then began to flare into open revolt. Having been ordered to the house of Prince Galitsin, the Russian ambassador, and given the galling command to present himself there to the archbishop's valet punctually at seven o'clock, he carefully arrived late, walked into the prince's presence unattended and addressed him. The Russian nobleman, who was a great lover of music and had heard of and known Mozart long before Colloredo paraded him at his house, took this independent behaviour in anything but bad part, much to the mortification of the archbishop, who promptly retaliated by forbidding Mozart to play at a charity concert for the widows of musicians. It did not improve the situation that the fashionable world at once took exception to such a procedure, whereupon Hieronymus had to yield, and the concert was given with enormous success. Next a concert of Mozart's own was prohibited by the petty tyrant.

So things fermented for a few weeks, and then came the inevitable outbreak. There was a great deal of shilly-shallying about the archbishop's return to his see, and in the meantime the Mozarts, son and father, had a somewhat agitated correspondence, Wolfgang wishing to know Leopold's views about his remaining independently in Vienna and the latter anxiously asking him not to take so rash a step. The obedient son, still quite ready to do as he was told at twenty-five, so long as it was not his employer who did the telling, on 28th April declared that he was prepared to return home. But on 9th May the storm burst. The archbishop, after having called Mozart such names as 'scoundrel,' 'knave' and 'scurvy fellow,' and asking him to give up his quarters without notice, ordered him through his valet to take a parcel back to Salzburg with him on Wednesday. For various reasons, partly a question of money and partly no doubt pure obstinacy, Mozart decided not to leave until the following Saturday, whereupon his serenity poured a torrent of abuse over him which ended only with a pointed suggestion that his services were no longer required. To which the obvious answer was that this was exactly what the young musician wanted. Mozart sat down at once and wrote to his father, telling him what had happened in a frame of mind composed of fury and satisfaction in equal parts. He had no doubts about his future in Vienna; indeed he had already been promised a German opera libretto by the younger Stephanie. His one anxiety was lest the archbishop should avenge himself on his father, in which case, however, he felt sure that they could all live comfortably in the capital, where he was made much of by the grandees. It was all quite simple—or so he eagerly assured himself as well as his father.

Leopold, who had good reason to fear that his son's affront to the archbishop would recoil upon himself, was terrified into imploring him to apologize and humbly ask to be restored to service. With this Wolfgang, quite apart from being fully aware that such an attempt would be fruitless as well as craven, was in no mood to comply. He replied in a persuasive but firmly dignified tone that he had no intention to dishonour himself in this fashion. He handed in a formal resignation to Count Arco, one of the archbishop's courtiers, who calmly refused to consider and forward it, on the ground that the young musician could not act thus without his father's consent. A second petition was ignored altogether. Mozart then proposed to submit a third to Colloredo in person, but could not do so over the head of Arco, with whom at last he came to high words. How far he forgot himself we do not know; but the nobleman was so far provoked as to forget the obligations of his nobility and send Mozart out of the house with a well-aimed kick. Seething with rage, he vowed to return it, though it should be in the open street. In deference to Leopold, who was quaking in his shoes at home, he gave up this rather childish plan of revenge before long. Besides, he was quite sensible enough to know that it was not he who had suffered a loss of dignity. Meanwhile the archbishop was recovering his, if indeed he had ever lost it to quite the extent Wolfgang, in his doubtless exaggerated letters, was anxious to make his father believe. At any rate, rather surprisingly, Leopold was kept on at court. But it had done with Wolfgang, and he with it. Except as a visitor, Salzburg was to know him no more.

CHAPTER X

TWO ELOPEMENTS

ALREADY before the final breach, at the beginning of May 1781, Mozart had been compelled to seek new lodgings on being turned out of the archbishop's quarters. He found them at a house called 'The Eye of God,' and, as fate would have it, with the Weber family he had met at Mannheim, of all people. They had left Munich for Vienna when Aloysia was offered an engagement in the Austrian capital, but soon found themselves in uncomfortably reduced circumstances. The father, Fridolin Weber, was dead. Aloysia had married an actor, Josef Lange, and left her mother's house. Her former lover had lost all his illusions about her, as his letters show:

> This girl hung round her parents' necks before she was able to earn money—no sooner had the time come when she could show herself beholden to her parents—*NB*: (the father died ere she had taken a groat here) than she left her poor mother, flung herself at a comedian, married him—and her mother has not—that much—from her.

Josefa Weber, now the chief breadwinner, was without an engagement and Constanze, who was past her eighteenth birthday, although a gifted vocalist enough, had not reached a professional standard. Maria Cäcilie, the mother, was thus only too glad to find a lodger, particularly a likeable young man whom they already knew and who showed signs of becoming a celebrity. She was a woman of low breeding and low principles, addicted to the bottle and, as it soon turned out, by no means averse from exploiting the attractions of her daughters in a way she no doubt regarded as wholly respectable. Perhaps it was, according to her notions. At any rate it combined expediency with a tender regard for honourable intentions in men where her own girls were concerned.

Mozart, who had already greatly annoyed his father with the resignation of his Salzburg service and had reason to feel that the experienced old man could not be expected to believe his accounts of the interviews with the archbishop and with Count Arco word for word,[1] was very careful not to alarm him further about his settling down with the Webers, which he knew would at once arouse the suspicions of Leopold, who had from the first regarded that family as a set of spongers. Thus, according to Wolfgang, they were all friendly in the extreme, Maria Cäcilie was most kind and obliging, they were intent only on his comfort and—most important of all—Aloysia was safely married and inaccessible. True, he was not so sure of himself there:

> With the Langin I was a fool, that is true, but what are we not when we are in love!—I loved her indeed, and feel, that she is not indifferent to me even yet—and it is fortunate for me, that her husband is a jealous fool, and never lets her go anywhere, and I therefore seldom have a sight of her.

---

[1] As most biographers have unquestioningly believed them, assuming as a matter of course that Mozart, being a great composer, must have been incapable of lying; as though it were not obvious that any son, however upright, who knows that he is going to annoy his father by a very disagreeable announcement, will naturally and half unconsciously paint the situation in such a way that his own faults become minimized and his grievances exaggerated as much as possible. It used once to be axiomatic to clear Mozart of any suspicion of guilt in this occurrence; on the other hand it has become the fashion lately to regard the archbishop's and even Arco's action as perfectly justified according to their lights; but the defenders of neither party to the quarrel seem to have considered the probability that the behaviour of Mozart's enemies was not quite what he represented it to have been.

But Leopold was not to be pacified, and the tone of the correspondence on both sides was one of increasing exasperation. Wolfgang grew more proud, defiant and independent. He was artful, too. In answering a particularly unpleasant letter he pretends that, of course, he has only been dreaming; that a father may have written such a letter, but not *his* father —not the best, most loving of fathers, who is always so concerned about his own honour and that of his children! What, he, Wolfgang, has shown no affection? No readiness to sacrifice anything? What advantages has he in Vienna, where he can do nothing but watch his purse? And so on and so forth. But he is determined: nothing will induce him to return to Salzburg; for the whole town knows that he has given notice, and why, and he is not going to disgrace himself by admitting that he has been in the wrong. He will give his happiness, his health, his life for his father, but not his honour.

By July 1781 musical Vienna had begun to gossip about Mozart's lodging at the Webers', and he thought it prudent to take his father's advice and move elsewhere. But it was difficult to find an excuse, and so long as nothing scandalous occurred these rumours were by no means unwelcome to his landlady, who saw her chance to make capital out of them. As soon as one of her daughters was sufficiently compromised in people's eyes, she would be able to lead her trump card. But which of the daughters?—that was the question.

Mozart had no idea of love-making, let alone marrying, or so he told his father on 25th July:

> I am sorry that I should be forced to do this [move elsewhere] because of stupid gossip, about which there is not a word of truth. I should truly like to know what pleasure certain people can take in talking thus into the blue without all reason.—Because I live with them, I am going to marry the daughter; of being in love there is no question at all; they skip that. But I lodge in the house, and I marry.—If all my life I ever thought of not marrying, it certainly is now! . . . God did not give me my talent to hang it round a woman's neck.

He then goes on to say that he occasionally indulges in a game with 'the *Mademoiselle* who has already been married to me,' but that, if he had to marry every girl with whom he has had some fun, he would easily have two hundred wives by this time. The *Mademoiselle* in question, with whom he protested that he was anything but in love, was Constanze.

Meanwhile he had begun to earn some money by giving lessons, though with little success, as all the wealthy Viennese had left town for their summer residences in the country, and he would not set up a bad precedent by taking pupils cheaply. He also tried his luck with publishing six violin Sonatas by subscription, four of them (K. 376–7, 379–80) newly written, with K. 296 and 378 added to them to complete the half-dozen. What mattered more to him was his German opera, for which Gottlieb Stephanie was supplying the libretto. This Stephanie was the younger of two brothers, an actor and inspector at the Burgtheater, where at the desire of the emperor the *Singspiel* had begun to be cultivated not long ago. This type of German opera or operetta immediately became popular with the production of the first essay, Umlauf's *Die Bergknappen,* in 1778, but the repertory consisted in the main of translations of foreign works, especially French comic operas. The one original work Mozart is sure to have heard in 1781 was *Der Rauchfangkehrer*; but the music was by an Italian—Salieri. He thus had a species to cultivate that was new not to himself alone.

What Stephanie wrote for him was *Die Entführung aus dem Serail* (*The Elopement from the Harem*[1]) (K. 384), a play with a Turkish setting based on a comedy by Christoph Bretzner and not unlike the unfinished *Zaide* in its plot, if one may judge from what has been preserved from that earlier piece. Mozart worked at it with delight. His unflagging interest in this task and his keenness of insight into such weaknesses of the libretto

[1] I propose to call the opera *The Elopement* hereafter, whenever I refer to it in English, although it is more commonly known in English-speaking countries as *The Seraglio* or *Il Serraglio.*

as he deemed it advisable to attend to and into the resources of musical characterization are revealed by the letters to his father in which he went into great detail about the progress of his composition.

Nevertheless, he was unusually long in completing this work, not only because he knew that he had to expend exceptional care on a specimen of a not yet too well established type of opera with which it was important that he should succeed in Vienna, but also because the second half of 1781 was filled with events calculated to distract him with a full measure of delight and vexation. For, having said that he would never consent to fall in love with Constanze Weber, he consented. It was too bad, but it could not be helped. And the calculating mother, who must have foreseen the inevitable very shrewdly, proceeded to lay her plans for the future with great relish. She had married off one daughter unprofitably; she would see to it that the next matrimonial deal should yield something for herself. In her circles one did not rear daughters for the benefit of other people.

Love or no love, however, Mozart would perhaps have proceeded with *The Elopement* quickly enough if it had really had to be ready for production in the autumn, as was at first planned. The first act was in fact written at great speed. But two visits to the court and the festivities they occasioned interfered. The Duke of Württemberg, Carl Eugen, arrived early in November to present his daughter, who had been chosen as consort for the Archduke Franz, and later in the same month came the Grand Duke Paul of Russia and his wife, in whose honour three of Gluck's operas were revived, much to the disappointment of Mozart, who thought that two serious operas would have been enough and felt that one of them might well have been his *Idomeneo*.

Love's path was more than commonly stony. When at last Mozart had found a lodging, it was a place fit only for rats and mice, he said. Then there was Josephine von Aurnhammer, the daughter of a gentleman who repeatedly asked him to his house. He first gave her good advice and finally lessons, and it was for her, and to play with her, that he composed the Sonata for two pianofortes in D major (K. 448). He wrote on 27th June that she was a monster to look at, but played fit to send one into raptures, except that she plucked everything to pieces. She told him, it appears, that

she would study honestly for two or three years, and then go to Paris, to make her *métier* with it.—For she says: 'I am not beautiful; *o contraire,* ugly. A hero from the chancellery with three or four hundred florins I have no mind to marry, and another I shall not get; consequently I prefer to remain as I am, and to live on my talent'; and she is right.

But by 22nd August the situation had developed astonishingly:

If a painter would paint the devil right naturally, he would have to resort to her face.—She is as fat as a peasant wench; . . . one is punished enough for the rest of the day if by a sad misfortune one has cast an eye on her—tartar is what one needs! . . . She is not satisfied if I spend two hours a day with her; I am to sit there all day long—and she acts such gentility!—But more than that: she is *sérieusement* enamoured of me.

It was enough to drive him into any one else's arms. At any rate it drove him into Constanze Weber's. He took a room in the Graben at the end of August, contenting himself with a gloomy outlook on to some courtyard, away from the handsome broad thoroughfare, with its fine mansions, its noble ornamental fountain and its sprawling baroque *Pestsäule,* commemorating the end of the plague long ago. The reason he gave his father was that he liked a quiet place; the real one may have been economy. But he had fled too late: he was still tied to the Weber household, had his letters addressed to the 'Eye of God' as before and went there daily.

In December another bombshell burst upon poor Leopold in the form of a letter dated the 15th. In spite of all his reassurances that he had not fallen in love, Wolfgang now announced that he wished to be married. He gave the best of reasons a young man who desired to live a respectable and comfortable life, not to say a happy one, could possibly have. But he knew his father and could not fail to anticipate a stern reminder that he had no settled income, and that if he had, there were domestic obligations at Salzburg. Indeed Leopold, whose salary was very meagre, had sunk considerably into debt to pay for his son's travels. Wolfgang was well aware that it would be hard to enforce a decision he had taken with his usual unfilial independence. The worst of his confession was this:

And now who is the object of my love?—there again, do not take alarm, I beg of you;—what, not a Weberish one?—Yes, a Weberish one—but not Josepha—not Sophie—but *Constanca*; the middle one.—In no *famille* have I seen such disparity of dispositions, as here.—The eldest is a lazy, rude, false person, who knows what 's what.—The Langin is a treacherous, evil-thinking person, and a *coquette*.—The youngest is still too young to be anything at all,—nothing but a good but light-minded creature! may God preserve her from seduction.—But the middle one, to wit, my good, dear konstanze is—the martyr among them all and, perhaps for that reason, the best-hearted, cleverest, and in a word the best of them.—She takes care of everything in the house—and yet cannot do anything right. Oh my best of fathers, I could fill sheets, if I were to describe the scenes to you, which we two have gone through in this house. . . . She is not ugly, although anything but beautiful. —Her whole beauty consists in two small, black eyes, and a handsome figure. She has no wit, but enough sound human sense to be able to fulfil her duties as a wife and mother.

It seemed, in fact, that Constanze was the perfect Cinderella, denied by an unjust mother what little her other daughters could be given, kept at home to do the housework, always ready to serve others and efface herself. Wolfgang was desperately anxious to conciliate his father, even promising him half of whatever certain income he might expect. Leopold's letters of this period are lost, but it is clear from his son's replies that this new 'Weberish' escapade drove him frantic. His frenzy must have reached a climax when three days before Christmas he received news that Wolfgang had been compelled by Constanze's guardian, Johann Thorwarth, inspector of the theatre wardrobe, to sign a marriage contract, undertaking to marry the girl within three years or, failing that, to allow her an annuity of three hundred florins. Apparently Winter, who was a member of the Munich orchestra and on leave in Vienna, had told Thorwarth various derogatory tales about Mozart, either because of some old grudge from the Mannheim days,[1] or with the idea to damage him as a rival, or else for the mere tattler's pleasure of being thought more knowing than anyone else. Other people seem to have made mischievous comments on Mozart's living in the Weber household. Thorwarth officiously took it upon himself to intervene, went to Maria Cäcilie Weber and, although she defended her daughter's and Mozart's conduct, insisted on the latter's signing the document. What we know of the mother's character from her subsequent conduct makes it safe enough to conclude that, for all her outward protestations, she was delighted with this turn of events, if indeed she had not secretly precipitated it herself. All the crafty instincts of the landlady who has eligible daughters to count among the slender assets of her trade were awakened in this unscrupulous hag, and it made no difference to the advantage of this welcome transaction that she did not for a moment believe that Constanze had any legal claim upon Mozart.

Neither need any one else believe it. When it was a question of averting his father's wrath, or even only of saving him annoyance, Mozart was capable of deceiving himself into stretching the strict truth a little now and again; but there is too candid and serious a tone about his letter in which he swears that he had 'never so far had anything to do with a woman in this way' for any one to doubt that this was the truth. He makes no hypocritical professions of any particular

[1] He had been a pupil of Vogler, for whom Mozart had shown no liking at Mannheim.

love of virtue and does not pretend that he has found continence up to the age of nearly twenty-six easy; he claims no more for himself than decent principles combined with prudence, which makes an asseveration he was after all not called upon to offer his father sufficiently convincing.

There had, we hear, been dramatic incidents in the Weber household; but the *scène à faire* occurred after the signing of this infamous contract. When Constanze's guardian had left the house, she asked her mother to give her the document. 'My dear Mozart,' she said, 'I need no written assurance from you; I believe your word as it is!' and tore the paper from top to bottom. This must have been worth watching, with the foiled maternal villainess standing by, unable to show open disapproval.

Joseph II was hard put to it to entertain the Russian visitors, who stayed until early January 1782. One of the diversions at court was a concert on 24th December at which Mozart was asked to play the clavier in competition with Clementi, who was on a visit to Vienna. The emperor, who had recently described Mozart as 'un talent décidé,' made a wager with the grand duchess that he would score over the Italian, who at the age of twenty-nine already had a great reputation as composer and pianoforte player. They both improvised, played works of their own, read sonatas by Paisiello at sight at the grand duchess's request, and finally extemporized on two pianofortes on a theme chosen from these works. The emperor was convinced that Mozart had won, for he agreed with Dittersdorf later that while Clementi had only art, Mozart had both art and taste. In one respect, however, Clementi did better: he enthusiastically expressed his astonishment at Mozart's genius, while the latter had not a good word to say about the Italian, or rather, one good word which he immediately qualified by a disparaging remark:

He writes *presto* over a sonata, or even *prestissimo* and *alla breve*, and plays it *allegro* in 4–4 time. I know, for I heard it! What he does very well, are his passages in thirds; however, he sweated day and night over them in London. Beyond this he has nothing—nothing whatever—not the least interpretation nor taste, much less feeling.

All of which did not prevent him from modelling the theme of the *allegro* in the *Magic Flute* overture on the very Sonata of Clementi's (B flat major, Op. 6, No. 2) which had formed part of the competition. True, this was nearly ten years later, and it may have been done quite unconsciously.

The engagement at court was probably obtained through Joseph von Strack, chamberlain to the emperor, who had met Mozart at the house of Baroness Waldstädten and heard his E flat major Serenade for wind instruments (K. 375), 'written somewhat reasonably,' Mozart said, on purpose to impress that influential courtier. There was a question a little later of obtaining an appointment at court, but he was determined not to give so much as a hint to Strack that this would be acceptable, 'for if one makes any effort, a smaller salary is at once fixed—and the emperor is in any case a skinflint,' he wrote on 10th April 1782. Nothing came of these vague hopes, mainly because the emperor greatly favoured Salieri, who saw no reason for recommending another musician. Neither did Gassmann and Umlauf, who occasionally appeared at the emperor's after-dinner music-makings. Haydn, whom Mozart met for the first time at the end of 1781 and who always showed the younger master great friendliness and interest, had himself no influence at court, being wholly tied to the house of Esterházy and rarely resident in Vienna.

Mozart gradually found more opportunities to earn money casually. For one thing, the pupils increased. Countess Rumbeck he had taught almost from the beginning, and we have met the embarrassing Miss Aurnhammer; but before very long he was engaged to instruct Countess Josepha Palffy, a niece of Colloredo's (which was to be kept dark at Salzburg), Countess Zichy and Therese von Trattner, the wife of a prominent bookseller who became a staunch friend, although not an over-generous one. Countess Rumbeck paid him even when she happened to miss a lesson, but 'the Trattnerin is too economical for that.'

On 3rd March he gave a concert of his own, at which he gave a selection from *Idomeneo* and his D major piano Concerto (K. 175) with a new final rondo (K. 382) that made a 'great noise'—among the audience. On 26th May he appeared for the first time at a concert at the Augarten, the Vauxhall of Vienna in those days and an open-air resort a good deal more fashionable than the Prater.

Die Entführung progressed more and more slowly, owing to various alterations Mozart induced Stephanie to make in the libretto, which he considered to be too weak towards the end.[1] The arrangements for the production at the Burgtheater were even slower. All sorts of procrastinations and intrigues deferred the day of performance again and again, until at last Joseph II commanded that it should be fixed for 16th July 1782. The house was crammed on this first night, and in spite of an opposing faction that did its best to ruin the composer's chances, the opera was received with rapture. There was frantic applause after every number and many pieces had to be repeated. The music was thought very novel and daring, particularly by the emperor, who prided himself on his solidly conservative tastes and told Mozart that the score was too good for Viennese ears and contained too many notes; to which the composer politely but firmly replied that he had put in exactly as many as were required. The opera was repeated many times during the season and always filled the house.

Although the German *Singspiel* that had been established in 1778 was of a comparatively low and light type, the chief

[1] It must have been feeble indeed in an original form that achieved the feat of being worse than the third act as it now stands. In this respect *The Elopement* is a true forerunner of the Viennese operetta of the nineteenth and twentieth centuries, where a poor, eventless and musically inferior third act seems to have become an honoured tradition.

singers engaged for it were artists of distinction, and it so happened that Mozart obtained the services of the best of them. Catharina Cavalieri, a young Viennese in spite of her Italian name, was a soprano of exceptional technical powers, and Therese Teyber, a member of a very musical family, was scarcely less accomplished. Valentin Adamberger was a tenor who delighted Mozart by his refined, musicianly style, while Ludwig Fischer was a *buffo* bass of uncommon gifts, among which was an unusual range of low notes. It was of him that the Archbishop of Salzburg had said that he sang 'too low for a bass.'

In July the Haffner family at Salzburg wanted to have another serenade similar to that composed for them in 1776. Mozart wrote it in a great hurry and sent it piecemeal to Leopold. Wolfgang at first suggested that the march attached to the old Serenade had better be used, but afterwards wrote a new one (K. 408, 2). Later the work was returned to Vienna, flute and clarinet parts were added to it, one of the two minuets was omitted, and it was performed as a new Symphony in D major (K. 385).

The composer's great haste is not difficult to understand—much less difficult than the fact that the 'Haffner' Symphony shows not a trace of it. That he had to write a new Serenade for wind instruments (C minor, K. 388) at short notice was perhaps no great matter, though the work turned out a significant and passionate one; but the day of his wedding was now rapidly approaching. It had all become more and more troublesome. Constanze's mother planned that the young couple should continue to live with her and pay for their keep, and it was all they could do not to let her know too soon that they intended to do nothing of the kind. For Mozart had pretty well seen through her by the time he was formally engaged to Constanze, and the latter had small reason for any particular filial devotion. The mother, no longer judging it necessary to dissemble, tended to become alcoholically abusive, so that by January 1782 Mozart felt that poor Cinderella must at all costs be saved from her home. In April the wretched girl sent a pathetically humble and ill-spelt letter to Nannerl, asking if she would vouchsafe her condescension and friendship ('o ja! ich Hoffees'), and in May she added a postscript to the same effect to one of Wolfgang's letters to Leopold. Her future sister-in-law was as gracious as she dared be under her father's stern eye, but Leopold remained adamant, choosing doubtless to be still further disquieted rather than touched by the illiteracy of this pitiful appeal.[1]

There was more trouble. The lovers had a quarrel because Constanze had allowed some young spark to measure her calf in a game of forfeits, a very common custom in the loose-mannered Vienna of those days and normally regarded as harmless by Mozart himself, who, however, in a rather annoyingly solemn letter assured Constanze that it was not to be tolerated from a promised bride. There was a loss of temper on both sides and perhaps a momentary feeling of dismay on Mozart's part at possible future discoveries of shallowness in his wife. That blew over, however. The incident had occurred at the house of Baroness Waldstädten, an excellent amateur clavier player and a lady of the world with a reputation by no means above suspicion, who had done the lovers a kindness by asking Constanze to stay with her when home had become quite unbearable. The irate mother thereupon threatened to send the police for her daughter unless she returned at once, and the grim figure of Thorwarth again loomed on the horizon.

The situation was not to be endured any longer. Mozart wrote post-haste to his father for his consent to a marriage he felt he would rather undertake with a paternal blessing than without, but could not delay any further. He did not wait for an answer to fix the day of the wedding, and married his Constanze on 4th August 1782, determined to feel happy in spite of some qualms. Leopold's grudging consent did not

[1] Not that anybody could spell German in those days; still, there were degrees, and they made for very rigid epistolary class distinctions.

reach him until the following day. The bride's mother, although she attended the ceremony, had not been asked for her sanction, much less her blessings. But that was all one to the young couple, who had cause to feel entitled to snatch happiness as best they could at last and were young enough—he twenty-six and she nineteen—to enjoy a runaway match. It was Mozart's second 'elopement' that year, and he felt that it was a second success.

CHAPTER XI

FROM HIS MARRIAGE TO FIGARO'S

WOLFGANG and Constanze Mozart settled down to a haphazard domesticity. They were happy in a way, without understanding each other wholly. It was fun to be man and wife; the new discoveries they made in each other did not often induce serious thoughts, but called up sudden gusts of tenderness such as cheat young people into an illusion of profound felicity. They lived from hand to mouth, with enforced frugality at times, in a higher style when a little money came in, with any chance friend to share a capon and a bottle of wine at moments of recklessness, if not of affluence. There was no great reason to fear poverty, even without an immediate appointment for Mozart, who felt too sure of himself to doubt whether he could go on for ever repeating his successes, large and small. His wife, without being clearly aware of his exceptional genius, believed in his power to charm the public. Did he not charm her? He had a way with him, as she found whenever her ill-controlled 'Weberish' temperament threatened a domestic squall.

They lodged now here, now there in the narrower, more crooked streets of the inner city, which became more and more cramped and crowded within its girdle of ramparts. Only once or twice did they rusticate outside, beyond the glacis, where wealthy people alone could afford to live in spacious comfort—Gluck and his rich wife, for instance, who invited the Mozarts to dinner after a performance of *The Elopement* which had been given at the aged and influential master's request.

Servants of various degrees of sluttishness came and left as circumstances dictated. Some of the less slatternly ones may have been sent about their business by Constanze in little fiery fits of jealousy, more or less justified. For oddly enough—and yet understandably in a way—the young man who before his marriage had prided himself on his fastidiousness, now began to play with paltry temptations to extra-marital diversions, some of them none too dainty. How far his little infidelities went we do not know at all definitely, but we hear that before long Constanze had to listen, half dismayed and half amused, to light-hearted and loose-tongued confessions from a husband who was so entertainingly frank and at the same time so sincerely repentant that she could never refuse him an impulsively affectionate forgiveness. This she could grant the more easily, one feels, because her upbringing had been anything but austere. Indeed her husband was not without his own anxieties lest her behaviour should give rise to talk.

The marriage, one gathers, was thus happy in so far as an indulgent mutual understanding could make it; but that there was a limitless comprehension between these two it is impossible to imagine. Mozart—there is no getting away from it—can never have known a love that was commensurate with his infinite capacity for it—the capacity of the supreme artist. It may be as well for the world that it was so: he gave much to his music that a perfect wife might have kept for herself; but it is heartrending none the less. Constanze, on the other hand, was probably as contented as she could ever have known how to be. She did her best, there is no doubt of that, though that best was not any too good. If she failed to penetrate deeply into his music, she was far from being as artistically detached a wife as Haydn, for example, was burdened with. She played the clavier tolerably and had the family gift of song, not as highly cultivated as Josefa and Aloysia, but developed to a degree that was unprofessional only for a period at which exorbitant demands were made of public singers. Her taste in music, too, was far above her breeding. When, before her marriage, she had gone with Mozart to the house of Baron Gottfried van Swieten, a diplomat who cultivated music passionately, and heard fugues by Bach and Handel, she earnestly exhorted her lover to exercise himself more assiduously in the composition of this severe form than he had done so far.

What the young couple lived on it is hard to imagine. Mozart, despairing of any sort of court appointment, thought in the very month of his marriage of turning his back on Vienna and emigrating to Paris or London. He even practised his French and took some lessons in English. But he rashly told his father of these plans, and poor Leopold, who had just begun to reconcile himself to a marriage which from his point of view he had been quite right in opposing, was once more maddened with anxiety, so much so that he wrote to the Baroness Waldstädten, imploring her to restrain his son. Was not Bonno, the court *Capellmeister,* a very old man? Would not Salieri succeed to his post and vacate his own? Was not Gluck aged too? If only Wolfgang would not expect everything to happen in five minutes! So all of a sudden it was the father who was full of confidence, now that it suited him. It might have been better if he had kept to his former scepticism about Wolfgang's prospects in Vienna. But, be that as it may, he succeeded in persuading his son to wait patiently until some appointment should turn up.

Nothing turned up; but by various means the young Mozarts managed to go on existing. Constanze could be economical when it was imperatively necessary, and her husband scraped some money together by giving subscription concerts and playing on Sunday mornings at van Swieten's private 'academies.' Lessons continued here and there, while friendly patrons like Prince Galitsin, Prince Kaunitz and Countess Thun did something to put advantages in Mozart's way. His fame was spread by performances of *The Elopement* at various Austrian and German theatres, as well as in Prague, though whether any money accrued to the composer from them is doubtful.

He was easy prey for swindling managers. In December 1782 he wrote three new piano Concertos (K. 413–15) for his own concerts, among which were private Sunday morning sessions at his lodgings, and on the last day of that year he completed the string Quartet in G major (K. 387), the first of the great set of six subsequently dedicated to Haydn. He also arranged five Fugues from Bach's *Well-tempered Clavier* for string quartet (K. 405), probably at the request of van Swieten or perhaps under the influence of his musically serious wife.

Mozart's great desire was to conciliate his father, whose letters remained distressingly detached in tone. All that was needed, he felt, was a visit to Salzburg with Constanze, who could not fail to impress herself favourably on his family and friends. But the plan did not mature until the autumn of 1782, and then his wife became pregnant. They postponed their journey. Mozart went on playing in public and composing. He also published the last three piano Concertos by subscription. In May he wrote a horn Concerto (K. 417), the first of three in E flat major, which seems to have been the key favoured by Ignaz Leutgeb, a Salzburg horn player who had settled in the capital and for whom all the horn music of this period was written.

On 7th June Mozart wrote to ask Leopold to stand godfather to his child, 'be it *generis masculini* or *faeminini*.' On the 17th his first son, Raimund Leopold, was born and the young father achieved the incredible feat of working at the composition of his D minor string Quartet (K. 421)—No. 2 of the Haydn set—while his wife was in the throes of a very different creative labour. True, one may understand that a work with so sinister a feeling in the first movement and so tender a note in the second should come of this unnatural occupation; but how a whole quartet could turn out so faultlessly organized at such a time passes all conception. One can only set down the whole strange incident as the strongest evidence in all Mozart's career of his amazing power of emotional detachment. If one had not a hundred other reasons for holding him to be the greatest artist among creative musicians,[1] this example of what may perhaps be called the callousness of genius—the faculty of momentarily subordinating all other interests to the preoccupation with a work of art, would surely be enough to substantiate such a claim.

The infant died two months and two days later,[2] to the great sorrow of the young parents, who were not yet used to this natural but wasteful and cruel form of birth-rate control to which nearly every family had to accustom itself at a time when civilization had other defects than its present ones.

Meanwhile, not knowing the grief that awaited them, Mozart and Constanze prepared to go to Salzburg. Leopold had allayed a fear lest the archbishop might have it in his power to arrest a musician who had left his service without a formal dismissal, and the young couple left Vienna at the end of July. Why the baby was not left in the care of his grandmother is not known, but he was sent to a home for infants, where he seems to have been fed with fatal carelessness.[3] At any rate, if the diagnosis of the death certificate is to be trusted, he died of dysentery.

[1] I have said elsewhere, and had better repeat it here, that when I say the greatest artist I mean just that and no more: not, for instance, the greatest craftsman or the greatest originator.

[2] Not in December, as has commonly been supposed because Mozart still refers to the child in a letter of that month, and as even Abert still repeats in his magnificent revised edition of Jahn's biography. The date, 19th August 1783, appears in the death-roll in the city archives of Vienna.

[3] The customs of child-rearing were as appalling as the hygienic conditions. It was considered vulgar for a mother to nurse her child, and Mozart said he was resolved not to inflict this indignity on Constanze. He would have liked the baby to be brought up on water, since this had been good enough for his sister and himself, and he forgot that it had not been good enough for his five dead brothers and sisters. It was only on being told that most children in Vienna succumbed to this treatment that he reluctantly consented to engage a wet-nurse.

Mozart took with him a portion of the Mass in C minor (K. 427), a spaciously planned work for solo voices, chorus, orchestra and organ, which he had vowed to write during an illness of Constanze's before his marriage, if she should recover and become his wife. He had ready the *Kyrie, Gloria, Sanctus* and *Benedictus,* together with a fragment of the *Credo.* Most likely he intended to finish the work at Salzburg, though one may perhaps suspect a mentally stipulated condition that the meeting between his wife and his father should turn out wholly successful. Providence seems to have compromised in this matter, and he compromised in return: the Mass was eventually finished, but not all of it was newly composed. He used some portions from older masses and repeated the music of the *Kyrie* for the *Agnus Dei,* a procedure which Süssmayr was later to adopt in completing the *Requiem.*[1] The Mass, whether thus pieced together or in a fragmentary form is not known, was performed at St. Peter's in Salzburg on 25th August. Constanze sang the soprano part, the considerable difficulties of which prove that she must have been no mean technician, though not, of course, that she sang them flawlessly. At any rate she must have worked at them, for part of the *Kyrie* is based on one of the *Solfeggi* (K. 393) Mozart had written for her in the year of their marriage.

Among the countless friends at home to whose approval poor Constanze was submitted was Varesco, whom Mozart had already approached from Vienna for a new Italian comic opera, the German opera having by this time proved a failure, probably because a sufficient repertory of original works was not to be obtained. Varesco submitted to him the first act, with a sketch for the remainder, of *L'oca del Cairo* (*The Goose of Cairo*) (K. 422), and the composer set the first six numbers more or less sketchily. After that the work was abandoned.

Another acquaintance whom they visited was Michael

[1] In 1785 Mozart made further use of the C minor Mass by converting much of its music into the cantata *Davidde penitente* (K. 469).

Haydn, with whom and whose wife the family was on fairly friendly terms, although Leopold had once said that Haydn would be sure to 'swill himself into a dropsy,' and they regarded 'the Haydin' as something of a mischief-maker. At any rate Mozart, who did find that Haydn was suffering from some illness or another, readily volunteered to write two Duets for violin and viola (K. 423–4) without any keyboard accompaniment which the archbishop had commissioned from his concert master.[1] They were duly submitted in Haydn's name and accepted as his work. If the archbishop had known! Well, he ought to have known, for these two duet sonatas—for that is what they amount to—are beautifully, and one would have said unmistakably, Mozartian.

It may have been Varesco's fault, it may have been anything, that stopped Mozart's work at *L'oca del Cairo.* But why was the C minor Mass not composed honestly right through? After all, a vow was a vow, and Mozart, who was still a good catholic, was not given to trifling with such matters. There is only one explanation: he had made that mental reservation about Leopold's reception of Constanze and found that the condition that it should be wholly favourable was not fulfilled. His father was polite, and that was all. Indeed his politeness was the trouble. Constanze did her best to please, but remained ill at ease all through the visit, and the worst was that her sister-in-law behaved like a sister in nothing else. There were no quarrels, no bickerings, perhaps not even innuendoes; but there was no feeling of simple heartiness, much less of affection. Wolfgang, who was attached both to his family and his wife, was naturally hurt and uncomfortable. He had hoped that some family trinket would be offered to Constanze as a token that she was now a Mozart in more than name; but nothing of the sort happened. The wonder

[1] He also wrote the slow introduction to Michael Haydn's Symphony in G major, the whole of which was until recently regarded as Mozart's work (K. 444), though significantly enough hardly ever performed.

is that he could endure such a situation for nearly three months. Perhaps more remarkable still is the fact that, so far as we know, there was no open disagreement between any of these four embarrassed people. But Wolfgang and Constanze were deeply disappointed, and left at the end of October.

On the way they stopped at one or two places and made a longer stay at Linz, where Count Thun received them hospitably. This old nobleman, the father-in-law of Mozart's exalted pupil in Vienna, was going to give a private concert on 4th November and asked Mozart to do nothing less than write a new symphony for it. The composer sat down and did so. What is more, he did it uncommonly well, for the work is no other than the splendid one in C major still known as the 'Linz' Symphony (K. 425). There is not a trace of haste in it. Mozart might have dispensed with a slow introduction, but he wrote one; he might have omitted a minuet, as he had done more than once before, but he supplied one.

Back in Vienna, he composed the Fantasy for pianoforte (originally pianoforte and violin) in C minor (K. 396), another in D minor (K. 397), a Quintet for horn and strings (K. 407) and another horn Concerto (K. 447), both in E flat major, the third 'Haydn' string Quartet (K. 428), in the same key, and he made some sketches for another comic opera, *Lo sposo deluso* (*The Deceived Husband*) (K. 430). Various concert arias also belong to 1783 (K. 416, 418–20, 431–33, 435), two of them being extra numbers for Anfossi's opera, *Il curioso indiscreto.* They and some others of these pieces were written for Aloysia Lange, with whom he was by that time on terms of a sincere but quite detached friendship. Perhaps she had learned to bridle her 'evil tongue'; at any rate as a singer she had what Mozart liked to call 'a glib gullet.'

A small work belonging to the end of that year calls for particular mention, not because it is musically of great importance, but because it is the first evidence left to us of Mozart's growing interest in freemasonry. It is the masonic cantata, 'Dir,

Seele des Weltalls' ('To Thee, Soul of the Universe') (K. 429). Ideals of universal brotherhood greatly engaged the finer spirits of Vienna towards the close of the century, and Mozart had a great capacity for disinterested friendship and—we should know it from his insight into the characters of his operas if we knew it from nothing else—infinite sympathy with human beings, good and bad, intelligent and stupid, high and low. He was, I repeat, still a good, orthodox catholic, and the fact that he ceased writing masses once he had left Salzburg is to be more satisfactorily explained by his holding no church appointment in the capital than by any change of heart in matters of religion. But he had liberal views of the most intimate concerns of conscience and was ready to be drawn into freemasonry by friends he liked and respected. He entered the lodge of 'The Crowned Hope,' converted in 1785 by order of the emperor, who insisted on a reformatory amalgamation of certain lodges, into 'The New-Crowned Hope.' An important work in this connection is the Masonic Funeral Music (K. 477), written in November 1785 on the death of two distinguished masons. It is scored for a dark-coloured orchestral combination that anticipates certain devices in *The Magic Flute*.

In the spring of 1784 a violinist, Regina Strinasacchi, a lively, attractive Italian girl of nineteen or twenty, visited Vienna, and Mozart hastily wrote a violin sonata for her concert of 24th April. It was the Sonata in B flat major (K. 454), a work that betrays no sign that the composer was able to finish only the violin part for the artist to study on the morning of the concert and that he played the piano part from memory with the aid of a mere rough draft hastily jotted down at the last moment.

Later in the year he met two eminent Italian composers, Sarti and Paisiello, who visited Vienna on their way, respectively, to and from St. Petersburg. Although he often had little cause to like his Italian rivals, many of whom were apt to be disagreeable when they could not conceal their jealousy and dangerous when they could, he found both these masters entirely friendly.[1] He gave Sarti pleasure by writing Variations for pianoforte on the air 'Come un agnello' from his opera *Fra due litiganti* (K. 460).[2] On a theme of Paisiello's, 'Salve tu, Domine,' he had already written Variations (K. 398) the preceding year. What interested him now was that master's comic opera *Il barbiere di Siviglia,* which had been produced at the court of Catherine II of Russia in 1780 and was brought out in Vienna during the composer's visit. There can be little doubt that it was this work which first gave him the idea of an operatic setting of another comedy by Beaumarchais, the sequel to *Le Barbier de Séville.* [3]

A much more lasting friendship was formed during the following winter, beginning about the time of the birth of Mozart's second son, Carl Thomas, on 21st September 1784. Haydn seems to have been in Vienna for an exceptionally long time that year and he gave a number of musical evenings at the town residence of Prince Nicholas Esterházy, at which he invited Mozart to play more than once. The younger master had an almost reverential regard for the elder, both as man and as composer, and he especially admired Haydn's string quartets. It must have been at this time that he conceived the idea of dedicating a set of six works in that form to one who had cultivated it so assiduously and successfully.[4] Three masterpieces were ready to hand, and he now completed the set within a few months, finishing the Quartet in B flat major (K. 458)

[1] Sarti, however, criticized him adversely for his string Quartets later, saying that he wrote like a clavier player who could not distinguish between D sharp and E flat; but this judgment appears to have been made in conservatively professional good faith, and from an academic point of view it is not incomprehensible. For a discussion of it see Ernest Newman, *A Musical Critic's Holiday* (Cassell, 1925).

[2] Used later in the little domestic concert of wind instruments in the final scene of *Don Giovanni.*

[3] We have already seen that in Paris he had made the acquaintance of the incidental music Beaumarchais had himself provided for this play.

[4] Forty-three Quartets by Haydn, written before 1785, are extant.

on 9th November 1784, that in A major (K. 464) on 10th January 1785, and that in C major (K. 465) four days later.

Haydn often came to Mozart's house to play quartets with Dittersdorf as second violinist and Wanhal as cellist, the host playing the viola. It was here that he met Leopold Mozart, who had come to return his son's visit, staying in Vienna from February to April 1785. (Leopold had made the journey alone, for his daughter had been married in 1784 to a nobleman, Berchthold zu Sonnenburg of St. Gilgen, where she lived in the very house where her mother had been born.) Haydn, who was thirteen years younger then Leopold, warmed his fatherly heart by saying to him, after a home performance of the three new quartets: 'I tell you before God, and as an honest man, that your son is the greatest composer I know, either personally or by name; he has taste, and apart from that the greatest science in composition.'

The other important works of this period, next to the Quintet for piano and wind instruments (K. 452), which Mozart himself felt to represent him at his very best, were several piano Concertos, a medium in which by this time he succeeded in combining perfect aptness to its special requirements with inexhaustible poetry and originality. The series includes the delicious B flat major Concerto (K. 456), written for the blind pianist Marie Therese von Paradies, who had been on a visit to Salzburg at the same time as the young Mozarts, the G major (K. 453), with the folksong-like theme in the finale which is said to have been whistled by a starling bought by the composer, the crisp little F major (K. 459) and three others (K. 449–51). It concludes with the passionately romantic D minor Concerto (K. 466), the first performance of which considerably astonished Leopold in February 1785.

The quartet playing did not always take place at the Mozarts', but often at the lodging of Stephen Storace, a promising English composer of twenty-two, who had come to Vienna with his sister Ann Selina, better known as Nancy, who at the age of nineteen was already an opera singer with a reputation in Italy and had just been engaged for the new Italian opera establishment which Vienna had substituted for the unsuccessful German venture. There was almost a musical British colony in the capital, for apart from the Storaces, Thomas Attwood, aged twenty, had come to be, like Stephen Storace, a pupil of Mozart. They soon formed a friendly circle round the Mozart household which was completed by the Irishman Michael Kelly, who, four years older than Nancy Storace, had also made his name as a singer in Italy and was engaged as tenor at the opera. Kelly became a particularly close friend. He visited Mozart almost daily, played billiards with him and received his advice about turning a gift for melodic invention unmatched by technical proficiency to the best advantage. It is to Kelly's attractive *Reminiscences* that we owe one of the best contemporary pen-portraits of Mozart that have been preserved:

He favoured the company by performing fantasias and capriccios on the piano-forte. His feeling, the rapidity of his fingers, the great execution and strength of his left hand particularly, and the apparent inspiration of his modulations, astounded me. After this splendid performance we sat down to supper, and I had the pleasure to be placed at table between him and his wife, . . . After supper the young branches of our host had a dance, and Mozart joined them. Madame Mozart told me, that great as his genius was, he was an enthusiast in dancing, and often said that his taste lay in that art, rather than in music.

He was a remarkably small man, very thin and pale, with a profusion of fine fair hair, of which he was rather vain. He gave me a cordial invitation to his house, of which I availed myself, and passed a great part of my time there. He always received me with kindness and hospitality.—He was remarkably fond of punch, of which beverage I have seen him take copious draughts. He was also fond of billiards, and had an excellent billiard table in his house. Many and many a game have I played with him, but always came off second best. He gave Sunday concerts, at which I never was missing. He was kind-hearted, and always ready to oblige; but so very particular, when he played, that if the slightest noise were made, he instantly left off.

Before long both Nancy Storace and Kelly, who was also known as O'Kelly and on the Italian stage as Ochelli, were to be artistically associated with Mozart as well as personally. For it was high time for him to tackle another work for the stage, and the German opera having come to grief, he was naturally looking out, without success at first, as we have seen for an Italian book. Beaumarchais, we know, attracted him, and about the middle of 1786 he found the opportunity to embark on an operatic version of the second comedy in the French author's trilogy—*Le Mariage de Figaro.* He had met the right librettist in Lorenzo da Ponte—the right one for him, at any rate, for da Ponte had worked with other composers like Salieri, Gazzaniga, Righini and the italianized Spaniard Martín y Solar with varied success. He was a Venetian Jew by birth, Emanuele Conegliano, but had been christened in his fourteenth year by the Bishop of Ceneda, whose name he adopted. He took holy orders, which did not prevent him from being a complete man of both the world and the half-world, a kind of minor Casanova, less abandoned but also less distinguished than that dangerously attractive model. He was no great literary genius, but an adroit craftsman and neat versifier. At any rate the Beaumarchais subject suited him, and he turned it skilfully into what, but for a weakness in the fourth act, has remained one of the world's best operatic librettos, excising the numerous political allusions in the revolutionary comedy, which did not suit the purposes of the musical stage, but leaving the polished intrigue of the original unimpaired. Moreover, he was shrewd enough to recognize a great composer and saw his advantage in being associated with a genius like Mozart, whose suggestions he knew to be sound and accepted without demur. The book was soon ready to Mozart's hand. He set to work on *Le nozze di Figaro* (K. 492) with avidity and—who can doubt it?—with none of the misgivings that may have stirred in his breast, almost unknown to himself, at his own wedding.

CHAPTER XII

WAXING POWER AND WANING FORTUNES

BEFORE *Le nozze di Figaro* was ready for production Mozart wrote several important works. There were two particularly lucky ones in his lucky key of E flat major: a violin Sonata (K. 481), finished on 12th December 1785, and a piano Concerto (K. 482), completed four days later. He had already earlier in the year produced another Concerto, the ostentatiously brilliant one in C major (K. 467), and two utterly different masterpieces of the kind, A major (K. 488) and C minor (K. 491), were to follow on 2nd and 24th March 1786. It was at this time, too, that he concocted the cantata of *Davidde penitente* (K. 469) from the unfinished C minor Mass dating from the Salzburg visit of 1783.

But even a work for the stage intervened, though a small one. It was the comedy of *Der Schauspieldirektor* (*The Impresario*) (K. 486), commissioned by the emperor and performed in the orangery at Schönbrunn on 7th February 1786, at a festivity in honour of the governors of the Netherlands. The actors and singers of both the German and the Italian stages took part, the latter in a piece by Salieri, *Prima la musica e poi le parole.* The score of Mozart's piece consisted of only five numbers, but masterly music in a frankly theatrical style, both comic and lyrical, had been lavished by him on the silly and long-winded topical play written for the occasion by the younger Stephanie. It is a feeble, witless satire on the theatrical conditions of the time, so tiresome as to be quite unperformable in its original form nowadays, the more so because the libretto contains a number of speaking parts and thus keeps the spectator waiting too long for the music, which shows Mozart at his maturest, dramatically and psychologically.[1]

Joseph II had always, more or less secretly, favoured Italian opera, and when he found that Vienna was not inclined to make a success of the German venture, he was only too glad to convene a new Italian company in 1783, though not disinclined to let the indigenous singers who were conversant with Italian operatic art be transferred to the new enterprise. His favourite composer, Salieri, was given the first chance to appear with a new work, *La scuola dei gelosi,* and a piece that shared its success was Sarti's *Fra due litiganti il terzo gode,* which we shall meet again in connection with Mozart. By 1786 an excellent company had been assembled. An ideal cast was chosen for *Figaro*: Steffano Mandini, a fine baritone, as Count Almaviva, a soprano named Laschi as the countess, Nancy Storace as Susanna, and a surpassingly good *basso buffo,* Francesco Benucci, as Figaro. It may well have been for the sake of Kelly, who was an accomplished character actor, that Mozart made a tenor part of Basilio.[2] Aloysia Lange was not in the running, although she had gone over to the Italian opera together with Cavalieri, Teyber and Adamberger; for it was of course for a production of Anfossi's *Il curioso indiscreto* at this new establishment that her brother-in-law had written the extra arias for her and Adamberger to sing in that

[1] Several attempts have been made to revive this little masterpiece with various new librettos. I venture to include in this volume (Appendix E) a version of my own in which I have endeavoured to keep to the original plot as closely as possible in the musical numbers, where indeed Mozart's astounding gift of delineation allows of no departure, and to fill in new connecting dialogue that tries to suggest the period and does not call for the inclusion of extra musical numbers culled from other works by Mozart, as other modernized librettos invariably seem to do.

[2] *Figaro* could thus not be performed with the same cast as a sequel to Paisiello's *Barbiere di Siviglia,* where, as in Rossini's later version, Almaviva is a tenor and Basilio a bass.

work (K. 418, 420). In 1785 he was asked to contribute a trio and a quartet to Bianchi's *La villanella rapita* (K. 479–80), and only then was he at last invited to supply an Italian opera of his own.

But *Figaro* was not to be produced without trouble. First of all the emperor, who had already forbidden the performance of Beaumarchais's play, would not hear of its presentation as an opera until da Ponte was able to reassure him that all political allusions had been eliminated. Then the court poet, Giovanni Battista Casti, who was not inclined to tolerate another librettist next to him, began to intrigue against Mozart and da Ponte, with the all too generous support of the intendant, Count Rosenberg, who tried to annoy the composer into withdrawing the work by cutting out the dance in the third act. But the emperor, who attended the rehearsal he had himself ordered, noticed the omission and commanded that it should be rectified. Mozart also suspected machinations on the part of other composers, notably Salieri and Righini, and he was fully upheld in his misgivings, as usual, by his father, who had spent a lifetime scenting mischief, real and imaginary. Kelly, however, confirms the Mozarts' suspicions:

> Mozart was as touchy as gunpowder, and swore he would put the score of his opera into the fire, if it was not produced first; his claim was backed by a strong party: on the contrary Regini [*sic*] was working like a mole in the dark to get precedence.—The third candidate was Maestro di Cappella to the Court, a clever shrewd man, possessed of what Bacon called, crooked wisdom.

The story that the singers themselves tried to jeopardize the work by deliberately making mistakes seems to be a pure fabrication of over-zealous biographer-partisans; at any rate the whole company, vocalists and orchestra, broke spontaneously into wild acclamations at one of the rehearsals when Benucci sang 'Non più andrai' in the most rousing manner, and the artists did magnificent work on the night of the production of *Le nozze di Figaro* (*The Marriage of Figaro*) (K. 492) on 1st May[1] 1786. Mozart conducted from the keyboard and, of course, accompanied the *secco* recitatives, a task which Joseph Weigl took over after the third performance. The house was crammed on the first night, and so many of the numbers had to be repeated that the opera lasted nearly twice its appointed time.[2] For all that, the work was withdrawn after the ninth performance on 18th December, the chief cause being Martín's *Una cosa rara,* which proved an immediate and easy popular success. That Mozart bore the Spanish composer no grudge for this will appear before long.

Figaro did very little to relieve Mozart of the material anxieties that beset him more and more sorely. Only nine performances were given in eight months for which he received nothing, having been paid a lump sum at the beginning. There were debts to settle, and he paid too much rent as it was for the first floor of the comparatively well-set-up house in the Schulerstrasse, and Constanze was once more with child. The third boy, Johann Thomas Leopold, born on 18th October, died on 15th November, so that pecuniary harassments were accompanied by emotional ones. The worried composer

[1] Have socialists ever noticed the date on which this class-subversive opera appeared? If not, a present may here be made them of the observation.

[2] Only those familiar with Gilbert and Sullivan audiences can have some faint conception nowadays of how undisciplined the opera public was in the eighteenth century. Even Mozart, though he wrote the loveliest orchestral perorations to his arias, which must have been ruined again and again by applause, took this insensitive responsiveness calmly for granted, though he did once say that what he liked most of all was approbation by silence. (But he confessed to Jacquin that he could not tell whether Paisiello's *Le gare generose* had been well performed in Prague or not, because he had been talking too much.) A characteristic decree was issued after the first *Figaro* performances: it was proclaimed by order that no musical number written for more than one voice would be repeated in future—which amounted to an encouragement to insist on repetition of the arias.

worked hard. But then, as soon as he set pen to paper, the usual miracle happened: trouble forsook him, and he turned out one exquisite piece after another. The E flat major piano Quartet (K. 493) was finished on 3rd June, the G major piano Trio (K. 496) on 8th July, the great F major Sonata for piano duet (K. 497) on 1st August, the Trio for clarinet, viola and piano (K. 498) on 5th August, the D major string Quartet (K. 499) on 19th August, another Trio, in B flat major (K. 502), on 18th November, a C major piano Concerto (K. 503), the one work among all these which betrays a certain laxity of spirits, on 4th December, and a Symphony in D major (K. 504), showing a possible trace of haste only in its lack of a minuet, on 6th December.

It was this Symphony which was performed in Prague during a visit in January 1787. Mozart had not intended to go there; his desire was to revisit England, perhaps to settle there if his prospects proved but a little brighter than those in Vienna, where by this time he despaired of ever making his way. For lessons were irksome as well as insufficiently remunerative, the court continued to be lukewarm, and he had too many enemies, perhaps not altogether without his own fault, for he had a sharp and none too well guarded critical tongue where other people's music was concerned. The English project came to grief because he was apparently unwilling to go without Constanze, and they could not take two babies with them. Just before the death of the younger boy he asked his father if he would take care of the children for him, in which case he would send them to Salzburg with the two servant wenches. Leopold's answer, dated 17th November 1786, must have been categorical, to judge by his account of it given to his daughter on the same day—more so than it would have been had he known that the younger child had just died:

To-day I was obliged to answer a letter from your brother which has cost me much labour in writing. . . . That I had to write a very emphatical letter, you may well imagine, since he proposed to me nothing less than that I should take care of his 2 children, as

LEOPOLD MOZART

Portrait by an unknown Salzburg Painter

half-way through the carnival he desired to make a journey through Germany to England, &c. . . . Not bad, to be sure!—They could travel in all tranquillity,—they might die,—might remain in England,—and I could run after them with the children &c.: or after the payment for the children which he offers me for wenches and children &c.—*Basta!* my excuses are forcible, and instructive, if he will make use thereof.

That was that. Leopold's letter had clearly been both forcible and instructive enough to keep the still obedient son of thirty at home. On the other hand there was no reason to interfere with a visit to Prague, indeed no need for Wolfgang to write home about it. He took Constanze with him, feeling perhaps that she could do with some agreeable distraction, poor thing. They found Prague seething with enthusiasm over *Figaro,* which had just been produced there with a positively explosive success. It gave them untold satisfaction to find at a ball that the tunes from the opera had been converted into 'nothing but *Contredanses* and *Teutsche,*' as Mozart wrote to his friend Gottfried von Jacquin in Vienna, and he was elated to discover that 'here they talk of nothing but *Figaro*; scrape, blow, sing and whistle nothing but *Figaro*; visit no opera but *Figaro*, and eternally *Figaro*.' Not only that, but *The Elopement* had charmed the Bohemians in 1783. When on 17th January they attended a performance of *Figaro,* the rumour of the composer's presence at once went round the house, and after the overture he was accorded a frenzied ovation. On the 20th he conducted the opera himself; but it was the day before, at a concert he gave in the opera house, that the new Symphony, now always called the 'Prague' Symphony, received its first performance.

Mozart and Constanze stayed at the house of Count Johann Joseph Thun during their visit, but they also saw much of Franz Dušek and his wife Josepha, whom Mozart had already met at Salzburg. Both were influential musicians, and it was largely due to their devoted friendship that Mozart obtained a commission to write a new opera especially for Prague. The impresario who had brought *Figaro* to the Bohemian capital, Pasquale Bondini, was eager to attach so successful a composer to himself, and when the Mozarts left in February Wolfgang had a contract for a hundred ducats in his pocket.

The work was to be produced the following autumn, so that no time was to be lost. Mozart went straight to da Ponte, who suggested, as though a new idea had just struck him, the tremendous subject of Don Juan, probably without in the least realizing its whole import, but taking it merely as an excellent excuse for good comedy, titillating situations and a fine theatrical thrill at the end. How much Mozart himself saw in it just then it is impossible to guess; but if he was unaware that he would make of it one of the few stage works in the world which have a claim to be called the greatest opera ever written, he must at least have felt that the completely new problems raised by this text, so far as he was concerned,[1] would make an engrossing task for weeks to come.

Da Ponte's *Memoirs* give an amusing and characteristic account of how this poetical busybody and worldling set to work, though he does not say that he modelled his libretto very closely on that used by Gazzaniga. He at least did not shun concentrated labour, while he knew how to make it highly agreeable for himself, if we may believe the glamorous old-age recollections of an adventurer who, not as abandoned as Casanova, may have been no less mendacious:

> I thought it time . . . to exert my poetic powers again. . . . The opportunity was presented to me by the three above-mentioned composers, Martín, Mozart and Salieri, who all came to me at once asking me for a play. . . .

---

[1] It was not in itself new. Gluck's *Don Juan* ballet had been produced in Vienna in 1761, and Mozart's music at some points very curiously resembles that of Gazzaniga's opera, *Il convitato di pietra* (*The Stone Guest*), produced in Venice early in 1787, though it is impossible to say definitely that he knew this work. He must, on the other hand, have been familiar with Righini's of 1777.

. . . I went to the emperor, put my ideas before him and informed him that I intended to write these three operas contemporaneously.

'You won't succeed,' he replied.

'Perhaps not,' I answered, 'but I shall make the attempt. At night I shall write for Mozart, and I shall regard it as reading Dante's *Inferno*; in the morning I shall write for Martín, and that will be like reading Petrarch; in the evening for Salieri, and that will be my Tasso.' He thought my parallel very good.

Directly I reached home I set to work.

I sat down at my writing table and stayed there for twelve hours on end, with a little bottle of Tokay on my right hand, an inkstand in the middle, and a box of Seville tobacco on the left. A beautiful young girl of sixteen was living in my house with her mother, who looked after the household. (I should have wished to love her only as a daughter—but——) She came into my room whenever I rang the bell, which in truth was fairly often, and particularly when my inspiration seemed to begin to cool. She brought me now a biscuit, now a cup of coffee, or again nothing but her own lovely face, always gay, always smiling and made precisely to inspire poetic fancy and brilliant ideas.[1]

Whether these conditions were the ideal ones in which to tackle Salieri's *Assur*[2] it is hard to decide, and they certainly do not seem to fit Martín's *L'arbore di Diana*; but it can scarcely be questioned that they suited a Don Juan opera to perfection, always provided that the volatile *abbate* wrote the truth.

Be that as it may, he wrote a sprightly libretto full of well-devised situations which make the spectator quite overlook the fact that his Don Juan, although there is much talk of his amorous escapades, is seen throughout the evening to be notoriously unsuccessful in their pursuit. There is, it must be confessed, an extraordinary confusion about half-way through the second act, which no amount of producer's ingenuity ever succeeds in clearing up satisfactorily; but it must be borne in mind that this may have arisen from subsequent manipulations of the text in which quite possibly

[1] Translation by L. A. Sheppard (Routledge, 1929).

[2] An Italian version of *Tarare,* produced in Paris in June 1787.

Mozart had rather more to say than da Ponte may have liked. What is extremely diverting is that old Casanova himself, who was just about that time writing the recollections of his own Don Juanesque career at the castle of Dux in Bohemia, where he had been charitably offered a librarian's post by an old acquaintance, and who was in Prague in the early autumn of 1787, seems himself to have had a hand in revising, and possibly muddling, da Ponte's libretto at that particular juncture, for a sketch in his handwriting has recently been discovered.[1]

In February 1787 Mozart lost his English friends all at once. The Storaces, Kelly and Attwood returned home, paying a visit to his father at Salzburg on the way, and he had a last flicker of desire to join them and try his luck in London. In the end it was cautiously decided that they should first look round for an opening for him, and that he might follow later. Then *Don Giovanni* intervened. It was not the only important composition of that period, though, for the two glorious string Quintets in C major and G minor (K. 515–16), the Serenade for strings, *Eine kleine Nachtmusik* (K. 525) and the grand-scale violin Sonata in A major (K. 526) belong to it. Also, two outward events occurred in May, one calculated to shake Mozart personally to his depths and the other a linking-up of musical history, as he had the foresight to discern. It seemed little enough to begin with: merely the visit of a sullen-faced youth of seventeen with a thick Rhenish accent, who was introduced to him by some acquaintance. But Mozart, after a somewhat frigid reception of the unprepossessing lad, soon pricked up his ears on being played to on the pianoforte with a startling power and originality, and said to some other visitors in the next room that this young man had better be watched, for he would make a noise in the world before long. The young man did: his name was Ludwig van Beethoven.

[1] See Dyneley Hussey, *Wolfgang Amade Mozart,* Appendix I (Kegan Paul and Curwen, 1928).

On 29th May Mozart heard that his father had died the day before, at the age of sixty-eight. He had not been quite unprepared, for on 4th April he had written home to say he knew that Leopold had been ill and to ask anxiously for news about his condition. But it was a blow to be suddenly told that the old man was no more. There had been estrangements between father and son; Leopold had been harsh and peremptory enough to cause bitterness in a young man who, while anxious to remain dutiful, chafed under restrictions; and Leopold's admonitions had been none the less disagreeable for being, as Wolfgang well knew, based on common sense and affection. But now the old filial tenderness welled up, and he was genuinely afflicted by his loss.

About the end of August the Mozarts left for Prague a second time, Constanze once again in an interesting situation. How far *Don Giovanni* was finished before their departure is not known, but it is certain that a good deal still remained to be done. They lodged at the 'Three Golden Lions,' but were half the time the guests of the Dušeks, who lived at a country house in 'Bertramka's vineyard.' There they enjoyed good food, cheerful company, games of darts and skittles and what not, and Mozart intermittently worked at his score on a stone table in the garden, surrounded by ripening grapes and facing the view from the slope.

There was a good deal of trouble with the singers, who, Mozart wrote to Jacquin, were not as accomplished as those in Vienna in catching hold of a new work quickly. The young baritone Luigi Bassi, who sang the title part, complained that he was given no great display aria, and it is said that Mozart composed the duet 'Là ci darem la mano' five times before Bassi was kind enough to say it pleased him. Then Caterina Bondini, the wife of the impresario, probably from fear of spoiling her voice, could not be persuaded to make Zerlina's cry behind the scenes sufficiently realistic. Mozart's remedy was simple: at a rehearsal he suddenly assailed her roughly from behind at the given moment, whereupon she gave forth a scream which he declared to be a perfect sample of what he wanted at the performance. To complete the traditional complications of opera rehearsals, gossip had it that Mozart, perhaps with a view to still greater realism, indulged in love affairs not only with his Zerlina, but also with his Donna Anna, whose interpreter was Teresa Saporiti, and with his Donna Elvira, sung by Caterina Micelli. Saporiti, it was said, had expressed surprise at Mozart's insignificant appearance, whereupon he transferred his affections in a pique. Some of this may be true; all of it certainly is not, since tittle-tattle always has a way of inflating the facts, if any; and as nobody does know how much is true, let us leave it at that, with a strong suspicion that these rumours emanated from those who can never believe an artist to be capable of creating a dramatic figure without having personally gone through its experiences.

Another set of stories is current, about the composition of the overture to *Don Giovanni,* which is supposed to have been written only the night before the performance and distributed to the players, with the ink still wet, to get through at sight as best they could. But Constanze told Nissen, her second husband, distinctly that it was on the last night but one before the production that Mozart wrote down the overture while she regaled him with punch and kept him awake with stories, so that the sight-reading can only, at the worst, have happened at the dress rehearsal. That the whole piece was fully composed in Mozart's mind, according to his astonishing habit, and only needed writing down, may be taken for granted.

That the music for Don Juan's dinner entertainment in the second finale cannot have been ready until quite late is shown by the original libretto, which does not contain the words sung by Don Juan and Leporello while these little wind octets are played. It appears that they were at first to be left to the players' choice, but in the end Mozart interpolated favourite melodies from three recent popular operas: Martín's *Una cosa rara,* Sarti's *Fra due litiganti* and his own *Figaro.*

At last, on 29th November 1787, *Il dissoluto punito, ossia Il Don Giovanni* (*The Debauchee Punished, or Don Juan*) (K. 527) was produced. Prague went mad with delight over it, in spite of Mozart's fear lest the public should be bewildered by the novelty of the music, which must have astonished even himself as it fell to him with the inevitability that makes genius after its highest flights stand amazed and ask: 'How did I do it?' He conducted the first performance himself, and the artists, anxious to do justice to a work and a composer of whose greatness they had been given ample opportunity to become aware, did the utmost in their power to make the production a success. Those not yet named were Antonio Baglioni as Don Ottavio, Felice Ponziani as Leporello and Giuseppe Lolli, who doubled the parts of the Commendatore and Masetto.

The Mozarts were in no hurry to return to Vienna and their everlasting domestic cares. For once they enjoyed themselves, and their hosts were reluctant to let them go. The new baby was not due just yet[1] and little Carl was no doubt taken care of by his grandmother. On 3rd November Josepha Dušek, who had been promised a concert aria, locked Mozart into a summer-house at Bertramka and declared that she would not let him out until he had written it down. He obeyed, but retaliated by refusing to give up the piece unless she could sing it at sight. It turned out a grand and extremely difficult thing, full of strange intervals and harmonies; but Josepha, who was a bit of a composer herself and a good clavier player, brilliantly acquitted herself of the task imposed on her by the composer, who dedicated this aria, *Bella mia fiamma* (K. 528), to her.

Two German songs (K. 529–30) were also written during the visit to Prague, but they were less important than one or two of a group composed earlier that year (K. 517–20, 523–4), among which *Abendempfindung* is particularly interesting as a

[1] It was to be a girl this time, Theresia, born 27th December 1787, died 29th June 1788.

true forerunner of the Schubertian *Lied* and only less so than *Das Veilchen* (K. 476) of two years earlier because that is the one evidence of Mozart's awareness of Goethe, who as a lad had attended his infant-prodigy display at Frankfort.

On 12th November the Mozart couple were back in Vienna. Three days later Gluck died of a stroke at the age of seventy-three, and by 7th December Joseph II, who could not help being rather impressed by Mozart's successes in Prague, appointed him chamber musician to the court in Gluck's place with eight hundred florins a year. The immediate effect seems to have been to drive him to the composition of various dances (K. 534–6) for the court balls and to inhibit him from writing larger works, the only one being the curiously empty piano Concerto in D major (K. 537)—the last but one. Still, though the new appointment amounted to little enough, it may have given the Mozarts some hope of being relieved of the nagging worries that seemed to plague them the more relentlessly the more the master's creative power grew and the more his fame spread beyond Vienna.

CHAPTER XIII

WORK AND WORRY

SOME time early in 1788 Vienna decided to hear the Prague opera. *Don Giovanni* was put into rehearsal with a notable cast—so notable that what Mozart had written for what they considered a set of provincial singers was not good enough for those in the capital. They cleverly attributed the failure of the work at its first performance, on 7th May, to the fact that they had not been allowed to shine sufficiently with solo displays. With the honourable exception of Aloysia Lange, who sang Donna Anna, Francesco Albertarelli, who appeared in the title part, and Francesco Bussani, who took the Commendatore and Masetto,[1] they all insisted on some extra number or another. Caterina Cavalieri was given Elvira's 'Mi tradì,' much too lovely a piece to be cut, but rather in the concert-aria style and difficult to fit in logically anywhere; [2] Francesco Morella received a second song for Ottavio, the beautiful though static 'Dalla sua pace'; while Luisa Mombelli and Benucci, the original Figaro, were fobbed off with a duet for Zerlina and Leporello that continues deservedly to be neglected as the one inferior number in the whole score.

The opera was given a mere fifteen times in the course of the year and did not reappear in 1789—indeed not until after Mozart's death, when it was revived in a lamentable German

[1] Masetto's 'Ho capito,' often indicated as an extra number in old editions, was in the original score; so was Don Juan's 'Metà di voi' in the second act, which is too often omitted.

[2] It is a wrong, post-Wagnerian and anti-musical principle to suggest, as German critics do almost with one accord, that so perfect a piece should be sacrificed because dramatically it is uncalled-for.

translation. Joseph II declared, according to da Ponte, that 'the opera is divine, perhaps even more beautiful than *Figaro,* but no food for the teeth of my Viennese,' on which Mozart's comment seems to have been: 'Let us give them time to chew it.'

The Mozarts had moved out of town again, to what was then the Währingergasse—quite a long way in those days. The rural surroundings pleased them, and they had a garden; but above all the lodging was cheap, and Mozart rarely had occasion—too rarely, unfortunately—to busy himself in the heart of the city. He was doing badly. The meagre court salary was swallowed up by the most urgent debts. In order to feel that he was earning it, he had to go on turning out dance music: minuets, *contredanses* and *Teutsche* of a peculiarly Viennese sort.

His power of concentration on important work was not leaving him, however, even during times of the greatest material vexation. At the very moment he began to write those pitiful begging letters to his friend and fellow-mason Michael Puchberg he performed one of the most miraculous feats of mental discipline that even his career was to show: he produced the last three Symphonies between June and 10th August. The work in E flat major (K. 543) bears the earliest date: 26th June; the G minor (K. 550) is dated 25th July, and the set concludes with the so-called 'Jupiter' Symphony, in C major (K. 551). How long these works had been shaping in his mind before they were actually put on paper it is impossible to tell; but in any case the wonder remains incomprehensible, for it is as much of a puzzle how music of such lucid complexity could be carried in a man's brain without an immediate written record as how three complete masterpieces, equally great and entirely different from each other, could have been committed to paper within so short a space of time during a period of acute anxieties of a particularly prosaic and disheartening sort.

But there the three works remain for all to wonder at afresh each time one of them is heard. Unhappily the letters to Puchberg also remain for posterity to blush over and for humankind to regard as a wretched token of its feeble hold on the world. They begin with a pathetic concealment of wounded pride, continue in a more and more desperate tone, and at times abjectly abandon all pretence at dignity in an urgent cry for immediate help. Mozart's demands were at times too great for Puchberg to meet, but he seems to have done his best to assist his friend without involving him in unbearable burdens of indebtedness and humiliation.

Once sunk in debt and worried into fatalistic indifference, Mozart floundered on helplessly, unable to master the situation. Occasional windfalls could do no more than bring temporary relief. One of them must have come as a godsend, all the same. Van Swieten had taken it into his head to cultivate one of his favourite masters, Handel, not only by study, but by performance. He gave private concerts to which many of the nobility subscribed, either in the large hall of the court library or at one of the subscribers' town residences; but as none of these places contained an organ, it was found necessary to provide additional accompaniments to replace the missing *continuo*. The conductor was at first Joseph Starzer, who had already arranged *Judas Maccabaeus* in this manner; but Starzer had died in April 1787, and for his next season van Swieten engaged Mozart, whose first arrangement was that of *Acis and Galatea,* performed in November 1788. *Messiah* followed in March 1789, and the following year he completed his versions of Handel with *Alexander's Feast* and the *Ode for St. Cecilia's Day*.

These isolated employments could not keep the wolf from Mozart's door. He was therefore glad enough in the spring of 1789 to accept an invitation from Prince Carl Lichnowsky to accompany him to Berlin. The journey, it is true, held out no immediate promise of material advantage, but he had nothing to gain by staying at home, and there was always a chance that some lucrative employment, temporary or permanent, might result from the new contacts he was sure to make in the Prussian capital. Besides, he had not, at thirty-three, become a stay-at-home. He never forgot his hankerings after England, and it was exciting to go anywhere abroad once more.

They left on 8th April, travelling in princely fashion in Lichnowsky's own coach. Thus Dresden was reached very quickly. As early as the 14th Mozart played before the Elector Frederick Augustus of Saxony—the D major Concerto (K. 537) among other things—and received a hundred ducats. He could do with them, for just before his departure he had been obliged to apply for another loan, this time to Councillor of Justice Franz Hofdemel, on whose imminent election to the freemasons' lodge he was compelled to presume with humiliating haste. What is worse, this was not an expedient to relieve Puchberg of his importunity, but evidently an additional loan, for he writes to Constanze from Prague asking her to convey 'all that is thinkable' to the Puchbergs and to tell his friend that he will write from Berlin to thank him. Thank him for what? We know but too well, alas!

To Constanze he wrote the queerest letters during the separations from her which now began to become frequent. They are tender, crudely amorous and childishly comic by turns, full of that punning, rhyming and word-playing fatuousness which people who are simply and frankly but not profoundly in love with each other indulge in to their hearts' content. He called her the most idiotic names and was touchingly solicitous for her health—sometimes, too, for her behaviour later on, when he had to send her to Baden [1] to be cured of various ailments and was now and again assailed by a sudden fear that she might, perhaps inadvertently, lay herself open to malicious talk. It is clear that he had never been able to forget the trifling yet distressing incident which had led to a brief but sharp quarrel before their marriage and was at

[1] The health resort near Vienna—Beethoven's Baden.

CONSTANZE MOZART, NÉE WEBER

Portrait by Hans Hansen, 1802

times haunted by a feeling that she was, not perhaps of questionable morality, but disposed to look upon moral issues too lightly for his liking. The impression that he never found it in his heart to love her quite unreservedly is strengthened by these connubial letters of the last years, although they leave no room for doubt that he had a genuine affection for her, which would at times gush forth without any sort of restraint.

Mozart had been received in several private houses at Dresden and greatly admired. It was much the same in Leipzig, where he arrived on 20th April; but what chiefly attracted him there was St. Thomas's Church and the organ on which Bach had played for over a quarter of a century. The great cantor's successor, Johann Friedrich Doles, an old man of seventy-four, received him with great kindness, invited him to play on the hallowed instrument and was much struck by the appreciative way in which the Viennese composer, in whom a very different direction of taste was to be expected, discussed Bach's music, for which indeed he had an admiration bordering on reverence. After a public performance on Bach's organ, with which Mozart had astonished a numerous assembly, Doles had the master's motet, 'Singet dem Herrn,' performed for him by the St. Thomas choristers, whereupon he exclaimed: 'Here, for once, is something from which one may learn!' He then asked for copies of Bach's other motets.

The Prussian court being at Potsdam, Mozart went straight there from Leipzig. He was soon presented to Frederick William II, who was a great lover of music and had learnt to play the violoncello from the Frenchman Jean Pierre Duport, who was attached to his court, and on a minuet by whom Mozart wrote a set of Variations for pianoforte (K. 573).

When Lichnowsky returned to Vienna at the beginning of May, Mozart took the opportunity to go back to Leipzig, where he was anxious to give a concert. It took place on the 12th. He conducted one of his symphonies, played the piano Concertos K. 456 and 503, and Josepha Dušek, who happened to be in Saxony, sang the aria 'Non temer, amato bene'

(K. 505). Those who were present saw to it that the concert was a success; but unfortunately there were none too many of them: he made no money to speak of. On the 19th he was back in Prussia, this time in Berlin itself, where on that very evening *Die Entführung* was given at the National Theatre.[1] Two stories are current of how Mozart attended the performance unknown to anybody, was recognized and dragged upon the stage to acknowledge the public's frantic applause; also one of a love affair with the coquettish singer Henriette Baranius which has every appearance of being untrue.

He gave no public concert in Berlin, Frederick William not being in favour of such condescensions on the part of those he protected; but he received a handsome present of a hundred *Friedrichsdor* from the king, which yielded him about seven hundred Austrian florins, as well as a commission to compose six string quartets for the royal violoncellist and six easy piano sonatas for Princess Friederike. That an appointment to the Prussian court was offered him which he refused in deference to Joseph II must be regarded as legendary. He had no reason for any such attachment to the emperor, and it is not conceivable that he would have refrained from mentioning so important an offer in his letters to his wife. Still less is it likely that he would have refused it.

In some inexplicable way—or can the fair Henriette be the explanation, after all?—his profits seem to have melted away by the time he was ready to return home. We only know that his princely host, Lichnowsky, finding himself short of money, had asked him for a loan which for obvious reasons he could not refuse to make. On 23rd May he wrote to Constanze: 'As regards my return, you will have to look forward to me more than to the money.' On 4th June, after a journey via Dresden and Prague, he was at home again.

In the course of that month he finished the first of the Quartets for the King of Prussia (D major, K. 575), for which

[1] *Figaro* and *Don Giovanni* were not yet known in Berlin.

he received a sum similar to that already bestowed on him by the generous monarch. That ought to have encouraged him to continue the series forthwith. But fate would not thus be cheated of its prey. It promptly hung a pall of depression over him which made work impossible. Constanze, once again in her usual condition,[1] was the convenient instrument. She became very seriously ill, and nothing would do but a cure at Baden. Decoctions, leeches, electuaries, ants' eggs and all the usual quackeries did no good. The Prussian money melted away, doubtless under the scorching eye of creditors. On 12th July a heartrending letter reached Puchberg, reflecting distraction in its shapeless sentences:

> God! I am in a situation that I would not wish my most wicked enemy; and if you, my best of friends and brothers, forsake me, I am *unhappily* and *innocently* lost with my poor sick wife and my child.—Only the other day I wished to bare my heart to you—but I did not find the courage!—and I should still lack it—it is only tremblingly and in writing that I dare—and I should not dare even in writing—were I not aware that you know me, know my circumstances, and are wholly convinced of my innocence in the matter of my most sad and unfortunate condition. O God! instead of thanks, I have but new entreaties for you!—instead of settlements but new demands. If you know my heart entirely, you must be able to feel the whole distress which this gives me.

And so it goes on. Constanze seems better one day, and the next her condition throws him into such despair that he cannot work; he has sent round a subscription list for a private concert, and it has come back with a single name on it—everybody is out of town; and then, most pathetic of all, he assures Puchberg, who must have long ceased to believe in anything of the sort, that all this embarrassment is only temporary, that he is sure to make money presently, that he will repay everything with interest very soon. The worst was, Mozart no longer believed this himself.

[1] A girl, Anna, was born on 16th November 1789 and died the same day.

It was dreadful: Puchberg did not answer. Mozart had to write him two more letters, more abject than the first. Perhaps the good man was away, like the rest of wealthy Vienna; perhaps he really had to begin to consider the situation, which may well have gone beyond his means, his good nature or his understanding by this time. However, he seems to have helped in the end, for Constanze did go to Baden and rapidly improved in health. But her holiday seems to have spoiled her in other ways, for no sooner had Mozart begun to rejoice at her recovery than he became worried over the careless way in which she managed to set tongues wagging in the health resort, where everybody was so accustomed to watch promiscuous affairs of all kinds that the slightest appearance of frivolity made the idle spectators jump to the most damaging conclusions. An acquaintance, who normally looked upon women most chivalrously, had 'written the most monstrous and the rudest *sottises*' concerning her, and Mozart complained that she was making herself cheap.

Figaro was to be revived on 29th August 1789, with Adriana Ferrarese del Bene as Susanna, and for her Mozart composed two extra arias: the concerto-like rondo, 'Al desio' (K. 577), which is usually regarded as a piece for the Countess, but was intended for Susanna disguised, in music as well as in dress, as the Countess, and the little arietta, 'Un moto di gioia' (K. 579). Mozart did not think much of this singer, but she had to be obliged because, for one thing, she was da Ponte's mistress, or rather—begging his pardon for this insinuation of singularity—one of his mistresses, and for another because she was to be in the cast of a new Italian comic opera which the emperor had commissioned from da Ponte and Mozart.

This time da Ponte meant to be original, although it was said that the gist of his plot for *Così fan tutte* came from an adventure that had shortly before happened to two pairs of lovers in Vienna, and he used stock figures and situations of the conventional *opera buffa.* However that may be, he wrote a very amusing and polished libretto, none the less good because the whole of the nineteenth century, with Beethoven at the head, persisted in condemning it for its supposed immorality —as though it mattered whether a purely theatrical fantasy of this sort was in the least moral or not. Indeed, adverse criticism extended even to the music: those who could not bear to think of Mozart as anything but a paragon of all the virtues, and could therefore not conceive the idea of his setting such a libretto except under pressure, hypnotized themselves into regarding music written in spite of an imagined protest as necessarily inferior in quality, without apparently listening to it at all.

The Viennese public was less squeamish and more sensible. It enjoyed *Così fan tutte, ossia La scuola degli amanti* (*That's what they all do,*[1] *or The School for Lovers*) (K. 588) on its first performance on 21st January 1790 and crowded its subsequent performances, which were interrupted by court mourning but resumed in June. The palpable absurdities of the libretto were taken simply for what they were operatically worth, and it should be remembered that the disguises of Despina as doctor and notary did not seem too incredible to a public still accustomed to the male soprano. Ferrarese del Bene sang Fiordiligi, and though Mozart was dissatisfied with her, she must at least have had peculiar accomplishments, for he wrote very difficult music for her including sudden skips over a wide range of voice. Louise Villeneuve was Dorabella, a tenor named Calvesi sang Ferrando, Benucci turned up once more

[1] The Italian title is untranslatable, mainly owing to the feminine inflection of the word 'all,' which can be rendered in English only by circumlocution—'Women's Ways,' 'Girls will be Girls,' etc. But, as Professor Edward J. Dent has suggested, the translation of the alternative title, *The School for Lovers,* might well be adopted once and for all: it is the librettist's own and might quite well be an English play-title of the period. The first English version given in London in 1828, with the music arranged (!) by Samuel James Arnold, was called *Tit for Tat.*

as Guglielmo, and Bussani as Don Alfonso completed the cast with his wife as Despina.

For Louise Villeneuve Mozart had already in the preceding year written three extra arias to be interpolated into other composers' operas: 'Alma grande e nobil core' (K. 578) for Cimarosa's *I due baroni,* 'Chi sa, chi sa qual sia' and 'Vado, ma dove?' (K. 582–3) for Martín's *Il burbero di buon core.* Also, in July 1789, he had composed the piano Sonata in D major (K. 576), said to be one of those intended for the Prussian princess, though it is anything but easy, and on 29th September of the same year he had produced the exquisite Quintet for clarinet and strings (K. 581), one of the works in which he showed an especial love for the clarinet towards the end of his life.[1]

The court mourning mentioned above was in reality a national mourning. Joseph II had died on 20th February 1790. If he had done little for Mozart, there was plenty of excuse: unusually heavy cares of state, a lonely and childless life after an early widowhood and an unhappy second marriage, and not, when all was said, any profound interest in music except as an object for fashionable cultivation. But if Mozart hoped for an improvement under Leopold II, who ascended the throne on 13th March, he was mistaken. He had once called Joseph a skinflint more or less playfully, but he might have applied the epithet to his brother with conviction. He hoped that perhaps he might now be appointed *Capellmeister* in the place of Salieri, who had enjoyed a long run under a very partial patron and forestalled a dismissal by withdrawing voluntarily; but Joseph Weigl was put in his place and Mozart ignored. He might be thankful to be allowed to retain his former post as chamber musician. When he handed in a petition for employment as second *Capellmeister,* as composer for the church, as instructor to the archdukes—anything

[1] In this, if in nothing else, he was emulated by Brahms a century later. Mozart's composing for Anton Stadler and Brahms's for Richard Mühlfeld are curiously analogous.

—he met with no success. When King Ferdinand of Naples visited Vienna in September, operas by Salieri and Weigl were paraded before him and Haydn was presented, with the result that the ageing master received a pressing invitation to Naples, which he neglected only for a more tempting one to London. Mozart, much to his mortification, was passed over as though he did not exist.

Indeed it became more and more difficult to do so. Constanze was still ailing and had to go to Baden again in the summer. He was unwell himself, suffering from rheumatic pains, headaches and toothaches. The faithful Puchberg helped again and again, though he must have realized that he poured money away without doing anything permanently useful for his hapless friend, who was now reduced to resorting to usurers, or at any rate to trying to move Puchberg by telling him that he intended to take this desperate step. In May and June, overwhelmed with cares as he was, he managed to write two more of the Quartets for the King of Prussia, B flat major and F major (K. 589–90); but he was obliged to dispose of them 'for a mere song' to raise a little money somehow. In August he became seriously ill. The other three quartets had to wait. It was hopeless to attempt any composition in these circumstances. Even Mozart's power of detachment was not proof against them. A great personal grief—yes, that would have set the floodgates of inspiration wide, would perhaps in these years of forcible maturing have called forth music of an even darker passion than that of the G minor Symphony, an even profounder human understanding, if that were possible, than anything in *Don Giovanni* showed. But this grinding, gnawing worry could only blight his spirit.

Something had to be done, something material, practical. A daring plan formed itself in his mind. Leopold II was to be crowned at Frankfort on 9th October, and although Mozart was not officially attached to the court for the occasion, he conceived the idea of going there on his own account and giving concerts while the imperial city would be swarming with people from all over Europe. Salieri and Umlauf were to go in state in the imperial retinue, and fifteen chamber musicians with them, but Mozart would show them that he had no need of such prestige, and so would his brother-in-law, the violinist Franz Hofer, husband of Josefa, who decided to accompany him. True, the silver had to be pawned first; but what of that. The old travelling fever was on him, the old optimistic confidence that, neglected though he might be at home, somewhere far off the best of fortunes was only waiting to be grabbed by him.

CHAPTER XIV

CONSUMMATION AND EXTINCTION

Off Mozart and Hofer went on 23rd September 1790, and all seemed to be miraculously well once more. At Ratisbon they took their midday meal 'with divine table music, angelic (*Englische*) attendance and a glorious Moselle wine.' In Nuremberg they breakfasted—'an ugly town,' Mozart wrote with characteristic eighteenth-century contempt for all that was 'Gothick.' Würzburg, on the other hand, was 'a fine, magnificent city,' and only at Aschaffenburg were they 'miserably swindled by mine host.'

At Frankfort the coronation absorbed every one's attention at first. Still, Mozart was 'wanted everywhere' and had to submit to being 'quizzed everywhere' in order to advertise his concert as widely as possible. It took place on 15th October, and he played the D major Concerto (K. 537), which has ever since been called, rather misleadingly, the 'Coronation' Concerto. (It had been written, we know, nearly three years before.) That his brother-in-law also appeared at this concert cannot be doubted. As usual, it yielded him much honour and little cash, and he left the same week. He went to Offenbach, where he met Johann André, who was later to become his publisher; to Mainz, where he played before the elector for a disappointingly small reward; and to Mannheim, where he heard a performance of *Figaro* on the 24th. But to see the old Mannheim friends, or those who were left, he had to go to Munich, where he arrived on the 29th. On 4th November he had the satisfaction of appearing after all before the King of Naples, who paid a brief visit to the Elector of Bavaria just then. A nice snub for the Austrian court, he thought.

Some time in November he returned to Vienna, not appreciably better off than when he had left. He found a letter from O'Reilly, manager of the Italian opera in London, inviting him to go there and compose at least two operas, and when Salomon came to invite Haydn to England in December, he promised Mozart that he should be the next to be asked to appear at his London concerts. For some reason or other O'Reilly's invitation could not be accepted, and Salomon's had in any case to wait. The old misery began again, punctuated by appeals to Puchberg and relieved here and there by a commission. Thus the two string Quintets in D major and E flat major (K. 593, 614), written in December 1790 and April 1791, were composed for a Hungarian patron, and a collector of curiosities ordered three works for a mechanical organ (K. 594, 608, 616), written in 1790–1 and, considering that they admittedly failed to interest Mozart, of an astonishing depth and originality. On 5th January 1791 the last piano Concerto, in B flat major (K. 595), was finished. Much dance music for the court was again turned out at this time.

He had a busy year in front of him. No less than three important orders were to come his way, and fortunately, although he did not feel any too strong and well, creative work was what troubled him least. He could always forget himself in it. The first task came from an unexpected quarter. Who should offer it to him but that shrewd man of the theatre, half artist and half charlatan, Emanuel Schikaneder, who had been befriended by the Mozarts during his season at Salzburg and in return admitted them free to his performances? He was giving popular pantomimes, farces, spectacular pieces and musical plays at the Theater auf der Wieden, a great barn of a place where a very mixed audience enjoyed his entertaining but none too fastidiously selected performances. Mozart was delighted to meet this amusing *farceur* again, especially as he turned out to be a fellow-mason, and he welcomed his suggestion that they should collaborate in a musical pantomime and call it an opera by courtesy. At any rate Mozart privately decided to see to it that it would be an opera, whatever catch-penny concoction the astute impresario might expect. So Schikaneder submitted him a libretto he gave out as his own, though he had merely pieced it together from various favourite plays. By the time he had finished with it an astonishing farrago of high-minded masonic symbolism, fairy-tale and farce emerged, full of ill-digested elements of poetry and philosophy, adroitly put together with an eye to theatrical effect and, for all its incongruities,[1] abounding in possibilities for the most varied and novel musical treatment, as Mozart was quick to see. At any rate he seized upon *Die Zauberflöte* with avidity and set to work at once.

The sooner the new opera could be produced the better, for Constanze, true to her regular habit, once more expected a baby. Moreover, she was in very poor health again and had to be packed off to Baden in June. While she was away, Mozart worked hard, felt lonely, beguiled himself by occasionally eating at Puchberg's and other friends' houses or sleeping at Leutgeb's, and Schikaneder often invited him to his dinners, which seem to have frequently ended in debauches. Whenever he could he went to see his wife and little Carl at Baden, and it was during one of these visits that he composed the motet 'Ave, verum corpus' for four voices with accompaniment for strings and organ (K. 618) on 18th June. This was the first piece of church music he had written since 1783. It seems almost as though fate were urging him to try his hand at a sketch for a much more important work of the kind he was to undertake shortly.

It was in July that the curious event occurred. One day a gaunt stranger dressed in grey presented himself at Mozart's

[1] For instance, according to the original plan, Sarastro was to be a force of evil and the Queen of Night the opposing force of good. Half-way through the first act this was changed to the opposite, but the three beneficent genii who accompany Tamino and Papageno are still supplied by the wicked queen, whose activities were said to symbolize those of the court faction which opposed freemasonry.

lodging with an order to compose a *Requiem*. It was to be called for at an appointed time and bought at a generous price, on condition that the composer should not tell a soul about this commission and the conditions under which it had been offered him. The transaction was in reality quite simple. The caller was the steward of a certain nobleman, Count Franz von Walsegg, who dabbled in music, wished to bestow a great work on the world as his own and, lacking the required invention and skill, conceived the idea of buying it ready-made from an acknowledged master, not realizing or little caring that its very excellence would make it impossible for any one with the slightest discernment to take him for the author. But to Mozart, who was probably far from well at the time and may have been in a feverish state when the stranger called, the incident seemed charged with the most sinister import. It threw him into a state of acute depression and foreboding. He set to work on the *Requiem* in a frame of mind in which, to judge by its music, a kind of febrile exaltation and fascination were uppermost.

Altogether July 1791 was an eventful month. *Die Zauberflöte* was as good as completed,[1] and on the 26th another son was born, Franz Xaver Wolfgang, who was destined to be the only child apart from Carl to survive his father and grow up. Long before Mozart had completed the *Requiem* the third commission arrived, this time from Prague. Leopold II had already been crowned as Emperor at Frankfort, but his coronation as King of Bohemia had still to take place, and for it Prague required a new festival opera, which had of course to be of a serious nature and, if possible, allusive in its subject. The theme of a magnanimous ruler seemed indicated, and so Metastasio's old and much-composed libretto of *La clemenza di Tito* was chosen, somewhat furbished up by one Caterino

[1] In order to keep Mozart under his eye Schikaneder had placed a little summer-house near the theatre at his disposal, in which most of the opera is said to have been composed. This modest shack is now on the Kapuzinerberg at Salzburg.

Mazzola. Mozart had no particular inclination to revert to the old, stiff, lifeless type of Italian *opera seria,* but he had no choice and was still less disposed to refuse an order that was both profitable and honourable. Prague had done much to further his reputation, so that, busy as he was, he could not think of turning a deaf ear to such an invitation.

No time was to be lost, for the coronation was to take place on 6th September. Mozart and Constanze set off post-haste, and he began to sketch his music in the stage coach, working out what he had done at the inns where they stayed for the night. No sooner had they reached Prague than he made the acquaintance of the singers in order to study their idiosyncrasies and acquaint himself with their caprices, as usual. The whole work, carried out in terrible haste, was completed and rehearsed within the space of eighteen days, an incredible feat even if it is remembered that Mozart's pupil Franz Süssmayr, who accompanied them, was given the *secco* recitatives to do. After a performance of *Don Giovanni* on the 2nd, *La clemenza di Tito* (*The Clemency of Titus*) (K. 621) was produced at the end of the coronation day, 6th September 1791, with a cast that was wholly new to Mozart with the exception of Baglioni, his original Don Ottavio, who sang the title part. The success of the work was lukewarm, and no wonder: it was in a style that no longer attracted the composer and had been written in too much of a hurry. Moreover, the evening's acclamations were not unnaturally reserved for the new king. Mozart received two hundred ducats, which hardly consoled him for his failure, more especially as he had been feeling far from well during this visit to Prague. Back in Vienna about the middle of September, he was completely exhausted and in very poor health.

He did not know what was the matter with him, and if he took any care of himself it was by the usual drastic and haphazard family remedies, which naturally made matters worse. Somehow his precarious state seems to be reflected in the hectic beauty of the clarinet Concerto in A major (K. 622), composed for Stadler and finished on 28th September. Two days later, 30th September 1791, *Die Zauberflöte* (*The Magic Flute*) (K. 620) was produced at Schikaneder's theatre, with that enterprising barnstormer not only announced in large type as the author, but appearing in the part of Papageno, so designed as to earn him all the evening's laughs and to put the catchiest tunes into his mouth.[1] Mozart's name was characteristically given only in a note under the cast:

> The music is by Herr Wolfgang Amade Mozart, *Capellmeister* and Imperial Royal Chamber Musician in Ordinary. Herr Mozart will, in deference to a gracious and honourable public, and from friendship for the author of the piece, conduct the orchestra in person to-day.

Evidently Schikaneder regarded the music as merely incidental. The programme resumes:

> The book of the opera, adorned with two copper engravings, showing Herr Schikaneder in the part of Papageno, engraved after the actual costume, may be had at the box office for 30 kreuzer.
>
> Herr Gayl, the theatre painter, and Herr Nessthaler as decorator, flatter themselves to have worked with all possible artistic zeal according to the prescribed plan of the piece.

The cast was not of any great distinction, as might be expected at a theatre of this sort. Still, Schikaneder had succeeded some time before in attaching Mozart's sister-in-law, Josefa Hofer, to his company, and it was for her that the composer wrote the exceedingly high and florid part of the Queen of Night. The Sarastro was Franz Gerl, an excellent bass, whose wife sang the small part of Papagena. The tenor Benedict Schack, who was also a flautist and a composer in a humble way, was the Tamino, while Pamina was sung by Nannina Gottlieb, who had advanced to that important part from the tiny one of Barbarina in *Figaro*.

[1] He is even supposed to have hummed one or two of Papageno's melodies to Mozart as he wanted them; but the rumour may be confidently dismissed as a legend.

The opera did not have a very great success at first, for music-lovers may well have found the pantomime too childish while the score was above the heads of the rabble. Still, it pleased better and better as the performances went on, twenty-four of which were given in the course of October alone. Mozart, who could be very angry with people who showed no response to music, did not take himself so seriously as to refrain from entering into the farcical side of *The Magic Flute*. At one performance he took it into his head to play the chime bells for Schikaneder behind the scenes during the song 'Ein Mädchen oder Weibchen,' where Papageno accompanies himself with their magic tinkle. He waggishly inserted an arpeggio in an unexpected place, whereupon Schikaneder looked round in surprise and the public, having found out that he was not striking the bells himself, began to laugh. The actor then paused in the next verse, waiting for the same trick to be played by the composer, and when the arpeggio resounded a second time without his having touched the instrument, he addressed it with a snappy 'Shut up!', whereupon the whole audience gave forth a great shout of laughter. Let this story be recalled by those who would like to regard *The Magic Flute* as a solemn ritual and who are unduly impressed by the fact that the great Goethe, who much admired the work, planned to write a libretto as a sequel to it—a project which, it should be remembered, he abandoned before it was more than half carried out.

In October, when Constanze was once more at Baden, this time with her sister Sophie, Mozart resumed his work on the *Requiem*. Not knowing that another would claim the credit for it, and perhaps with some obscure feeling that this mass for the dead must represent him as worthily in the domain of church music as the last opera, the last three symphonies and the last chamber music did elsewhere, he feverishly lavished all his inspiration on this task. He had days of terrible dejection on which he could not work, and when he did he was sometimes interrupted by fainting fits. Dread premonitions haunted him day and night. When Constanze returned from Baden she found him strange, melancholy and rapidly weakening. She did her best to keep him from work, but he returned to the *Requiem* again and again in a sort of terrified desperation. In his fevered state he began to believe that he had been poisoned,[1] a suspicion that may well have been confirmed by his inability to account for his illness by any natural causes. In November, when he felt somewhat better, he himself confessed that it had all been pure imagination, and he was able to compose the *Little Masonic Cantata* for male voices and orchestra (K. 623) for which Schikaneder had supplied the words. It was dated as finished on 15th November, and he even contrived to conduct it. But the recovery was deceptive. Before long he felt worse than ever. His gloomy moods returned, he grew ever weaker, his hands and feet swelled, his body became rigid and he had appalling attacks of sickness. Towards the end of November he was overwhelmed by one of those minor bitternesses which make a lingering death more dreadful than physical pain: he had to ask them to remove his beloved canary because he could no longer endure its singing. The distracted Constanze was faithfully helped by her sister Sophie Haibl, who had married and outgrown the stage of flapperhood once none too favourably described by her brother-in-law. She proved a gentle nurse.

He was happy to hear of the growing success of *The Magic Flute,* but drove tears into the eyes of those around him by holding his watch in his hand on the evenings it was performed and working out the time at which this or that favourite passage would be sung and played. He still tried to work at the *Requiem,* discussed it with Süssmayr and asked his friends to hold little rehearsals for him, singing in four parts with keyboard accompaniment. But on 4th December, just as they were beginning the 'Lacrymosa,' he broke down. Some

[1] There is not the slightest evidence that he himself suspected Salieri of an attempt upon his life, and all subsequent rumours to that effect must be energetically rejected as hysterical fancies.

kind of partial paralysis set in. A priest was called to administer extreme unction. The *Requiem,* however, occupied him almost to the last.[1] Even after he had said his last farewell to his family and to the world its strains still seemed to haunt him, and he tried to sing them. Towards midnight he turned to the wall, as though inclined to go to sleep. The first hour of 5th December 1791 had nearly run its course when Wolfgang Amadeus Mozart breathed his last, not quite thirty-six years of age.

As in the case of his mother, nobody knows what he died of. Of the countless diagnoses it has been attempted to establish that of uraemia is the most convincing. Perhaps it was only by a happy accident that he had lived at all, just as five brothers and sisters had died in infancy by a sad one. There can be small doubt that he must have carried the seeds of this or that disease about with him all his short life. He had suffered from many illnesses as a child, and so had his surviving sister, who became blind in later years. Some say he was loved too much by the gods, but that may be too much like bitter irony, and it is not rational to suppose anything of the kind. Still, one hardly sees how he could have carried on his work much longer or what more he could have done. His music, one of the richest, most abundant and many-sided heritages ever bequeathed to the world by any artist, is fully matured—indeed almost over-ripe, one is inclined to think, in a few of the last works, which have the unearthly quality of music one cannot imagine to come from any human being but one facing extinction.

Constanze broke down in a wild, undisciplined agony of grief that may not have deserved all the sympathy she needed; but it is none the less distressing that she received so little help

[1] Constanze at first gave the work to Eybler to finish, but the task was afterwards turned over to Süssmayr, who knew more of Mozart's intentions than anyone else. The facts show it to be a mistake to believe that Mozart actually expressed a wish that Süssmayr should complete the score.

from those who had professed to admire and love Mozart. Van Swieten, who could very well have afforded to assist her in giving her husband a funeral such as would have at least granted her the comfort of self-respect, contented himself with offering good advice as to the cheapest way of burying him. Numb with sorrow, she could make no decision for herself, but did as she was told. So on 6th December the master was given a third-class funeral in a paupers' grave, with a dozen or more corpses of people who had nothing in common with him but the fate of having perished at the same time.

No monument stands over the resting-place of the artist who has left us an inexhaustible treasury of works without which the art of music would not only be a gloomier, a more cold-hearted, a less varied thing, but without which that art is simply not conceivable to those who know and love it—which is the same thing. Even the exact location of his grave is not known; his remains have vanished, and the skull now in the Mozarteum at Salzburg is far from being definitely ascertained to be his. But does it matter? The treasury remains.

CHAPTER XV

VOCAL MUSIC

AND now this treasury has to be explored. It is difficult to know where to begin. Still harder will it be to make an end where there is so much that tempts to discussion and not nearly enough room to say all that Mozart's music in its many aspects entices one to write.

To clear the ground, a whole large section of music that is of relatively small importance to the modern world may be reviewed in one single chapter: all the vocal music except that for the stage. Of small importance? It sounds odd, for is it not a commonplace to say of Mozart that he is primarily a vocal composer? Yet, come to think of it, how much of his non-operatic vocal music is of any use to practising musicians to-day? The masses are not readily adaptable even to the use for which they were originally intended, for the catholic service nowadays resorts either to more austere music less tainted with the fashions of a period or else, where the resources for such music are not available, to smaller and flimsier works. In any case the orchestra is not only no longer available in the catholic church, but no longer allowed, and Mozart's masses are useless without their more or less lavish orchestral accompaniments.

The concert arias are neglected for reasons that may emerge from their discussion a few pages farther on; the songs for the very obvious one that, as a species, they have been superseded by later achievements and thus suffer from the usual incapacity of most performers and listeners to judge a type of music according to the standards of its own time. The choral works were even in their days mostly reserved for special purposes, masonic or dramatic, and they include an arranged work and an early oratorio of no great value; the unaccompanied canons are mere *jeux d'esprit* almost impossible to fit into any scheme of performance; and the remaining miscellaneous pieces—duets, trios, short choruses and so on—have mostly lost their justification with the occasions for which they were composed.

Thus, considering the vast bulk of Mozart's vocal music, little remains for singers to pay attention to, and one must come to the conclusion that, if he really is a vocal composer, he is a vocal composer of instrumental music. It is true, he wrote incomparably singable music, but he wrote it more often than not, and more successfully on the whole, for instruments and combinations of instruments. Wagner drew attention to the fact that in the symphonies all the instruments sing, sing continually and gloriously, even the double basses.

In church music, for one thing, it may fairly be said that Mozart was not especially interested. It is significant, at any rate, that after 1780—that is after Salzburg, where the composition of music for the archbishop's services was incumbent on him—he wrote only three works of the kind. More than that: the most important of them, the *Requiem* (K. 626), was turned out to the order of another, a would-be composer. The second extensive one, the C minor Mass (K. 427), was prompted by a vow and, be it observed, never completed. The third is a small piece, the motet 'Ave, verum corpus' (K. 618), which musically falls into the category of Mozart's masonic music rather than of his church compositions proper.

The sixty works or so, large and small, produced for the Salzburg services, neither can nor need be discussed one by one in a small book. I do not, in any case, propose to review Mozart's music systematically by giving each species an equal amount of space, or even always the amount of space it deserves. It would be futile to pretend, for instance, that the five supremely important operas, let alone all the dramatic works, can be adequately dealt with in the single chapter it is possible to reserve for them. On the other hand a short survey of the church music as a whole, with merely a casual reference to a particular work here and there and special consideration of the two large post-Salzburgian compositions will have to be deemed sufficient, although some readers may happen to be more interested in that phase of Mozart's work than in the piano concertos, which have nearly a whole chapter to themselves. However, if any excuse beyond paucity of space is needed, it may well be urged that the concertos are far more representative of Mozart as a musical personality than the church music. Many other composers of the period wrote masses artistically almost as good as Mozart's, if stylistically as inappropriate to their purpose, whereas his orchestrally accompanied display pieces, and especially those for the pianoforte, are unique.

But perhaps no apology is really necessary. The concertos call for a good deal of discussion because they are alive and actually tend to come into a wider currency again than they enjoyed in the nineteenth century, whereas the church music is as good as useless, as it does not conform to the modern practice of the Roman liturgy. That, of course, is not Mozart's fault, though it is fortunate that the more sober traditions which revert to the unaccompanied music of the polyphonic masters and, so to speak, to the Gothic style, have swept away along with Mozart a great deal of trashy orchestrally accompanied music often more fit for the opera house than for the church.

Mozart's own masses, indeed, are too often operatic, though operatic in his own sterling way. That was exactly what they were expected to be, and if they are superseded to-day, that is their misfortune rather than their fault. All the same, they date more than any other music of his, which is another reason for suspecting that they were not written spontaneously. The mere fact that they were done to order proves nothing, of course, for so were Bach's cantatas, than which no music could be more personally expressive of religious devotion; but taken as a whole—for they have exceptional moments—they are as quaintly old-fashioned as the rococo architecture of Salzburg which they resemble. As delightful too, no doubt, but as little habitable or suitable for emulation.

They come out of the baroque mass that flourished from Fux to Hasse and was represented at Salzburg with some distinction by Eberlin. It was a grandiose affair with extended solo and choral subdivisions of the main liturgical rubrics, accompanied by large, festive orchestras as well as by the organ. With Mozart the instrumental body was sometimes confined to strings and organ, but it could be as full as the Salzburg band would allow on important occasions. Drums went with trumpets as a matter of course and trombones were used now and then. Mass sung at high festivals, at an installation or some such ceremony, was as dressy and flashy at Salzburg as the production of a new opera in Vienna. At the cathedral the archbishop's bodyguard attended with helmets and halberds, the vestments of clergy and choir were as splendid as the dresses of the fashionable ladies in the congregation, and the music was as ostentatious as was compatible with devotion —in fact, according to the ideas of other times, a good deal more so. The chancel was packed with singers, including the court soloists, and on four galleries that circled half-way round the pillars supporting the dome were perched the orchestral musicians, who could thus play antiphonally with as good effect as in concert, probably better, indeed, for they must have been difficult to keep together.

Mozart's first piece of church music was a *Kyrie* in F major (K. 33), written at the age of ten. It was probably intended to grow into a whole mass but, like other more normal boyish efforts, such as model battleships, theatres and carpenter's benches, had to be abandoned as too ambitious. The first complete masses were written in Vienna in 1768, one a *Missa brevis* in G major (K. 49) and the other the full Mass composed for the orphanage church in the Rennweg—said to be the work in C minor-major (K. 139).[1]

Mozart was the most natural genius born into the most

[1] Wilhelm Kurthen conjectures so in *Studien zu Mozarts kirchenmusikalischen Jugendwerken,* and he is supported by Robert Haas. But see footnote on p. 41.

artificial time. But here, in his church music, he was content to reproduce the artifice of his period without readily giving rein to his creative nature, or if not content, at least he did not rebel so long as he was obliged to supply this kind of work. So at least one gathers directly it is realized that he left church music alone the moment he had revolted against serving the archbishop. It made no difference to him whether a mass contained the kind of polyphony which the baroque age considered liturgical, as in the fugues to which he generally set certain portions of the text, such as 'Cum sancto spiritu' in the Gloria or 'Et vitam venturi saeculi' in the Credo, or whether it approximated to the operatic aria. The Kyrie[1] in the C major Mass (K. 317) of 1779, for instance:

will return as Fiordiligi's aria, 'Come scoglio,' in *Così fan tutte* eleven years later, and the 'Agnus Dei' in the same work:

[1] It is used again as the 'Dona' at the end of the Mass, thus creating a precedent for Süssmayr, who adopted the same procedure on completing the *Requiem*.

turns up again, in another key and time, as the Countess's 'Dove sono' in *Figaro*. Then again conventional formulas will serve him as well as anything else for a mass. The venerable tag:

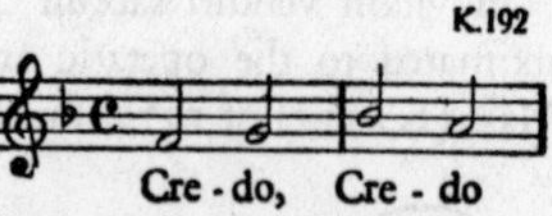

will do for the Credo in the *Missa brevis* in F major (K. 192) as it does for one of the subjects in the finale of the 'Jupiter' Symphony. Another conventional figure of this sort in the G major *Missa brevis* (K. 49) we know from the second Kyrie in Bach's B minor Mass:

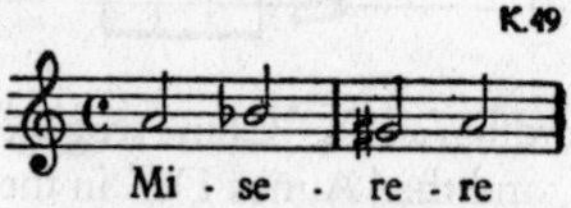

And a figure in the 'Dona' of K. 192 becomes an imploring phrase for Elvira in the second *Don Giovanni* finale:

That the composer could be quite daring at an early, tender age, even in a form of music that asked for restraint by convention, may be judged from the 'Cum sancto spiritu' fugue in that C minor-major Mass (K. 139), with its bold step of an augmented fourth—the tritone, the *diabolus in musica* in a mass, forsooth:

though it is immediately attenuated by the tonal answer, in which the interval becomes a major third. In this work, by the way, an original treatment of trumpets and trombones already asserts itself (in 1768, if we may really believe that this work was written by a boy of twelve, unaided by his father!).

Next to the masses Mozart's catalogue shows a large collection of smaller church pieces: offertories, graduals, litanies and the like, as well as several separate kyries, not all of them to be regarded as abandoned masses. These pieces show much the same characteristics as his church music on a larger scale, which may now be a little more extensively studied with the aid of an interesting and, although unfinished, representative work of the kind: the Mass in C minor for four solo voices, chorus, orchestra and organ (K. 427)[1] intended as a thanksgiving for the recovery of Constanze, and perhaps for his hoped-for reconciliation with Leopold.

We know that this Mass is patchwork, but it is doubtful whether we should have guessed as much had its history never become known, for it is by no means the only work of this type that exhibits fluctuations of style bordering on inattention and worldliness dangerously resembling irreverence in music for the church as we conceive it to-day. However, I need perhaps not reiterate that our own aesthetic reactions are irrelevant, though I am tempted to say that they are not likely

[1] I use for the purpose of this analysis the edition by Alois Schmitt in which the work is completed by five pieces taken from earlier masses, for it is in this form, if at all, that the reader is likely to hear it.

to disturb Mozart's ghost. The sensible thing to do, then, is to examine the C minor Mass in the light of the conceptions of its time and to see what good we can find in it from that point of view.

We find a great deal. It is true that even for the eighteenth-century Roman church some of the solo vocal pieces must have been almost too frivolously operatic. At one of the most solemn moments, the 'Et incarnatus,' the soprano sings a florid slow aria with concerto-like *obbligati* and a long cadenza that puts one in mind of the mad scene in Donizetti's *Lucia di Lammermoor* and Bishop's 'Lo, here the gentle lark' far more than of anything even remotely connected with divine service. At the same time, regarded with complete critical detachment as a piece of finely fashioned artificial music, this number is flawlessly beautiful, as is also the soprano's 'Christe eleison.' This is rather less operatic, less at any rate than the 'Laudamus te' for the mezzo-soprano, which might be one of those stiff arias—stiff in two senses of the word, both formally and technically—for Arbaces in *Idomeneo*. Here is a specimen:

It is difficult to imagine what this may be supposed to glorify, unless it be the singer.

The 'Kyrie eleison,' on the other hand, may be mentioned as a splendidly serious movement in C minor, which with much originality weaves into a freely contrapuntal pattern melodic material that is quite unaffected by the usual dryness of academic themes devised for polyphony. The rubrics of the Gloria and the Credo are set to series of separate numbers of such disparity of style that these larger sections cannot be said to hang together, though the Credo does so rather better, thanks to a repetition of the opening section, which the editor presents in a different key and time (C major, 3–4 at first, then E flat major, 4–4).

The opening chorus of the Gloria goes with a tremendous swing and has a beautifully transparent vocal texture. It makes one think of a Handel who has lost weight and become nimbler of foot. The contrast of 'Et in terra pax' is wonderful and still more so is the overlapping of its close with the re-entering 'gloria' phrase, as though the singers, concerned for a moment with earthly cares, could not turn back to the praise of God soon enough. Even finer are the short five-part choral 'Gratias' and the 'Qui tollis' for double chorus, both of them as nobly fashioned as anything in Bach's B minor Mass, while remaining distinctly Mozartian. The intervening 'Domine Deus' duet for the two women soloists suddenly and strangely reverts to an ecclesiastical manner of about a century earlier and also in some sort to the learnedness so gracefully worn by Steffani in his chamber duets. The two singers are joined by the tenor for the 'Quoniam' trio, which continues in something like the same vein. A brief 'Jesu Christe' is quite in the rococo style of the Salzburg masses and merely an introduction with a half-close to the 'Cum sancto spiritu,' a marvellously managed double fugue on two well-contrasted subjects, and a real, not a tonal fugue, which is rare in Mozart. Both stretto and inversion are used with consummate skill, and a sudden patch of harmonic writing into which the music veers unexpectedly, with tenors and basses kept high, has an inexplicably exciting effect:

The 'Crucifixus' shows less personal concern than Bach's, which is the expression of the truest devotion, or Beethoven's, which has a greater share of humanity, but in an only very slightly too theatrical way it is magnificently expressive all the same. The 'Et resurrexit' is frankly worldly. It contains earlier material, and so does the rapturously mellifluous 'Et in spiritum sanctum' for tenor solo with choral refrains. Not a suitable tune, perhaps, for the austerities of church service, but an unforgettably heart-easing one. This number leads, in Schmitt's edition, by a G major-E flat major transition to the renewed choral exclamation of 'credo' already referred to. This comes by way of the relative minor to the C major fugue of 'Et vitam venturi saeculi,' written in 1776 (K. 262) a tonal fugue this time, going almost at once into hair-raising strettos, with 'amens' of various shapes thrust into the texture nearly the whole time: an exhilarating piece of work.

The 'Sanctus' for double chorus is only introductory to the

'Osanna,' but suitably grandiose; the latter is a double fugue for eight-part chorus of a staggering intricacy on paper, but perfectly lucid as well as dazzling in effect. The 'Benedictus' for solo quartet has an archaic flavour again. There is neither solemnity nor tenderness in it, but its fluent writing and unfailing beauty of sound compensate amply for a certain emotional aridity.

One work written for the church still remains to be mentioned: the *Requiem* in D minor (K. 626) which Mozart left unfinished. Perhaps it is wide of the mark to say that he did write it for the church, for we know that it was commissioned by a stranger; but it would be equally false to suppose that he composed it only for the man represented by that mysterious person clad in grey. The truth is that he wrote it for himself. Not for his own funeral, be it understood. Let us not take any share in the kind of anecdotage that afflicts the history of music like an eruptive disease, of which responsible people vainly endeavour to cure it.

That the *Requiem* is an intensely personal expression is certain, and the constant interruptions that kept Mozart from it were more than a cause for worry: they were a tragedy. There is a strained, nerve-racked quality about this music at times, found quite like that nowhere else in his work. The very opening, with its restless syncopations and suspensions, is in its way as unhappily agitated below a surface of slow and subdued notes as any incident in Wagner's *Tristan and Isolde* three-quarters of a century later:

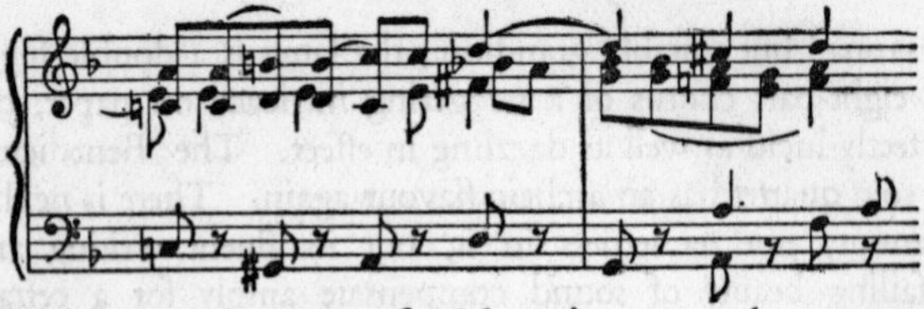

At the same time, even for Mozart's century the manner is archaic: it points back a hundred years or so and might be that of Fux or Caldara; yet an indefinable flavour of individuality is there. Without any manuscript evidence one would swear that this is Mozart, not Süssmayr or any one else. For the rest, it is not always easy to decide merely from what the ear receives where Mozart leaves off and Süssmayr begins, and without having room to go deeply into the matter here, I may as well draw attention to the fact that nobody will ever be able to decide with the aid of the autograph score either, even if Süssmayr's handwriting were less disconcertingly like Mozart's own. For it must be borne in mind that we cannot possibly know how many sketches on loose sheets of music paper may have been made by Mozart and destroyed by his pupil when he had worked out the score fully. All that can be said is that most probably there is more of genuine Mozart in the work than the manuscript discloses. While many of the earlier portions were merely outlined in melody and bass by Mozart and later filled in by his disciple, we know that the 'Sanctus,' 'Benedictus' and 'Agnus Dei' were missing altogether. But while we are aware that Süssmayr went back to the music of the opening number for the 'Agnus Dei' (not without Mozartian precedent, as I have already pointed out), we have no right to declare roundly that the master himself did not invent the 'Sanctus' and 'Benedictus' simply because nothing of them is preserved in his hand. We might as well say that it cannot be true that Bach wrote a Passion according to St. Mark.

On the other hand there are sections in the *Requiem* which, although known to be by Mozart, might well have been ascribed to Süssmayr, Eybler, Stadler or some such minor master.

The fugue in the first number, for example, shows but one original feature in giving the words 'Kyrie eleison' to the first subject and 'Christe eleison' to the second, these two rubrics, which tradition separates, thus appearing simultaneously. The fugal treatment itself is conventional, though not academically 'correct,' and the material seems to be deliberately derivative. The first subject is, in fact, one of the stereotyped patterns used by contrapuntists over and over again: the theme we all know best from the chorus 'And with His stripes' in Handel's *Messiah.* The 'Dies irae' is a fine dramatic but at the same time rigidly shapely chorus.

The 'Tuba mirum,' orchestrated at first by Eybler, whose scoring Süssmayr did not take over, is endangered at the opening by the trombone solo which is always on the point of taking the next step down from the sublime; but the vocal solo quartet here enters for the first time and joins in part-singing of the most heavenly beauty, with some of those cadences, fit to melt a heart of stone, that occur frequently in the course of the work. Even quite ordinary Mozartian mannerisms take on the aspect of miracles in the context. Here are two of them, quoted from the close of the 'Tuba mirum':

The vocal phrase is one of Mozart's most common musical full stops; the instrumental one the kind of female close he favoured particularly in the piano sonatas.

After a majestic chorus, 'Rex tremendae,' comes another quartet, 'Recordare,' beginning rather in the old polyphonic style of the 'Domine Deus' and the 'Quoniam' in the C minor Mass, but growing more harmonic as it goes on. And what harmony! It is all utterly simple, but I cannot resist giving a lengthy extract to show what celestial heights Mozart could scale merely by an infallibly judicious piece of quartet writing:

K 626

So it goes on: noble grandiloquence alternates with heart-searching supplication and occasionally with ecclesiastical stiffenings which just raise the ghost of a doubt whether the *Requiem* is all of a piece as a work of the highest inspiration. Perhaps not, indeed; but then its peaks are so elevated that exultation cannot be lost during the brief descents. And never let it be forgotten: we cannot be sure how far we hear it as it was intended to be. No wonder the tone of a work produced in such difficulties and perturbations is sometimes hysterical, as in the 'Lacrymosa' with its melody almost too limpid for choral singing, and sometimes a little formal, as in the double fugue 'Quam olim Abrahae.'

If the 'Sanctus' with the suspiciously short 'Osanna' fugue are really wholly by Süssmayr, they are at least successfully in the vein of Mozart's worldly-ecclesiastical manner of the Salzburg period. On the other hand it is hard to believe that the 'Benedictus' was not at least extensively sketched by Mozart. Surely only he could have devised so simple and yet so thrilling a cadential climax as that at the end of this number. At any rate it takes a greater master than Süssmayr to do this, one would think. And a greater one—just one—did do it much later in another *Requiem.* His name was Giuseppe Verdi.

A very different category of vocal works is that of the arias written either for concert performance or for interpolation into operas, his own or other people's. They are in a measure for singers what the concertos are for instrumentalists, though they have never won the same currency, partly because they are too much of a technical problem for the degenerated modern art of singing and partly because, with some notable exceptions, they are less satisfactory as music. To begin with, a good half of them was composed before Mozart had reached maturity in his operas—and most of them are, very naturally, frankly operatic. Like the early operas, the early arias cling obediently to the current devices of the time. Diminished sevenths and German sixths, those never-failing expedients, abound[1]:

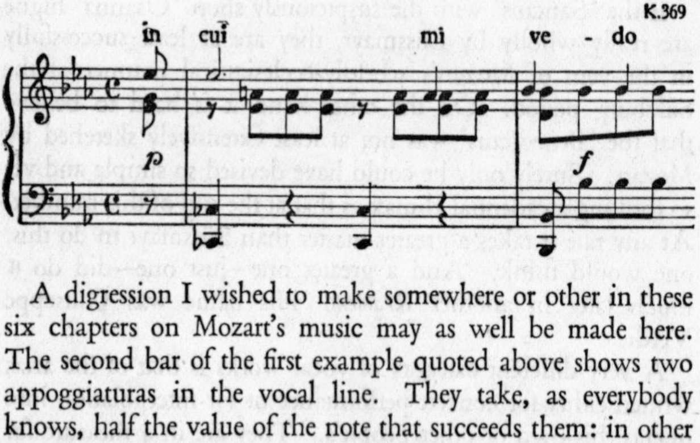

A digression I wished to make somewhere or other in these six chapters on Mozart's music may as well be made here. The second bar of the first example quoted above shows two appoggiaturas in the vocal line. They take, as everybody knows, half the value of the note that succeeds them: in other words, this phrase is sung in even quavers. But what every reader of this book may not know is why Mozart did not write them so. The explanation is that he acted simply

[1] It must, of course, be remembered that in the eighteenth century they were nothing like the outworn currency they are now. They were still fresh enough to be used with good effect, at any rate by masters, and in Mozart's mature work they remain convincing because they infallibly stand in the right relation to the rest of the music.

according to the fashion of his time, which decreed that composers should, when a dissonance produced itself by a melodic suspension on a strong beat of the bar, pretend that the really important note was that following the suspension and actually belonging to the chord. It was all merely a polite fiction whereby an intruding note was made to appear as harmless as possible, just as it was imperative in polite society that however daring the conversation might be, it should always be wrapped up in decorous phraseology. These appoggiaturas were nothing else than the musical equivalent of elegant circumlocutions used in the place of 'strong language.' Which did not, needless to say, prevent composers from sometimes forgetting themselves and speaking out: hence any amount of inconsistency in notation.

It is curious to note that when Mozart supplied additional arias to his operas, they fell out of the frame of the work as a whole and assumed very much the character of his concert arias. He was entirely absorbed in the atmosphere of an opera while engaged upon it, but his versatile and volatile genius immediately changed its whole disposition once a work for the stage was finished. That is why among the afterthought-arias such as Elvira's 'Mi tradì' for *Don Giovanni* and Susanna's 'Al desio' for *Figaro* (they were composed in that order), beautifully polished and harmonious pieces of work as they are, the first does not fit the stage character particularly well and the second is an almost grotesque misfit, so much so that, as I have already shown, this aria is generally regarded as having been meant, not for Susanna at all, but for the Countess. How Mozart could have remained unaware of this incongruity is a mystery, unless one can really believe that he intended to show Susanna in the Countess's dress. But perhaps he knew quite well. Was that why he used basset horns in 'Al desio,' instruments which otherwise do not appear in *Figaro*? Did he wish to make sure that it would be found too inconvenient to include this aria in the opera after it had satisfied an exacting singer?

That even the best of the concert arias should show this detachment from any too individual expression is just as well. They may thus really be sung by artists in evening dress without making them look like opera singers at a rehearsal. Some of the best of these works are vocal concertos of the finest quality which it is a great pity to neglect, and any gifted singer, next time she or he intends to drag an aria out of a Mozart opera for performance at an orchestral concert, will do well to look up the master's more suitable vocal pieces. Even some of those who would like to achieve the apparently impossible compromise of singing with an orchestra without doing their accompanist out of an engagement will find their problem solved, for there is a fine *scena,* 'Ch'io mi scordi di te,' with the rondo, 'Non temer, amato bene' (K. 505), for soprano with a solo pianoforte part. Sopranos have altogether the widest choice, though tenors had better consider if some of the pieces in high tessituras not specifically written for them will not suit them all the same. However, the aria that was good enough for Adamberger to sing in Anfossi's *Il curioso indiscreto* (K. 420) ought to be good enough for them. Basses should look at K. 432, 512 and 513,[1] but particularly at the fine aria originally intended for *Così fan tutte,* 'Rivolgete a lui lo sguardo' (K. 584).

For contraltos there is only one single item, and that an early one (K. 255), while their (in this respect at least) more fortunately voiced sisters are confronted by a veritable *embarras du choix.* One may point out the very beautiful, warm-toned rondo of K. 374 and the nobly decorative K. 416, the latter of which will do well for the singer who boasts a high E flat (the F is not quite indispensable), not to mention those few other accomplishments which may happen to be still considered desirable in a modern soprano. But the crowning work is the magnificent 'Bella mia fiamma' (K. 528) written for Josepha Dušek just after *Don Giovanni,* as fine as the grandest

[1] Where numbers are given without titles, the works may be identified by a glance at the catalogue (Appendix B).

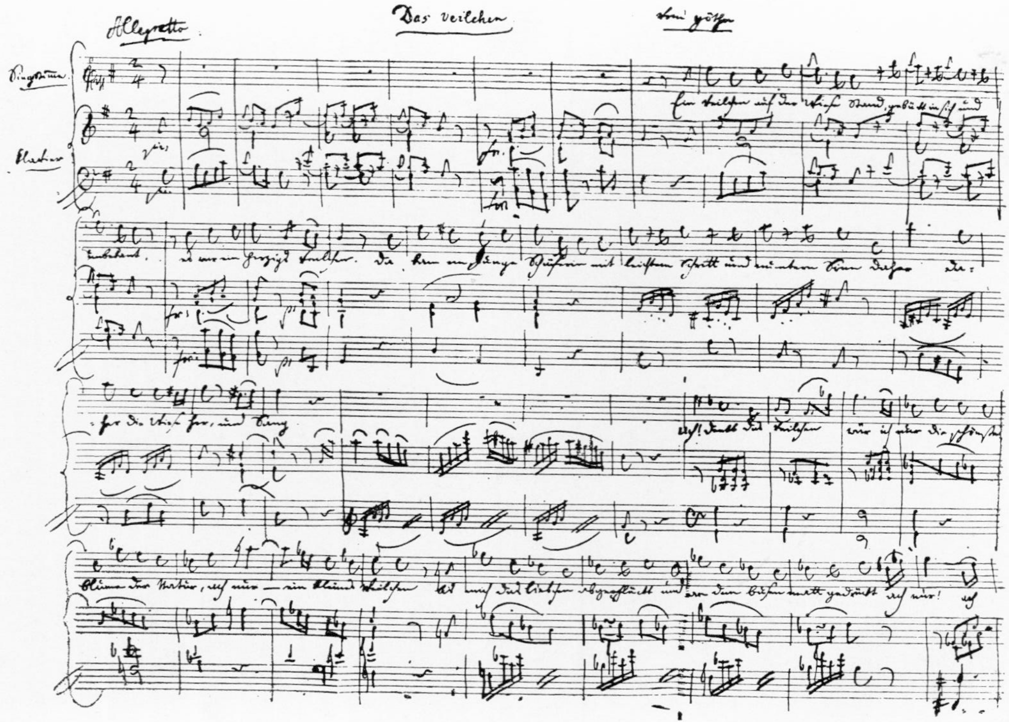

FACSIMILE OF THE MANUSCRIPT OF 'DAS VEILCHEN'

expressions of Donna Anna in that work. The way in which Mozart turns the difficult intervals, primarily intended to tease the singer, to unfailing artistic account is nothing short of miraculous.

Mozart's songs, like Beethoven's, are very much neglected, some of them deservedly enough, but by no means all. On the whole this disregard is due to the fact that they have been obscured, as representatives of a species, by the work of Schubert, Brahms and Wolf. Lovers of music, there is no getting away from it, will pay no heed to the conditions under which this or that form of the art was produced and expect to find developments of such a one as that of the *Lied* in work of a period at which it could not possibly have shown them. It was for Schubert, who was Germanic through and through, to bring the German song to its maturity, not for the cosmopolitan Mozart. Nevertheless, in two at least of his songs Mozart gave the younger master a lead towards a polish and poetry he would have sought vainly in Zumsteeg or Reichardt or Zelter.

Many of the songs are simple strophic ditties, but the more developed ones, even the best among them, are the outcome of a dramatic, sometimes frankly theatrical impulse, not a purely lyrical one. Even the Goethe song, *Das Veilchen* (K. 476), an exquisite and perfectly shaped little thing in its way, still has an operatic touch in that recitative-like passage which is so wonderfully welded into the whole. The song of Luisa's burning of the letters from her faithless lover (K. 520) is plainly a dramatic scene in miniature, contrived very briefly with one or two grand gestures that seem to come from the later and greater of the two pianoforte Fantasies in C minor. The bewitching *An Chloë* (K. 524), again, is in the vein of the concerto-like arias interpolated into the operas, only on a less grown-up scale, so to speak. It might be an extra song for Cherubino, whose enthusiastic and at the same time swaggering and yet well-bred exuberance it has. Then *Das Lied der Trennung* (K. 519), a strophic song with large aria extensions, is a passionate lament in F minor that might very well come from any of Mozart's heroines in a lovelorn mood. A difference is, though, that while on the stage Mozart gives all the most touching expressions of this sort to women, this is actually a man's song; in fact it is its being concerned with one particular person—another Luisa—which puts it in the company of the romantic songs of Beethoven and Schubert, who are fond of singing subjectively about Adelaidas and Lauras and Theklas.

These four are Mozart's great songs. But the greatest, because the most purely a song as distinct from an aria, is that lovely lyric, *Abendempfindung* (K. 523), the more marvellous in its avoidance of all that is theatrical because the rather vapid words by Campe contain a far-fetched reference to 'a curtain falling on the gaudy scene of life.' A cadence that recurs in various forms and keys is very Schubertian indeed.

Some of the simple strophic songs contain good tunes. The best-known of them, *Sehnsucht nach dem Frühlinge* (K. 596), recalls the tune of the rondo in the B flat major piano Concerto which had just preceded it. Others have more distinctive melodies, however, such as the rhythmically attractive *Der Zauberer* (K. 472) and that striking little portrait of an old woman, *Die Alte* (K. 517), which is rather in the manner of certain character pieces in Grétry, Philidor and other writers of French comic opera. Actually French are the two ariettas composed at Mannheim, of which the first, 'Oiseaux, si tous les ans' (K. 307) is merely a flimsy *chansonnette,* while the second, 'Dans un bois solitaire' (K. 308), is a more extended piece with engaging modulatory turns and discreet dramatic inflections.

The most distinguished poet, apart from Goethe, upon whose work Mozart drew is Hölty, the setting of whose *Das Traumbild* (K. 530) is one of the most appealing of the strophic songs. As a curiosity may be mentioned the song with mandoline accompaniment, 'Komm, liebe Zither' (K. 351), which is like a rather weak study for Don Juan's serenade, 'Deh vieni alla finestra'; and as a warning it may be pointed out, as indeed cannot be done too often, that the *Wiegenlied,* 'Schlafe, mein Prinzchen,' still frequently sung as a song by Mozart, is not by him at all, but by one Bernhard Flies, a composer otherwise so obscure that it would be cruel to withhold the credit for this pretty but quite un-Mozartian trifle from him.

The choral works with orchestra other than those intended for the church service may be briefly dismissed. Mozart's one oratorio, *La Betulia liberata* (K. 118), is an early effort made in response to a commission. It imparts nothing new to the species and does not add anything of especial distinction to the accepted conventions. As for the cantata of *Davidde penitente* (K. 469), we already know that it is largely an arrangement from the C minor Mass (K. 427), and cannot therefore be regarded as an inspired setting of its new text. More interesting are the two masonic cantatas, *Die Maurerfreude* (K. 471) and *Eine kleine Freimaurer-Kantate* (K. 623), which exhibit the qualities of simplicity and solemnity peculiar to the priests' choruses in *The Magic Flute.* So already does, curiously enough, the earlier cantata, 'Dir, Seele des Weltalls,' of which two differently scored versions exist (K. 429A and B). It makes one wonder whether that entirely peculiar style was not due as much to Mozart's setting of German words as to his freemasonry, for it is to be noticed that he wrote in quite different veins in his German stage music, not only that of the masonic *Zauberflöte,* but also that of *Die Entführung,* the unfinished *Zaide* and the incidental music to *Thamos.*

The unaccompanied music for several voices is, I repeat, of no importance. The English madrigal (so-called), 'God is our Refuge' (K. 20), is merely curious as a piece written by a clever child of nine, and the numerous Canons are the occasional jottings of a master who delighted in the ready exercise of his astonishing technical skill. They are often written to nonsense words the explanation of which may be some lost friendly or domestic joke, as is doubtless the case also with the comic quartet, 'Caro mio, Schluck und Druck' (K. App.5) and, we know, of the pretty trio in Viennese dialect, 'Liebes Mandel, wo is's Bandel?' (K. 441), the occasion for which was Constanze's inability to find a ribbon she wished to wear when Gottfried von Jacquin called for her and Mozart to go for a walk. The trio is the colloquy between the three of them on this world-shaking incident, Constanze being the soprano, Mozart the tenor and Jacquin the bass.

CHAPTER XVI

ORCHESTRAL WORKS

FORTY-NINE symphonies by Mozart are extant, if four isolated finale movements are counted as well as a work (K. 161) of which the first two movements are identical with the overture to *Il sogno di Scipione.*

The first three symphonies, dating from 1764–5, were written in London and performed there at the concert series begun by Abel and J. C. Bach in January 1765. They show the influence of these two composers, so much so that an 'Overture' in E flat major by Abel, now known to be his Op. 7, No. 6, actually got itself included in Köchel's catalogue as Mozart's work No. 18, whence it went unchallenged into the complete Mozart edition. K. 17 also is a spurious work whose author has, however, not been identified. There is no reason why he should not be J. C. Bach; in fact one hopes that he may one day be discovered as its author, for it would be convenient to have works by the boy-composer's two immediate exemplars so readily available for study among his own youthful efforts.[1]

These two were not, of course, the only symphonists who influenced Mozart, though the nearest. The Mannheim school, with the elder Stamitz at the head and Filtz, Holzbauer, F. X. Richter and others grouped round him, could not but

[1] Meanwhile Symphonies by Abel (Op. 10, No. 3) and Bach (Op. 21, No. 3), newly edited in score and parts by Adam Carse (Augener), offer a convenient opportunity for comparative study. They are scored for two oboes, two horns and strings, with a supporting *continuo.* The Bach work is particularly interesting because it has a rudimentary working-out section between the first and second subjects in the recapitulation instead of in the usual place after the exposition.

affect him indirectly, especially, of course, through Haydn, and Italian influences, particularly those of Sammartini and of Toeschi, the one Italian member of the Mannheim group, also played their part. It must be remembered, too, that the Bach influence itself is largely Italian.

The finales of the London symphonies are rondos in triple time. It is not until we come to the symphonies composed in Vienna and Salzburg in 1767–8 that we find the minuet in its dance form taken up by Mozart as a relic of the older suite. His outlook was then enlarged by composers of the Viennese school such as Wagenseil, Gassmann and Monn, though Haydn naturally continues to reign supreme. As in that master's early symphonies, there is no clear distinction in Mozart's from the operatic overture of the time, which had lost Lulli's fugal form of the *allegro,* but not its division into several movements. The connection of this early symphony type with that of the overture is indicated by the fact that the latter was called *sinfonia* in Italy. Thus it was possible for the young composer to transfer a Symphony (K. 45) bodily to the opera of *La finta semplice* as an overture, though without the minuet. It will be judged from this that these works were quite brief, with the merest episodes in the place of what later became the important working-out section in Haydn's and Mozart's hands. Gradually, too, the principal theme in the first movement tends to reappear after the recapitulation, which means nothing less than that Mozart is beginning to become aware of the importance of a coda, a peroration to clinch the argument of a sonata movement.

It would be interesting to follow the gradual formal development of Mozart's symphony throughout the numerous works in that form written during the Italian tours and at Salzburg, but interesting more to the writer and his colleagues than to the general reader, perhaps. Which is as good as saying that in a book which must needs concern itself with the living body of a master's work and not with the reconstruction of its skeleton, a short cut had better be made to the first work that is still likely to show vitality if any one should exhibit it in a concert room, though with the mere intention of producing a historical curiosity.

Passing over the numerous works—no less than sixteen complete symphonies and four separate finales—of the years 1770–2, the first arresting Symphony we come to is that in G minor (K. 183) of 1773. It is also the first in a minor key, after all these essays in the form. As will be observed elsewhere, Mozart's rare use of that mode is more than once like the sudden shedding of a repression. These romantic, personal outpourings, for which he chose for preference the minor keys of C, D or G, seem to have been generally held in check by the polite musical phraseology of the eighteenth century and by his father, who urged him to defer to the taste of his environment, which meant to him a desirable artistic discipline. The minuet is particularly striking, and that not only because one is surprised at the 'gloomy discontent and agitation' of such a movement, though there is no need to go as far as Jahn in finding that mood indulged to any great extent in it.[1] However, Mozart did have ample occasion for depression and discontent at Salzburg, and the first and last movements certainly do express an unhappy restlessness. They also contain interesting developments of the working-out section, which the composer begins both times with an immediate expansion of the final strain of the exposition.

The next work, in E flat major (K. 184), reverts strikingly to the operatic overture type. Its three movements are connected by modulatory bridge passages and the whole takes only some ten minutes to perform. But from now on the symphony as a form grows more and more interesting in Mozart's hands. The C major of 1774 (K. 200) begins with

[1] Wyzewa and Saint-Foix consider that Mozart's model for this work was Haydn's so-called 'Mourning' Symphony (No. 44) of about 1771. It is remarkable, at any rate, that Haydn too expressed himself more intimately in a minor key, and almost as rarely as Mozart.

the usual peremptory gesture, the typical eighteenth-century call to attention telling a chattering audience that the music has begun and something of interest may presently be expected; but the next, in A major (K. 201), a delicious little work, at once sets out with what is a real theme, as characteristic as though one of Mozart's unforgettable opera personages were speaking to us:

In the former work, the C major, there is, by way of a working-out, some striking development of a single figure from the first subject, with the arrangement of its notes reversed after a while, and the nine-bar phrase in the finale (seven bars *piano* for violins alone followed by a loud outburst of two by the whole orchestra) is as entertainingly original as the well-managed *crescendo* of the short coda. The 'whole orchestra,' however, consists of oboes, horns, trumpets and strings only. Trumpets without drums are exceptional, and even here this widowhood of these hardly ever unmated instruments was clearly due to special circumstances, for drum parts not given in the score afterwards turned up in manuscript, only to disappear again for ever. In the A major Symphony even the trumpets are dropped; but oboes and horns are enough to support the strings in this particularly lovely music, in which the interval of the octave yields extraordinary meaning and even the old-world device of the sequence is used with freshness.

The Symphony immediately following, in D major (K. 202), is a good deal less attractive. It has trumpets again, but no drums, much less flutes, bassoons or, of course, clarinets, which were not to be had at Salzburg. Bassoons seem to have been called for only on special occasions at this time and flutes appear to have been played by the oboists, for the two species do not as a rule appear together, but alternately.

No symphony came from Mozart's pen for four years after

K. 202, and then it was not until Le Gros in Paris promised to produce such a work at the *Concert spirituel* that Mozart ventured to compose one. It was the work in D major (K. 297) in which, as we have seen, he humoured the Paris fashion of the *premier coup d'archet* by introducing the music with it, and for which he agreed without demur to write a new slow movement after the first performance. For the first time he was able to score a symphony for what was then a full orchestra, including clarinets, which had never previously figured in any symphony of his. It is odd that he did not enjoy the new experience more: on the whole this Symphony falls flat, and even the second middle movement is not much of an inspiration. There is a good deal of pomp about the whole, though also a maturing Mozartian grace and wit.

The next two Salzburg Symphonies of 1779, G major (K. 318) and B flat major (K. 319), are even less distinguished in material. The former, however, deserves attention for its curious organization, which once more points back to the Italian overture or, if you like, forward to a procedure adopted by Mozart later in the overture to *The Elopement* and very nearly in that to *Figaro* as well, though he changed his mind in the latter case. The Symphony consists of two movements only, one fast, one slow, and the *andante* is wedged into the middle of the *allegro spiritoso* at the place where exposition and working-out normally join. The final portion of the *allegro* curiously partakes both of working-out and recapitulation without being a normal form of either. The B flat major Symphony, not otherwise remarkable, is well adapted by its gentle chamber style to the limited orchestra of oboes, bassoons, horns and strings. Truly, the archbishop ought to have appreciated a musician so capable of making the most of a limited musical establishment, with which he liked to cut as much of a figure in the great world as was compatible with moderate expense.

The first of the Symphonies to have achieved any degree of permanence, as far as concert practice goes, is that in C major

(K. 338) of the following year—and very justly, for it is a lovely work and, though formally on a small scale,[1] fully matured and typically Mozartian with its capricious changes between a variety of humours. The musical ideas are mostly the current coin of the time, but their treatment is in the nature of an ironical commentary. Mozart loves the musical *clichés* of his century and at the same time laughs at them up his sleeve, and never more wittily than in this little but captivating and very finished symphonic work.

I may as well say it here as anywhere else: his melodic invention is seldom very original. He is generally content with what has served a hundred other composers, or something very like it. You may put your finger on a tune and say that it is plainly Mozart's and nobody else's. But that is only because you do not know anybody else among his smaller contemporaries. If you did, you would be inclined to declare that they too are Mozartian—and even then you would be wrong. It is the simple truth that he was not one of the great melodic originators, much less so than many a smaller composer. His melody appeals, but does not smite or exact attention forcibly. It is not what he says that makes him the incomparable artist he is, but the incredibly finished, apt and well-ordered way in which he states, strings together and expands his ideas. Among all the great composers he is the one who keeps the secret of his genius most closely guarded. It all seems so simple, so easy to do—until one tries to do anything whatever, even the smallest sketch or the shortest improvisation at the piano, in his way. Anyone can write a few lines or play a few bars that are quite prettily Mozartian, indeed in isolation quite as good as a thousand things he wrote himself. But try to extend the fragment in what you think would have been his procedure, and it immediately turns into the shallowest commonplace imaginable. You may go on doing precisely what it seems to you he would have done, but it all refuses to take wing, let alone to take

[1] A sketch for a minuet was never completed.

fire. It may turn into tolerable Gyrowetz or Kozeluch, but somehow or other it will not convince any musician of some degree of experience that it is even passable Mozart. So that, while on the face of it he is the most obvious of musical inventors,[1] he is in the last resort the most enigmatic of creators.

Perhaps one may go part of the way towards an explanation by saying that his music need mean nothing tangible in order to be expressive. Like Lewis Carroll's 'gyring and gimbling,' it somehow conveys an immense amount of imaginative experience without giving away anything that can be understood literally. Even in the operas you do not always know what it does mean: his characters are shown to us very lucidly so far as their personalities are concerned, but his own attitude towards them finds musical expression in an enormous wealth of afterthoughts which trouble you in some new way every time you hear one of the great stage works, and that is the reason—yes, I do think that is the true secret of it all—why they never cease to have some fresh experience to offer. They are as inexhaustible in giving rise to new impressions in the hearer as the plays of Shakespeare, only in a different way—a musical instead of a literary way.

But his instrumental music does not even necessarily suggest afterthoughts, though the profounder symphonies, concertos and chamber works certainly do. You may enjoy them in complete emotional detachment. They may give to you exactly what you like, though that has nothing to do with the absurd notion that he is an 'objective' composer, set afoot by minor musicians who have no feelings to express and like to make the pretended example of a great master their excuse. The fact is rather that his music has an infinity of meanings.

[1] As to that, it is noticeable throughout musical history that secondary composers are often the greater originators, the more distinctive personalities; which is also the reason for their being more popular. People like Gounod, Tchaikovsky, Bizet or Puccini, to mention the first that come to mind, and not to descend to third-raters, are more strikingly individual melodists than Mozart.

Mr. W. J. Turner has suggested that you cannot tell whether in the last resort Mozart's music is sad or merry, and the observation is perfectly just. The one thing you can tell, it may perhaps be added, is that it is never purely joyous in the way that, for instance, Haydn's finales so often are. It may be *expressive* of joy, to be sure, but it is never *productive* of it without some alloy of sadness, not to say bitterness. Listen to anything of his that is apparently purely pleasurable—the bubbling finale of this C major Symphony last mentioned is as good an example as any other—and you may at any moment feel like bursting into tears. And the more perfect the composition happens to be, the nearer will you come to that strange well of bitter waters. But then, could anything be more poignant to human beings than perfection, unattainable in life even by such a being as Mozart himself, but magically conquered by him in art?

We now come to the last six great symphonies, which spread themselves over the years 1782–8 and begin with the so-called 'Haffner' Symphony in D major (K. 385) which, we have already seen, was planned as a second serenade for the Salzburg burgomaster. The discarded second minuet appears to be lost. It can hardly be that in C major (K. 409), called by Köchel a minuet for a symphony, though it might just possibly have been transposed later. Not that it matters.

As a symphony this work is in some ways unique and, if it comes to that, as a serenade too, or as anything else. The first movement distinguishes itself from any similar one in Mozart, though not in Haydn, much less in the Mannheim masters, by being based entirely on a single subject, and the reversion to an older type is accentuated by the fact that the theme might very well be a tag devised long ago by some ingenious contrapuntist:

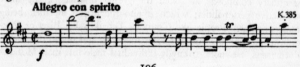

But he would probably have been more self-consciously cunning than Mozart, who performs all sorts of astonishing polyphonic feats with this melodically quite fruitless theme, but never anything whatsoever that is clever without being at the same time expressive. The whole movement is a model of technical accomplishment beautifully tempered by impeccable taste. At one point a miracle happens. The key has verged to the dominant, in which a second subject should appear in any well-conducted symphony of A.D. 1782. Well, something in the nature of such a contrasted subject does come forward, but not anything melodically too striking to conceal the fact that the violas continue persistently to maintain the first subject:

In the working-out section the main theme is marvellously combined in canon at various intervals. The serenade character of the work comes out in the slow movement and in the minuet with its lovely pastoral trio. In the final rondo, which Mozart said ought to go as fast as possible, he sent the Haffners a little personal message by using as his subject what is as nearly as makes no odds a quotation from Osmin's great aria of malicious triumph in *The Elopement,* the opera he had finished just before this serenade-symphony. All the spirited frolic of comic opera is here blended with the grace of the two women in the stage work he wrote so lovingly in the year of his wedding (one feels that he was more deeply attached to Belmonte's Constanze than to his own), and he fell so much in love with the enchanting first episode of his rondo that he could not let it go, but developed and restated it until it became a second sonata subject. Which is another special feature of this work.

There is no doubt that the next two symphonies are wrongly numbered by Köchel, for unquestionably Mozart must have written the slow introduction for Michael Haydn's G major Symphony, the whole of which the compiler of the catalogue assigned to Mozart as No. 444, during the visit to Salzburg in 1783, whereas his own C major Symphony numbered 425 we know to have been composed hastily at Linz on the return journey to Vienna. That work, dedicated to old Count Thun, is festive and brilliant, with trumpets and drums retained even for the slow movement, and flutes and clarinets omitted, we may be sure, only because they were not available at the provincial nobleman's establishment. In the energetic slow introduction[1] there is a momentary falling into one of those sudden fits of melancholy that can make Mozart so disquieting just when apparently he set out to give sheer delight; but the *allegro* that follows is untroubled and in fact contains one of Handel's 'brave hallelujahs' of which Horace Walpole wrote so derisively:

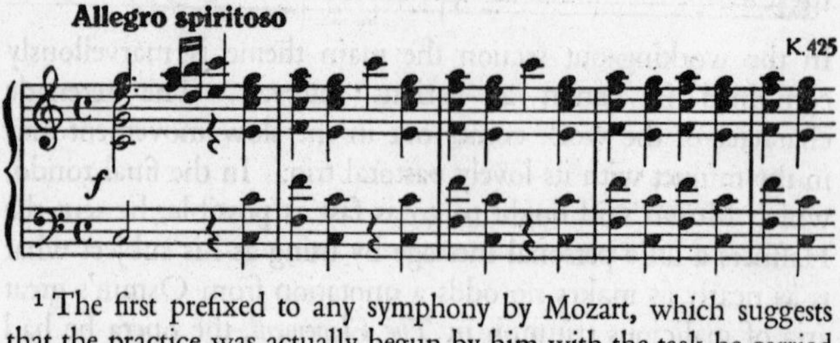

[1] The first prefixed to any symphony by Mozart, which suggests that the practice was actually begun by him with the task he carried out for Michael Haydn.

Very uninteresting, to be sure, looked at thus in isolation; but, like everything else in this Symphony, it stands exactly in the right place and gives edge to the more eventful thematic notions, of which there is abundance. Once again even the mechanical device of the sequence is made attractive by the kind of functional importance it is a great composer's knack to impart to it, and compared with such a conventional procedure the sudden drop from G major into E minor and back again is positively startling.

The slow movement is a thing of exquisite tenderness in spite of the trumpets and drums, which only deepen the colour of what always seems to me the perfect musical interpretation of Correggio's 'Nativity.' A new episode in the middle is most delicately and not too artfully worked. After a convivial minuet there is a *presto* finale the constant witty inventiveness of which makes one shiver with pleasure from start to finish, and not least when, at the beginning of the working-out a waspish sting reveals Mozart as the first propounder of Wagner's Beckmesser music:

After the 'Linz' Symphony there was a longish interval, and then came the 'Prague' Symphony, in D major (K. 504), in 1786, between *Figaro* and *Don Giovanni,* of the character of both of which it partakes to some extent, and the greatness of which it certainly shares in its own line. It was, as we have seen, not composed in or even for Prague, but taken there and performed by the composer. It is often distinguished from other works of his as the 'Symphony without Minuet,' which means nothing at all to those who know more than the last famous six symphonies, since a great many of the earlier ones are also devoid of minuet movements. It is as though Mozart had sometimes doubted whether this survival from the older form of the suite could justifiably find its place in a symphony, at a time, that is, before it had developed into the more modern scherzo form, the first traces of which were to appear in the G minor Symphony in 1788, but which Mozart never developed further.

The portentous and extended slow introduction of the 'Prague' Symphony is charged with the graver aspects of *Don Giovanni*; the half-close leading to the *allegro* is practically identical with that at a similar juncture in the great sextet of the opera, and an ominous figure in the finale almost makes one think of the stone guest appearing among a riot of mirth, though the grace and the laughter of Susanna are there too. The slow movement makes us dream of the idyllic summer-night stillness in Count Almaviva's invitingly artificial garden. The wonder of the Symphony is, however, that in spite of the variety of the visions it may suggest to the hearer, it is a perfect whole. Every structural part and every thematic feature is exquisitely proportioned. No separate incident is allowed to engage attention independently of the scheme in which it is assigned its function, even where it is as incredibly beautiful as the second subject of the first movement, which is surreptitiously introduced by a passage that is apparently merely transitional, or as engagingly spritely as the second subject of the finale with its bubbling bassoon accompaniment.

The last three symphonies, composed so close together in 1788, are the crown of Mozart's orchestral work. One does not know at which to marvel more, the equal perfection of the three masterpieces or the utter difference between them. Each is so detached from the others in procedure and mood that it is rather as though the same man had written Shakespeare's *Twelfth Night,* Racine's *Phèdre* and Goethe's *Iphigenie* within whatever period may be equivalent for the rapid execution of three plays as compared with three symphonies. This unfailing adjustment to and crystallization of three different frames of mind in so short a time is surely unequalled in the history of art.

The first of the three is the E flat major Symphony (K. 543). It is the most limpid and lyrical of them, not to say the most limpid and lyrical music in existence. Indeed, if one were asked to consider which work by any composer is the most serenely, the most consistently and continuously beautiful, and one only considered long enough and without regard to what is sensational rather than appealing, I think one could not possibly fail to arrive at this work. Once again, or rather more than ever, everything is displayed in precisely the right way to give proper value to everything else. The slow introduction, for instance, at once shows how admirably Mozart understood the art of creating tension in music. Taken by itself this short *adagio* might be regarded as rhythmically monotonous and harmonically extravagant, but by contrast with the more diversified motion of the *allegro* and the ampler proportions of its key distributions its directness and concentration are astonishingly apt. The harmony acquires pungency by suspensions, by stabbing diminished sevenths and even, at one point, by the (for the eighteenth century) unheard-of audacity of a semitonal clash (C in first violins, D flat in seconds). The last four bars may be quoted as a magnificent example of Mozart's supreme genius for raising expectation by means of a touch of artfulness (note the canon between treble and bass) that has to the ear an appearance of inevitable simplicity:

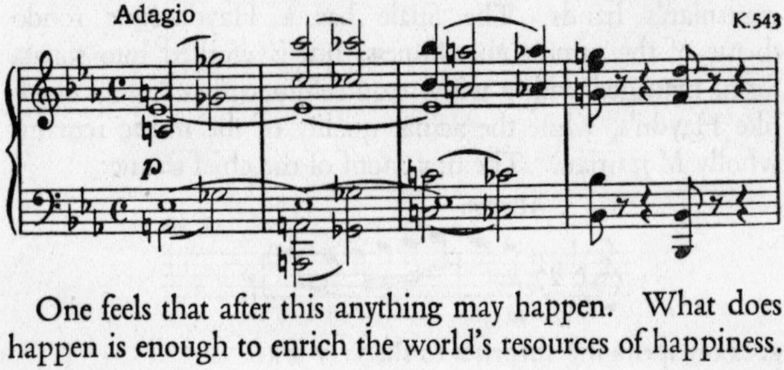

One feels that after this anything may happen. What does happen is enough to enrich the world's resources of happiness.

The music, after hovering tantalizingly round the dominant most of the time, settles down definitely to the tonic for the *allegro,* the prevalent feeling of which is a mysterious tranquillity of spirit with a distinct undercurrent of melancholy. It does not make us sad, but we feel that we take gladness but from transitory things of beauty. The poignancy of bright autumn days hangs about it, and indeed it is Mozart's own autumn of which we are conscious. It was in music such as this, we may be sure, that his contemporaries found evidence of his being a passionate, profoundly melancholy composer. And indeed they were right, for they saw what such writing meant when it was new, as we should endeavour to see it, regardless of the more highly seasoned or more hysterical music of later times.

The slow movement, in A flat major, is one long discourse, with very few digressions, on a single theme of extreme simplicity. Some wonderful variations are built on it, with incidents of heart-melting beauty, and although the chief material is used at considerable length, the unexpected concluding phrase—one of the most original final cadences ever devised by Mozart—comes all too soon. The minuet is one of his most familiar. Trumpets and drums are used in the stately first part, but dropped for the trio, which might be an Austrian country dance heard by the composer during a walk. Even the delicious gurgling accompaniment in the second clarinet hints at the most naïve people's music, though its barrel-organ effect becomes etherealized in the subtle craftsman's hands. The finale has a Haydnesque rondo theme of the utmost cheerfulness, but is worked into sonata form, managed with a witty resourcefulness that is very much like Haydn's, while the actual quality of the music remains wholly Mozartian. The tiny motif of the chief theme:

goes on springing surprises to the very last.

The wonders do not grow when we come to the G minor Symphony (K. 550). That would be impossible. But they change. It is a transformation scene not from a cave to a fairy garden, but from one fairy garden to another, utterly different one. We have now come to Mozart's pathetic symphony, as I venture to call it undeterred by the knowledge that a work by Tchaikovsky has, let us not be so unkind as to say vulgarized that term, but certainly distorted its meaning. For Tchaikovsky's B minor Symphony is in reality tragic or dramatic, not to say melodramatic, rather than truly pathetic: pathos is a quality not displayed consciously, as his feelings are, but impressing itself on the hearer without any volition on the composer's part. Mozart's G minor Symphony is full of unhappy agitation, but it reveals it because the composer's genius could not help producing this particular expression, and not because he intended to impress his hearers with his private concerns.

The G minor Symphony might also be called romantic. It would be an understatement to say that in it we first behold the dawn of romanticism in music, for there were composers groping their way in a romantic twilight side by side with classical ones all through the history of music as we understand it as an art. No, it is the full flood of romanticism's sunrise which bursts upon us in this work. Later poets in sound have developed certain special characteristics of romanticism of which Mozart never dreamt: Weber and Berlioz its fantastic aspects, Schumann and Chopin a lyrical expansiveness that led to indefiniteness of form, Liszt its glitter, and so on; but the individual expression which distinguishes it from the detached, formal perfection of classicism has never been more strongly felt in any musical work than in this Symphony. The wonder is only that Mozart contrived to achieve classical perfection of formal balance at the same time. In fact it may be said that the G minor Symphony is the work in which classicism and romanticism meet and where once and for all we see a perfect equilibrium between them, neither outweighing the other by the tiniest fraction. It is in this respect at least the perfect musical work.

The miracle is performed with extremely restricted means. The version more usually heard is scored for only a flute, two oboes, two bassoons, two horns and strings; but one is bound to agree with Sir Donald Tovey when he pleads for preference of the later one, carefully revised by Mozart to include two clarinets in addition, for it is quite clear that this represents his real intention. It is difficult to see why conductors should so persistently overlook this obvious fact, although the clarinet is too good a woodwind not to blow somebody harm: the oboe parts are greatly impoverished by the new version.

At the very outset a dark and restless quality is imparted to the music by the broken-up accompaniment of the middle harmony (divided violas):

K 550

The sudden entry of the woodwind at a cadence with a pathetic German sixth has a most moving effect, and an auxiliary subject of great structural importance represents the energetic aspect of the movement, or one might say the energizing one, since it is much used in the development later on. The second subject, in B flat major at first, is one of the most wonderful inventions in all music, a thing of the purest and most serene classical beauty imaginable, as perfect in shape as the Grecian Urn of Keats:

The slow movement is in E flat major. In symphonies cast in a minor key a slow movement in the major generally makes for some sort of alleviation. This, however, does nothing of the sort. There is a kind of brooding restlessness about it, produced by various devices, such as strong accents on weak beats, little fluttering, detached figures and more especially by semitonal clashes as well as a cross-rhythm of 3–4 against the prescribed 6–8. In the second part the music glides chromatically towards a resumption of the opening theme with a peculiarly dragging, joyless effect. The tranquil end, which would be heart-easing in its loveliness in another context, here achieves just that quality of pathos which is characteristic of the symphony as a whole.

Even the minuet is far from carefree, and nothing could be farther from a courtly dance. The intricate polyphonic texture suddenly dissolves into one of those chromatic droopings which are such a fascinating feature of this work. The trio, in G major, is the one smiling section of the whole symphony, a little pastoral piece of perfect Arcadian grace and simplicity.

The finale, in sonata form, has an unquiet first subject, the two contrasting rhythms of which yield material for very complex developments:

The second subject is comparable in beauty only to that of the first movement:

and if it is perhaps a little less striking at first, nothing could be more poignantly lovely than its final cadence, which once more makes use of those expressive chromatic descents:

The beginning of the working-out startles the hearer by its curious rhythmic gesture that leads to an elaborate polyphonic presentation of the opening figure of the first subject. All this is still further complicated by a new counter-subject which is also contrapuntally handled. But Mozart's skill in this kind of contrivance is so great that it does not even draw attention to itself, for in spite of the bewildering complexity his musical texture attains at certain points, he never ceases to write music that is beautiful apart from the wonderful workmanship that goes to its making. In the recapitulation the second subject is, of course, in G minor and, incredible as it seems, made even more seizingly beautiful by some new touches. One of these is the Neapolitan sixth, which seems to insist on the retention of the minor mode by a kind of extra depression that is most eloquent.

By whom the last Symphony, in C major (K. 551), was first called the 'Jupiter' Symphony nobody knows for certain. In any case, whoever invented the sobriquet is better forgotten. It could only have been someone who looked for sublimity of subject rather than of treatment in a work of art, who would have declared Rubens to be a greater painter than Constable or Chardin because he painted gods and they did not. Although this Symphony is the most 'classical' of the final group of three that is the apotheosis of Mozart's symphonic writing, there is nothing of divine detachment at any rate in its first three movements. The sudden outbursts in an unexpected minor key in the first, the strenuous syncopations and displaced accents in the second and the sighing chromatic descents in the minuet are all evidences of penetrating human feeling, and no doubt Mozart would have been the first to point with amusement to the fact that there is nothing Olympian in the little auxiliary G major theme in the first movement which he borrowed quite shamelessly from a comic aria of his, 'Un bacio di mano' (K. 541), of which the words run: 'You are a little dense, my dear Pompeo; go and study the ways of the world.' Supposing that one might imagine the name of the inventor of the fatuous 'Jupiter' nickname to have been Pompeo, one would like to sing this air to him, or to his memory, substituting 'the way of composers' for 'the way of the world,' but leaving the observation quoted above intact.

Only the last movement may be regarded as being Jovial, if one accepts the adjective in its original sense of godlike. There is no suggestion here of 'Jupiter, the Bringer of Jollity,' as in Holst's *Planets,* where we are, of course, concerned with the star, not with the god. What Mozart gives us is an awareness of the wonders of divine creation. Jove, if he appears to us at all in this crowning finale, does not do so as the thunderer, but as the maker of a world. There is a mystery in this music not to be solved by analysis or criticism, and perhaps only just to be apprehended by the imagination. We can understand the utter simplicity; we can also, with an effort, comprehend the immense technical skill with which its elaborate fabric is woven; what remains for ever a riddle is how any human being could manage to combine these two opposites into such a perfectly balanced work of art. There are five subjects, each of them a mere stock phrase such as any professor of composition might give to a student to work out as a fugue. Mozart does not work any of them into a fugue, but all of them into a sonata movement with a fugal texture of incredible elaboration, combining now any two of the subjects, now a single one in canon, and again mixing both procedures together. The dizzy culmination comes in the coda, where all five themes appear together in various juxtapositions. Here is a specimen (only the first four notes on the third stave are an independent theme):

We may leave the Symphony at that, I think. What more could be said? Either nothing or else too much for the present purpose.

Far too little room is left, even so, for detailed discussion of Mozart's miscellaneous orchestral works, most of the more important of which are in the nature of a form half-way between the suite and the sonata, be they called serenades, divertimenti or cassations. There are also a large number of separate movements, especially marches and minuets, which may or may not have been intended for incorporation in larger works. At Salzburg, where most of this kind of music was composed, Mozart clearly set down what came into his head whenever he found himself at leisure and had a few sheets of music paper to his hand.

A good many of these works are, accordingly, not of any great importance; but then it must be remembered that industrious composers of the eighteenth century, like Haydn and Mozart, would have been highly astonished if anybody had suggested to them that the entertainment music they were expected to write ought to be devised with an eye on the possibility of their inclusion in a complete edition a century later. In their own view, it cannot be sufficiently emphasized, they were craftsmen, not classics.

For want of a more thorough examination of this section of Mozart's catalogue we may take the well-known 'Haffner' Serenade of 1776, in D major (K. 250), as a typical example. It is elegant music and fills the moulds of sonata, rondo, minuet and so forth always admirably; but although gracious and euphonious, it has little character, and the familiar rondo with the solo violin part, which is excessively long, has about as much meaning as a kitten chasing its tail—a fascinating thing to watch, when all is said. The one movement of outstanding interest is the minuet in G minor, which, major trio and all, distinctly foreshadows that of the great symphony in the same key. The work as a whole is as much too long as the rondo is individually: eight movements including three minuets; but that was no defect in a serenade most probably never intended to be played straight through, and certainly not written for a concert. At the wedding, we may be tolerably sure, separate movements were played between the courses of dinner, and very likely the minuets, in this work as in others of the kind, were meant to be actually danced.

Very often these works, the first of which (Cassation in G major, K. 63) appeared as early as 1769, make use of cheerful, folksong-like material that proclaims Mozart, for all his Italian culture, a true child of Austria. The Divertimento in

D major for oboes, horns and strings (K. 251), for example, is full of such homely, sometimes almost yodelling tunes:

And so on. In the finale, however, the irrepressible cosmopolitan leaning of the typical eighteenth-century artist comes out: it is called *Marcia alla francese*.

The scoring of the works of the serenade type is more diversified—or shall I say that of the divertimenti more diverting?—than that of the symphonies. The use of individual solo instruments in this or that movement is frequent; sometimes a work is scored for wind only and may include English horns, as does the Divertimento in E flat major (K. 166); or we may find such freakish combinations as that of the C major Divertimento (K. 187), which is for two flutes, five trumpets and drums. The *Serenata notturna* (K. 239) is for two separate small orchestras and the *Notturno* (K. 286) for four, rather as though these works were studies for the ballroom scene in *Don Giovanni,* though nothing like the astonishing combination of three different dance rhythms occurs here. On the other hand, in the latter work the effect of a threefold echo is used with an almost fiendish ingenuity, the more surprising because the music played by the first orchestra, performed separately and without the intermittent pauses, make a complete musical piece in itself. Thus, although the whole composition is one continuous feat of technical dexterity, no constraint on the composer's imagination is noticeable.

A favourite medium was that of strings with two horns. It is that of the Divertimento in D major (K. 334), containing a favourite minuet and another which abounds in harmonic audacities that must have struck Mozart's hearers as extremely modern. The way in which the horns sustain the tonic while the strings diverge to the sub-dominant at the opening (with a semitonal clash, too) is remarkable (*see opposite page*), and the interrupted cadence preceding the little canon in a remote key is almost startling even to-day.

With the emancipation from the Salzburg servitude comes a very remarkable and beautiful Serenade, in B flat major (K. 361), for twelve wind instruments, including two basset horns, and a double bass part. It was probably written for members of the Munich orchestra during the time *Idomeneo* was prepared for production there. It is far removed from the world of Mozart's usual polite musical diversions and belongs rather to that of his grandest chamber-music style, like that of the string quintets[1] or the F major Sonata for piano duet.

After 1780 there are no more orchestral serenades, cassations, and divertimenti. Their place is taken by the slighter minuets, country dances and German dances composed for the court—slighter, but in their way very characteristic, for these pieces

[1] It was actually arranged as a string quintet later, and as such it appears in Köchel's list under the misleadingly early number 46. It is obvious that he could have invented nothing like this at the age of twelve or so which that number indicates.

grow straight out of the peasant dance tunes of Austria and lead in a direct line to the *Ländler* and scherzos of Schubert and thence to the waltzes of Lanner and the Strauss family.

Only three works of the Vienna period need be mentioned here, and one of them, the *jeu d'esprit* of *Ein musikalischer Spass* (K. 522), contains little beyond the joke of distorting popular music in an artistic way in order to suggest how a village band would do it naïvely, and a dig or so at the incompetent fellow-composer. The piece is, one must suppose, an affectionate recollection on Mozart's part of his father's descriptive musical diversions of the same kind.

Much more important, though quite short, is the impressive *Maurerische Trauermusik* (*Masonic Funeral Music*) (K. 477), composed in 1785 for the funeral of two distinguished free-masons and curiously scored for two oboes, one clarinet, three basset horns, double bassoon, two horns and strings, an orchestra very similar to that employed for some of the solemn numbers in *The Magic Flute.* The music, in C minor, with a major *tierce de Picardie* at the end, is gloomy and consolatory at once in a characteristic late-Mozartian way. It is also hauntingly beautiful.

After all, one orchestral serenade was written in Vienna—in 1787—apart from the two chamber works for wind of 1781–2. Only Mozart called it by a modest German name: *Eine kleine Nachtmusik* (K. 525). Well, little it may be, but it is by far the most familiar and favoured of his mixed orchestral works. The reason is perhaps partly that it is scored for strings only and thus easily accessible even to small orchestras. But it is certainly a singularly perfect worklet, thoroughly polished in a classical way—the first movement is a faultless sonatina—and out-and-out romantic in some of its aspects. The slow movement is actually called a romance and it has a mysterious middle section with ejaculations suggestive of subdued passion in treble and bass over and under a strangely agitated murmuring of second violins and violas. The theme of the wonderfully managed final rondo is the naïve Viennese popular song to the very life of Schikaneder's Papageno in *The Magic Flute*:

CHAPTER XVII

CONCERTOS

HERE we enter a world of enchanted artificiality. The concertos, like the concert arias, are frank display pieces. Mozart, who lacked the giant strength of Handel to hold a *prima donna* out of the window until she complied with his instructions, had many a diplomatic wrangle with his performers; but it would never have occurred to him to question the ingrained eighteenth-century notion that they made their appearances in their own right. Indeed, where the piano concertos are concerned, he was more often than not his own interpreter and by no means averse to showing what he could do as one of the most gifted keyboard players of the age.[1] What he wrote for solo players, therefore, was unblushingly set forth so as to bring out their accomplishments. The first movements of his concertos are sonatas, of symphonic proportions, certainly, but always sonatas for the exercise of brilliant individual qualities. The slow movements are arias, sometimes very operatic arias, transferred to an instrumental medium with an unfailing ear for the compensations required to make the metamorphosis acceptable. The finales were either sonata movements again or rondos, or, once or twice, sets of variations, all of them more lavishly spread than the corresponding movements in a solo sonata.

This expansion was, of course, due to the participation of the orchestra. The element of virtuosity alone did not satisfy Mozart; he also wanted a symphonic element to enter into

[1] Like Bach, who was widely known as an organist in his day, Mozart was too often undervalued as a composer because his genius was obscured by his more immediately noticeable executive gifts.

these double-purposed schemes of his, and so he effected the kind of glorious compromise between solo performances and symphony which, when all is said, conditions also other species of his music where the virtuoso has to be considered —the concert arias and above all the operas. With a kind of beneficent slyness that is unique in music he made his performers fancy that they were having things done for them all their own way while in reality he compelled them to enter into his own designs and, whether they chose or not, to yield him the utmost of poetry in the interests of the music itself. And for the most part they did choose, and still do, for it is possible only to the utterly insensitive, unsympathetic or self-centred to withhold a loving and enthusiastic participation in his work. He has such a way with him that even normally vain singers and players for the moment feel passionately that the music is more important than the audience while they are interpreting his arias or concertos. Mozart can make poets and connoisseurs of all but the very worst of them.

The share taken by Mozart's orchestra is extraordinarily enticing to the soloist. It supports ideally, but also irresistibly demands support in exchange. Any player will be happy just to fill in a bass or sustain a bare shake while two clarinets or a bassoon or what not contribute a captivating fragment. And such fragments are always in some inexplicable way part of the whole. Mozart's power of organizing melodic scraps instead of merely superimposing them as smaller composers do in concertos never ceases to surprise and delight. His orchestral parts, however incidental in appearance, are always found to drive somewhere.

The orchestra is as a rule quite small. No clarinets until after the Salzburg time, of course, and by no means always then. The violin concertos are all scored for two oboes, two horns and strings only. Trumpets and drums come in only in special cases, bassoons are often absent. A pair of horns, on the other hand, is the invariable rule, and Mozart's treatment of them, in spite of the disheartening limitations that restricted them in his time, always delicious. But stay! Not so much in spite of the limitations as because of them. The supreme artist is not discouraged by the shortcomings of his media: he is urged to make the most of his resources, such as they are. In Mozart's time and until a good deal later, when painters had to grind their own water-colours, certain tints—reds in particular—were not available. Well, the art of the water-colour has never been quite so enchanting as it was in those days.

With perhaps one or two exceptions the piano concertos are by far the most important. The violin concertos, imperishable treasures though they are for the fiddler and perennial delights for all lovers of music, are all early works written before the relinquishment of the Salzburg appointment. Five of them (K. 207, 211, 216, 218, 219) came very close together in 1775, and two more followed in 1777 (K. 271A) and (?) 1780[1] (K. 268). In 1776 a *Rondo concertant* (K. 269) was also composed, possibly as a movement for some unfinished work. The simple and rather superficial *Concertone* for two violins (K. 190) is earlier (1773) and after Salzburg came only two incomplete violin works, a Rondo in C major (K. 373) in 1781 and an *Andante* in A major (K. 470) in 1785.

The best known of the violin concertos show the young Mozart as the impartial cosmopolitan he was, in spite of his occasional avowals of Germanic patriotism. Next to Italian influences, unmistakably French models are betrayed by the *rondeaux* (so called by Mozart) in the G major Concerto (K. 216) and the D major (K. 218); there is even the kind of Hungarian gipsy music familiar in Haydn but strange in Mozart in the A major Concerto (K. 219):

[1] This may not be genuine, but C. B. Oldman ('Music and Letters,' April 1931) thinks it is at least based on Mozart and suggests the date 1780–1.

and in the same work we find the mock-Turkish music of *The Elopement* and the A major piano Sonata (K. 331) anticipated.

For all their slightness, the violin concertos have a tender fullness of emotion which makes some of the slow movements unforgettable, and the composer's economy in construction is at times most remarkable, as in the A major Concerto, where the tiny figure:

K.219

performs a most fascinating organic function and so becomes quite important enough to clinch the first movement without any further peroration.

We have already seen that the first four piano concertos (K. 37, 39–41) are arrangements from other composers' works. They may thus be disregarded here, together with the three Sonatas by Johann Christian Bach which Mozart arranged as piano Concertos (K. 107) with string orchestra. The series of original works begins in 1773 with the Concerto in D major (K. 175), where the young composer of seventeen begins the first movement with a theme foreshadowing the opera of nine years later (*The Elopement*) and starts his finale very artfully with a canon. The next Concerto, B flat major (K. 238), was written at the age of twenty. It is very endearing, full of tenderly playful gestures in the first and last movements, and has a deeply tranquil slow movement with curious little gusts of agitation, like an affectionate woman who is quick to be hurt but remains loyal. The other concertos of the same year are not so good. That in F major for three pianos (K. 242) is slight and somewhat marred by the inequality of the solo parts, one of the Lodron ladies for whom it was written having clearly been a player of no great proficiency. The C major (K. 246) is not especially memorable, and the rondo in minuet form at the end conforms to a convention that was becoming old-fashioned and never seems to have interested Mozart as it still did Haydn.

It is in 1777, with a work in E flat major (K. 271), that the series of truly original concertos began. Those preceding that work might still have been written by anybody else, but here is the unmistakable Mozartian quality. Its refinement, its polish, no less than those strange undercurrents of pathos, belong to him, and to him only. The scoring is still for the small Salzburg combination, oboes, horns and strings, but the music is spacious and moves forward from one pithy idea to the next in a way that must have kept his hearers, who were accustomed to regard music as an accompaniment to other distractions, very strenuously engaged. It was that which led to their regarding his music as overcharged and too full-blooded, more than any inherent strangeness in the idiom as such, though of course he sprung plenty of surprises in that direction. Modulating passages (with crossed hands) in the first movement of this work, for instance, which get the music to remote keys in no time, must have been only less startling than the very curious forms of the slow movement, which adapts not merely the operatic aria but the recitative as well to instrumental purposes, and of the finale, a very vivacious and difficult rondo with cadenzas and a piece in minuet time by way of episodes, to say nothing of a characteristic abbreviation of the subject at its last return.

Two years later came the Concerto in E flat major for two pianos (K. 365), not a great work, but technically a most attractive one by reason of the composer's joy in the special problem of co-ordinating two keyboards. His effects are sometimes quite unlike what could have been obtained from any other combination, as though they came from some transfigured, heavenly barrel-organ:

This double Concerto is a joy for two pianists to play even without an orchestra: it is singularly engaging to participate in those surprisingly rich figurations one seems apparently to be producing all oneself without any corresponding effort.[1] It is also pleasant to change over parts, as the two instruments by no means play exactly the same themes. The slow movement is fastidiously ornamented, and the final rondo abounds

[1] All the concertos, it may be said here, are delightful to play on two pianos with a second piano part arranged from the full score.

in good humour. The way in which Mozart makes the cadential phrase at the end of the subject take different harmonic turns is irresistibly comic as well as infallibly artistic.

In 1782, apart from two separate Rondos (K. 382, 386), came a group of three Concertos (K. 413–15). The first, in F major, which again has a minuet finale, is distinguished by a very lovely slow movement and has at least one salient point in the first: an exquisite overlapping of the end of an orchestral phrase with the entry of the solo instrument. The third, in C major, is not especially arresting. The second, in A major, on the other hand, is perhaps the most endearing of the whole collection; less grand or brilliant or passionate than others, but a thing of imperishable charm. The first movement has a caressing suavity, the second a deep tenderness and the third a gracious gaiety that smiles but never bursts into a laugh. The whole has a kind of feminine, virginal good breeding, a reserved poetry that makes it in some ways unique among all the piano concertos. It recaptures the adolescent tone of the violin concertos, but transcends them by a greater maturity of feeling.

Two years go by and then, in 1784, come no less than six piano concertos. First comes an interesting and unaccountably neglected work in E flat major (K. 449), in what is distinctly a new manner. It could not be said that Mozart's hand was getting heavy, for it never became that; but clouds begin to pass over his brow at times. There is something dark and melancholy about this Concerto that we have not yet met in this type of work. Although the first movement is marked *allegretto vivace,* it never shows the least vivacity in spirit. It moves along in large steps of wide intervals, with frequent turns into minor keys, and the 3–4 time has a restless effect that is unusual. There is a spacious opening symphony and the solo part is more expressive than brilliant. The recapitulation is approached by way of an almost tortured chromatic modulation. The slow movement, full of a troubled beauty, is so much too little known that I cannot resist quoting from it:

The pathetic turn which this phrase takes near the end is worth showing, too:

The finale has a Haydn-like main theme, but is full of typically Mozartian touches. It teems with inventiveness and again has troubling deflections into minor keys the gloomy impression of which even the final transformation into a dance-like 6–8 cannot quite dispel. A remarkable work which pianists ought to revive.

The next, in B flat major (K. 450) is much better known, but more conventional. The first movement is brilliant and difficult, the slow one a beautiful tune with variations, or rather embroideries, and the finale a somewhat superficial rondo with pianistically interesting features, some of which are very hard to play. A cross-rhythm akin to that in the finale of Schumann's Concerto is an occurrence of extreme rarity in Mozart. (The detached semiquavers are played by the left hand over the right):

The next number, in D major (K. 451) is friendly but rather uneventful music. Only two numbers ahead, however, we come across another delightful work, as different as possible from the last few: the G major Concerto (K. 453). This is music of such happiness as Mozart, who is never quite untroubled by conflicting emotions, could produce—gently cheerful in the first movement, filled with a quiet gratitude, not without twinges of reminiscent pain, in the *andante,* which opens rather like Schubert's song 'Du bist die Ruh,' and full of a cocksure chirpiness in the finale, which might be a set of variations on a song for Papageno in *The Magic Flute.* Here again the temptation comes to show that similar ideas came to Mozart in similar keys, for we find the same kind of Austrian folksong flavour in other things in G major: Papageno's birdcatcher song and the finale of *Eine kleine Nachtmusik,* for example. A song of the same sort which Mozart borrowed from Gluck for a set of piano variations, to be reverted to later, is also in that key.

The slow movement of the B flat major Concerto (K. 456) that follows might serve the same argument. It is in G minor and has the gentle pathos of many other pieces in that key.

Its tune, however, twists most engagingly into B flat major in the middle. The movement is one of the finest examples of Mozart's power to intensify emotion by a process that looks on the face of it like nothing but a gradual elaborating of the figuration. The first movement is crisp and light, full of dear little tunes and a kind of fragile poetry, with oboes making fairy trumpets. The finale is an Oberon's hunt, with neither Puck nor Titania far away, and there is a brief quarrel of rhythms.

The same transparent quality distinguishes the Concerto in F major (K. 459). Every strand of its airy traceries is distinctly heard. The delicately sprightly first movement is one of the most subtly designed, with its many small figures arranging themselves as if by some natural law into a perfect whole. The second movement is for once an *allegretto,* a piece of placid summer-evening poetry which Mozart seems to have recalled when he wrote Susanna's tender air in the garden in the last act of *Figaro.* The playfulness of the finale is strengthened by some intricate and miraculously lucid polyphonic writing. As in many of his last movements Mozart lets the solo instrument begin before he embarks on the expository orchestral symphony. Beethoven's similar procedure in the G major and 'Emperor' Concertos was thus a novelty only so far as the opening movement was concerned, and indeed even there not altogether, for in K. 271 Mozart lets the piano take part in the opening, though not actually make the first gesture.

Very little later he suddenly takes the piano concerto into an alien territory. In the D minor Concerto (K. 466) he is a futurist composer, a romantic before what historians conveniently but loosely label as the romantic period. He even prophetically calls his slow movement a *Romanze*—in German, be it noted. He is in the mood already into which Beethoven dropped temporarily and Schumann permanently, not to say in that of Wagner when he wrote his diatribe against 'wälschen Dunst mit wälschem Tand.' He got over it again, of course: he had too much traditional artistic breeding and was too much a citizen of the whole civilized world in his tastes to grow for good into a German of the *Sturm und Drang* direction; but here is this evidence of his fitful leaning towards it, the most striking though by no means the only one. For the first time in a piano concerto, for almost the only time in any concerto, he had chosen a minor key, and the particular key in which he was later to express Donna Anna's agitated grief, the ghostly appearance of the stone guest and the vengeful passion of the Queen of Night.

The Concerto begins with a shudder, and the first movement is full of unhappy commotion. Even the convention that the second subject in a sonata-form movement in a minor key should at first appear in the relative major and later in the tonic minor helps to intensify the drama: it is as though a false promise of relief were mockingly revealing itself as a tragic delusion.[1] The romance is in rondo form, with its beautifully suave tune turning up again and again, rather too often for those who have become very familiar with it, but with tastefully unemphatic differences in treatment. The wild middle episode in G minor is like a sudden fit of raving despair. Even in the rondo-finale the music remains stressful. It has a kind of unhappy restlessness, relieved by a major second subject of ineffable grace. This again proves a delusion when it returns in the minor; but only a temporary one, for presently, in an enchanting coda, the music clears into D major and the second subject triumphs in a sunny outburst of happiness, with woodwind, horns and trumpets answering each other with a supplementary phrase of the utmost good humour. After all, Mozart remembered, this was a concerto, a piece meant to entertain, and feeling that he had done enough to startle his polite hearers with his most impassioned music, he relieved them at the end and let them go away emotionally relaxed, as he was to do again a little later with an opera in

[1] This does not mean that music in a major key is necessarily always bright and that in minor always gloomy, but it happens to be so in this case.

D minor (*Don Giovanni*) that also has a cheerful coda in D major.

The very next work, C major (K. 467), which flourishes trumpets and drums in much gayer fashion, was again a more normal display concerto. The first movement, in fact, is grandly ostentatious and the finale full of pleasurable dash and daintiness. The slow movement, however, must again have made Mozart's hearers sit up by its daring modernities. Although by muting the strings and dropping the trumpets and drums he gave it a suave tone, there is a suppressed feeling of discomfort about it. Here is a whole bunch of audacities, quoted from the orchestral introduction:

A diminished seventh and a swooping skip in the first bar, an unexpected transition to the tonic minor in the second, discordant suspensions in the next three and a grinding false relation (B flat against B natural) in the last.

The E flat major Concerto (K. 482) retains drums and trumpets, but replaces the more usual oboes by clarinets, which give it quite a new colour, for Mozart always knows how to make the most of wind instruments. This work is many people's favourite among the piano concertos—until they hear one of the others. For it is with these works as with all serial artistic products that shine as much by variety as by quality: the one you happen to be confronted with at the moment always seems the best. Greatness has not necessarily anything to do with this, for it is as true of, let us say, Sullivan's operettas as of Shakespeare's sonnets or Hogarth's sequences of pictures.

However, the Mozart concertos are great art, and they became more and more surprisingly varied as they accumulated year by year. The first movement of this work in E flat, with its stately grace, is particularly enchanting in its new instrumental colour devices. The sequential passage for horns and bassoons just after the opening, for instance, or the overlapping of wind and string phrases a moment later, are the height of cunning contrivance resulting in what is apparently quite simple and obvious, but what could have occurred to nobody else. What is it that makes shivers of delight run down one's back at Mozart's mere notion of thrusting a little extra figure into the repetition of the following little tune?

The slow movement is a miracle, with woodwind, horns and muted strings giving the tenderest support to the piano, It is in C minor, but can never be held for long from turning lovingly into the flat major keys near it. Presently the strings and the piano withdraw, leaving the wind instruments to play some truly Mozartian serenade music, the second clarinet making celestial play with the stale trick of the Alberti bass. Even more exquisite, if possible, is a C major section where flute and bassoon have a little concerto of their own. The rondo in 6–8 is more commonplace, with its hunting horns and pealing *tutti,* although Mozart most knowingly applies his art of making unique values out of music's stock-in-trade. But he has a staggering surprise still in store. One of his rondo episodes turns out to be another quiet serenade movement, an *andantino cantabile* of the most heart-seizing beauty, as lovingly fashioned as the 'round' in the second finale of *Così fan tutte,* and not only very much in the same vein but—once again one is struck by this fact—in the same key: A flat major.[1]

The year 1786 again brought three concertos, two of them great works and as different as possible from each other. The A major (K. 488) is as sunny in the first and last movements as the use of that key would lead one to expect from Mozart, though the sunniness is by no means of a mild sort. The music can scorch and sting at times. Again clarinets are used most tenderly, but there are no brass and drums this time. The slow movement, in F sharp minor, is one of Mozart's most passionate expressions. It is in 6–8 time, a kind of tragic *Siciliana,* or rather *Napolitana,* it might be said, for the pathetic Neapolitan sixth plays a great part in making it more intensely plaintive. The finale is irrepressibly gay, though not without that after-tang of sadness which is always liable to make one

[1] An even more remarkable coincidence, if it really can be that, is that both these movements are written with the key signature of E flat major, the extra flat required being marked in casually wherever the note D occurs.

suddenly feel that Mozart, even in his most lighthearted moods, is fundamentally never a singer of ingenuous happiness.

That he can be quite gloomy, though without ever sacrificing the most limpid euphony, is shown by the next Concerto, in C minor (K. 491), the work immediately preceding *Figaro* and as different from it as a rainy day from a cloudless one. However, it is almost equally unlike the only other concerto in a minor key Mozart ever wrote. Less dramatic than the D minor, it is more declamatory. It has a more classical repose of gesture, more poise and shape, more unity of atmosphere. There is nothing like the unexpected happy ending of the earlier work: it closes, as it began, in the dark key of C minor. The one resemblance is the rondo form of the slow movement, with rather too frequent recurrences of a subject of very much the same type. There is no dramatic episode here, however, for Mozart again takes to a serenading tone with concertizing wind instruments, and there is another *Così fan tutte*-ish episode in A flat major. The finale is a set of very original variations on a shapely and sorrowfully elegant C minor *allegretto* theme. If tunes really can be portraits, as Couperin wished them to be, this would be one of a well-dressed and perfectly mannered widow who lets the world guess her grief without consciously showing it. There are two beautiful incidents in major keys, but the final variation in 6–8 not only keeps to the minor to the end, but has Neapolitan depressions.

The third work of that year, C major (K. 503), is a disappointment. It is interesting for some special technical problems which make it on the whole the most difficult of all the piano concertos, but the performer is not sufficiently repaid by the effort of overcoming them, for it is all rather frigid and comparatively unoriginal. The same is true to a smaller extent of the so-called 'Coronation' Concerto, in D major (K. 537), a polished work on a large scale, but making a rather static impression because the invention is not as abundant as elsewhere.

The last of the piano concertos, in B flat major (K. 595), is a truly valedictory work, with a kind of chastened mood occasionally verging on a feeling of oppressive foreboding. The following curious approach to a Neapolitan inflection is very poignant in its mixture of originality with simple spontaneity:

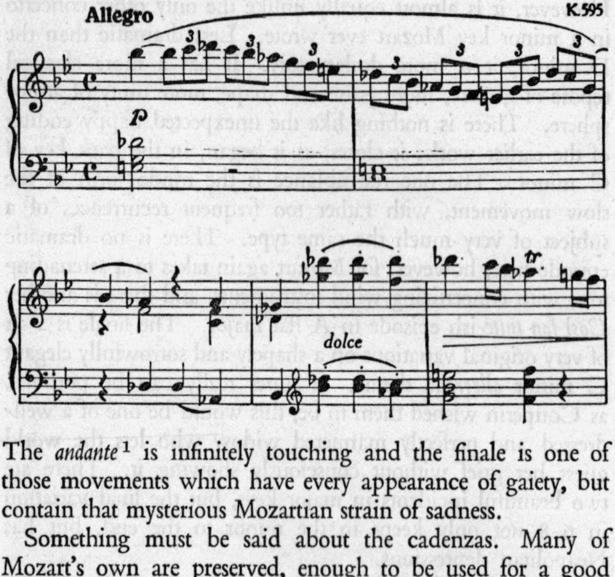

The *andante*[1] is infinitely touching and the finale is one of those movements which have every appearance of gaiety, but contain that mysterious Mozartian strain of sadness.

Something must be said about the cadenzas. Many of Mozart's own are preserved, enough to be used for a good number of the concertos and to provide models for other people to work on. For most of the cadenzas played by pianists in the concert-room are, in association with the music they draw upon, so much rubbish, even those by otherwise reputable composers. Nearly all of them are far too long and

[1] It is emphatically not an *adagio,* and a famous pianist quite mistakes its character in playing it very much more slowly in a recent gramophone record than any one with the slightest feeling for Mozartian expression can possibly feel that it should go.

all without exception do a great deal too much in the way of thematic developing. This is neither historically nor aesthetically the function of a cadenza, and concert-giving suffers from no abuse more offensive than these pretentious excrescences. There was originally no difference, as etymologically there is none, between the cadenza and the cadence. The former was simply an ornamental extension of the latter, inserted at first into arias and later, by analogy, into concertos as a concession to the technically gifted performer. It must therefore be a decorative feature and nothing else. The composer, at any rate a great composer like Mozart, has already worked out his thematic material exactly as much as he wished, and later musicians who take it upon themselves to show what more might have been done in that direction are guilty of an impertinence even when, as happens very rarely, they do not plaster a monstrous stylistic incongruity upon a perfectly organized structure. A glance at Mozart's own cadenzas shows that they are only very slightly thematic and tactfully keep to the subsidiary function of a desirable but not fundamentally vital embellishment.

The more important of the concertos and kindred works for other instruments than the violin and the pianoforte have already been referred to, and there is too little space left for their detailed discussion. The most valuable are assuredly the *Sinfonia concertante* for violin and viola (K. 364) and the touchingly beautiful clarinet Concerto (K. 622). Next come the horn Concertos (K. 412, 417, 447, 495), which show an astonishing grasp of the instrument's character and endless ingenuity not only in the surmounting but the turning to account of its eighteenth-century limitations. The early bassoon Concerto (K. 191), with its amusing quips that suit the instrument to perfection, is an attractive light piece of work, and so are the compositions for flute (K. 313–15), the finale of one of which (K. 314) anticipates Blonde's merry G major aria in *The Elopement.* The Concerto for flute and harp (K. 299) is rather weak, and the latter instrument is written for in a manner which more recent exploits on it have superseded. The same must be said of Mozart's treatment of the organ in the numerous Salzburg sonatas for that instrument with accompaniment for orchestra or string band, official music of the concerto type, though it keeps to one movement and glances back at the older species of the *sonata da chiesa.* These sonatas, written as voluntaries for performance during mass, show no lasting vitality.

Violoncellists have the misfortune of having been left no concerto by Mozart. Indeed he does not seem to have favoured this instrument particularly. The *obbligato* part in Zerlina's 'Batti, batti' in *Don Giovanni* does not amount to very much, and its favoured position in the quartets for the King of Prussia is quite evidently due to the fact that Frederick William himself played the cello parts in those works.

CHAPTER XVIII

CHAMBER MUSIC

MOZART cultivated chamber music in practically all its most current forms as well as with several unusual instrumental combinations, and if it is considered that many of the divertimenti originally intended for orchestra may very well be played with single instruments to each string part, the richness of his chamber repertory greatly exceeds that of normal modern performing practice. More 's the pity. Much of his finest and profoundest music thus lies almost wholly neglected, especially the chamber music containing parts for wind instruments, and even the magnificent string quintets requiring two violas are far too rarely heard at concerts and in private.[1] They are, in their fundamentally different way, quite as important as the string quartets, but as the latter are far more accessible to players and listeners alike, at any rate the last ten fully matured works in that form, a beginning had better be made here with a somewhat closer study of them than it will be possible to devote to the rest of the chamber music.

Nobody will ever determine quite conclusively whether the string quartet first reached perfection, both as a form and as a mode of expression, through Haydn or through Mozart. Their reciprocal influences are so inseparably entangled that a decision as to how much must be ascribed to the one and how much to the other will always in the last resort depend upon prejudice in favour of this master or that. But prejudice is the last thing that will do in criticism, and an attempt

[1] Viola players being scarce, it is worth while drawing the attention of amateurs to the fact that the quintets do admirably for domestic purposes in a good arrangement for piano duet.

must at least be made to unravel the facts. Dr. Ernest Walker established a good working theory in his famous epigram about Haydn's first showing Mozart how to write string quartets and Mozart then showing Haydn how quartets should be written. Epigrams too, however, though they agreeably enliven a discourse on aesthetics, are fraught with some danger. They may find too ready a currency as easily remembered generalizations. Thus, while we may accept Dr. Walker's pithy aphorism with grateful amusement as broadly true, it is as well to examine the subtle interaction of these two composers in greater detail. This can be done only in outline here, for nothing short of an exhaustive investigation of their whole quartet output can do justice to this absorbingly interesting subject.

The most striking fact in the string quartet activities of both Haydn and Mozart is that each of them, at an important period of his career, ceased to produce works of this kind for about a decade, and roughly the same decade. Haydn wrote no quartets between 1772[1] and 1781, when the so-called 'Russian' Quartets (Op. 33) appeared, and Mozart produced his last quartet preceding the ten great ones in 1773, resuming the form at the end of 1782. Now Haydn, in bringing out the 1781 set, announced that these quartets were written in quite a new and unusual style, which in fact they were. Their close thematic workmanship was all but absent from the three dozen or so[2] of quartets written by him before 1772. In justice to Haydn it must therefore be pointed out that wherever the incentive for such workmanship came from, it cannot in

[1] It has been proved by Adolf Sandberger (in *Gesammelte Aufsätze zur Musikgeschichte,* Munich 1921) that Pohl was wrong in assigning Haydn's Op. 20 to the year 1774.

[2] The number of quartets written by Haydn can never be quite definitely ascertained, as the early examples are not always clearly differentiated from cassations, divertimenti and even symphonies for string instruments. But see the reasonably conclusive list in the *Haydn* volume of this series, Appendix B.

the first place have come from Mozart. For it is not likely that a man of nearly fifty should have even looked at quartets written by a boy of seventeen, however great his genius, and quartets which are manifestly immature.

The influence seems rather to point the other way than Dr. Walker implies, at any rate as far as the first of Mozart's quartets dedicated to Haydn is concerned. This work (G major, K. 387) is quite obviously Haydnesque almost throughout, and especially in the light and yet taut fugal texture of the finale. On the other hand it is indisputable that Haydn continued to develop considerably after his Op. 33, that is, after he had come to know and admire the quartets inscribed to him by Mozart. Nor does it seem likely that Haydn's quartets were the first to stimulate Mozart to write similar works. His earliest Quartet (G major, K. 80), written at Lodi during the Italian tour of 1770, at the age of fourteen, seems derived from the divertimenti of Sammartini and the *sonate a quattro* of Tartini rather than from German models. The latter, in their primitive form, originated from and tended for a long time to revert to the form of the suite, and this was followed at first by Haydn, while the Italian species, to which Mozart at once began to lean, took the line of the indigenous chamber sonata.

After this mere hint at the fascinating complexity of the problem of Haydn's and Mozart's artistic inter-relations, it is time to make this study more immediately relevant to the latter's mature quartet style. We have already seen that it has not fully emerged in the first of the quartets dedicated to Haydn, for whom it is evidently intended to be a compliment verging on the sincerest form of flattery. But even here it is with difficulty repressed, and the composer's individuality asserts itself the more energetically in the D minor Quartet (K. 421), which is in fact perhaps the most characteristic of the ten works under discussion. It is the only example written in one of the minor keys which Mozart used so sparingly, but nearly always with a force of significance rarely equalled by any of his works or movements in major tonalities. Dyneley Hussey points out in his book on Mozart that the composer's contemporaries looked upon his music as charged with profound melancholy and an intense personal expressiveness. Fastidious artist that he was, and keenly aware of the importance of moderation in all things, he may have felt that in the gloomier minor keys he gave away almost too much of himself for an age that was courtly and hedonistic, an age not interested in individuals and knowing nothing of psychology. He may therefore have consciously assigned them a smaller share in his work; but that does not alter the fact that when he did use them they revealed the dejection that underlay his habitual gaiety the more poignantly. The suppressed passion of the opening movement of the D minor Quartet, the intense, almost hectic beauty of the *andante* with its unprepared transitions from key to key, and above all the finale with its curiously fitful gleams of intermittent minor and major, its allusions to the Neapolitan sixth, which makes a kind of redoubled minor by its depression of yet another note of the scale, and especially the violent *sforzandi* off the beat—all this amounts to a personal confession that is kept within the bounds of pure art only because its expressive intensity is matched by the utmost tact and the keenest discernment of a perfect balance between technique and design. The febrile intensity of the slow movements will also be observed in the B flat and C major Quartets (K. 458 and 465), and more especially in that in E flat major (K. 428) with its almost *Tristan*-like chromaticisms. The *sforzandi,* which are the lion's claw hidden under the lithe feline charm of Mozart's eighteenth-century idiom, even betray themselves occasionally in his minuets (K. 458).

The tendency to lay stress on the finale is one of the novel features of Mozart's treatment of the string quartet. The sonata form, at the stage it had reached in his time, still tended to maintain the supremacy of the first movement that had been a feature of all its predecessors. The *sonata da chiesa* and the French overture opened with a ponderous slow introduction

o, and the suite almost
vement, preferably the
traditional lively gait
s, but he stresses their
ensification, as in the
n exceptional triumph
major (K. 387, 464).
ant of the suite form,
n in Mozart's hands.
rely pace of the dance,
mic element can be
the F major Quartet
quare metrical pattern
e minuet and five-bar
a caustic note in some
scherzos of Beethoven,
s in the minuet of the
hromatic inner part of
—where one thinks of
in dance movements,
is noticeable that the
t perhaps, very often
e—the kind of feeling
s *Ländler*-like minuets
could not resist the
ubstance uninfluenced
by the incomparably

as of all his chamber
a form, which had by
ings of Carl Philipp
ool. But though it is
es, there is apparently
ting it to fit mood and
example, the influence
daring working-out

section is distinctly felt to extend to the recapitulation, its significance being balanced at the close by that of the coda.

None of the quartets starts with those empty, fanfare-like calls to attention which initial almost every symphony of Mozart's down to the last. A great difference between the chamber and the concert styles was inherent in the musical conditions of the eighteenth century: only in the family circle would people listen collectively, while in the concert room and the theatre the frivolous audiences had to be elaborately warned, not that the music was about to begin, but that it had begun. No one understood this difference better than Mozart, who was not too proud to act as his own announcer when there was need, but could plunge at once into an arresting discourse without preliminary flourish.

Neither has more than one of the last ten quartets a slow introduction.[1] The exception is, of course, the C major Quartet (K. 465), with its mysterious preamble, which has set people guessing ever since the work appeared and was the chief provocation of Sarti's adverse criticism.[2] It is possible to feel that this introduction satisfies ear and sense as a kind of deliberate enveloping of the musical substance in a mist in order that the radiant C major subject of the *allegro* may appear the more sunny. But, the procedure occurring in Mozart, the riddle remains, for though he is often curiously ambiguous in his moods, he is perhaps never, with this single exception, so in his methods. It is not the early appearance of pungent discord:

[1] And only two of the earlier works in that form.

[2] See p. 128, footnote.

that surprises and puzzles, for we may find much greater audacities of harmonic clashes and false relations in the Italian and English madrigalists, in Purcell, in Bach, in a hundred other composers older than Mozart. What astonishes is the fact that it does not fit in with the limpid style of the rest of the Quartet. However, enigma or not, stylistic blot or otherwise, one could not do without the sharp sting this passage never fails to give to one's emotions or even without its ever-new incitement to one's curiosity.

Mozart no more ends his quartet movements—and for that matter his quintet and other chamber-music movements—with emphatic full closes than he begins them with formal flourishes. There is no clinching his matter with a prolonged hammering at tonic and dominant. In the mature quartets he finds more cunning ways of enhancing the effect of the perfect cadence, of which he never tired to the end of his life. The cadences themselves, it will be observed, remain comparatively conventional and restricted in range of disposition, but Mozart's manner of approaching them is infinitely varied. He is particularly fond of announcing them in chamber music by means of elaborately chromatic passages which seem to waver for a moment, to point this way and that, only to be suddenly resolved in some entrancing way into full closes that may be ordinary, but spring their surprise because they come at an unexpected moment (*see next page*).

The curious thing, which indeed may be observed in all music that has a true vitality, is that the astonished delight at Mozart's deceptive preparations of the cadence does not wear off with close acquaintance. There never was a composer familiarity with whom bred greater love and respect.

One of the most simply effected yet greatest of these perennial surprises in the string quartets is that of the opening of the E flat major Quartet (K. 428), with its theme stealing upon the ear in unobtrusive octave unison:

and then suddenly bursting into dissonant harmony:

The most amazing fact about this never-failing thrill is that it is gained by means of what has since become the stalest of all tricks in the whole harmonic resources of music—the chord of the diminished seventh.

A way of effecting modulation that is peculiar to Mozart in its refined ingenuity, and more frequently found in his chamber music than elsewhere, is that of combining it with quasi-fugal imitations such as the older polyphonic composers kept more strictly within one key. He will sometimes change from one tonality to another at each successive entry of the four instruments, thus giving the hearer a series of delicate shocks in order to make the settling down to a new key the more luxuriously comfortable. This harmonic heightening in the string quartets and quintets is quite evidently intended to compensate for the evenness of instrumental colour. These media, it is true, are handled to perfection only so long as they are allowed to rely primarily upon design; but Mozart saw that it need not necessarily be a design in black and white. His quartets and quintets have delicate flushes of colour-wash which, so far from impairing the line-drawing, enhance its purity.

The treatment of the instruments grows more and more interesting in Mozart's hands. The individual responsibility of the chamber-music player, as distinct from the orchestral musician, is recognized by a much more equal distribution of the musical interest along the parts. We have only to compare the cello parts of the quartets and quintets with the basses in the score of, let us say, *Figaro,* to become at once aware of the difference. In the opera the basses are plain and solid, frequently marked by the fundamental progression of the perfect cadence (sub-dominant, dominant, tonic—frequently preceded by sub-mediant), while in the chamber music they are adjusted to the lighter upper structure, more continuous and varied, and frequently concerned in the conduct of the melody. The viola parts show a similar emancipation, and in the quintets, where there are two of them, they weave inner strands of a dark, saturated colour into the structure with a peculiarly heart-smiting effect.

The instruments are not used to their fullest range of technical possibilities, yet always required to give the greatest force to any intended idea. Only the flatteringly elaborate cello parts in the quartets written for the King of Prussia occasionally disregard a wise imposition of economy; but it must be remembered that they were written for an exalted cellist who plumed himself not a little on his skill. That is doubtless also the reason why these three quartets (K. 575, 589–90) are more superficial in expression than the six dedicated to Haydn, though no less finished in their own way. But although these last quartets have not the depth of the earlier set, nor quite the wonderfully adjusted craftsmanship and polished grace of the separate Quartet in D major (K. 499), and do not reveal the composer so intimately—which indeed might have seemed to him an impertinence in the circumstances—the wonder is that they come so near to Mozart's high-water mark in quartet writing, for all that they were written under the constraint of poverty as well as that of a royal mandate. And that high-water mark, though Beethoven's later quartets are greater human documents, indicates also the summit as yet reached by this musical species at any point of its history, so far as the most finished art of writing and the perfect adjustment of matter and manner are concerned.

I have not discussed each of the ten great quartets in as much detail as, for example, the piano concertos, partly because I chose to fill the space allotted to them with a different discussion, designed to avoid the monotony a work-for-work analysis of the whole of Mozart's catalogue could not fail to produce, and partly because in this case the present study can be easily supplemented by the writings of others.[1] A few words must

[1] e.g. Thomas Dunhill's essay on the quartets, which fills two books of the 'Musical Pilgrim' series (Oxford University Press).

be said, however, on the earlier quartets, of which thirteen are extant. They begin, with the G major Quartet (K. 80) written at Lodi at the age of sixteen, in a style that makes them differ no more than Haydn's early *quadri* do from music of the divertimento or serenade type. Their often elementary treatment of the viola and cello show that Mozart in his youth could not at once emancipate himself from the convention of the figured bass, which had long tended to stiffen the bass line of any music in which it was employed or allowed to exercise its influence, perhaps unnoticed by the composer. This rigidity of the bass and lack of independence in the viola continues throughout the first of two sets of six quartets (K. 155–60), dating from 1772, though it is occasionally relieved by signs of greater initiative. The movements are still quite short and those in sonata form have episodic working-out sections. That in the first movement of the fourth Quartet, in C major (K. 157), for instance, is quite independent of the thematic material until it makes a tiny but significant allusion to the first subject in the minor and so leads to the recapitulation in a way that hints at the composer's later practice. The fifth Quartet, in F major (K. 158), glances back at the older dance-suite form by introducing a minuet-like first movement.

Another set of six quartets (K. 168–73), written during the sojourn in Vienna in 1773, shows very clearly that the boy of seventeen was anxious to impress his learning on the musicians of the capital. They are no doubt the fruit of his contrapuntal studies under Padre Martini, though the actual incentive may have come to him from the provocative example of the more learned masters of the Viennese school, with Haydn at the head, but his brother Michael, Wagenseil, Gassmann and Georg Monn also playing their part. The F major Quartet of this set (K. 168) has an *andante* in F minor which begins very intricately with a fourfold canon and continues with elaborate canonic formations; the E flat major (K. 171) has a more studiedly polyphonic first movement than any quartet so far, and the D minor (K. 173), an interesting work and the first in a minor key, has a fugal finale on a chromatic theme with all the complex devices of pedals, strettos, inversions and so on applied with unfailing resource and skill.

The string quintets, as I have already hinted, differ entirely in character, though not in depth and finish, from the quartets. There are five of them, strictly speaking, with two arrangements in addition. It was not Mozart himself, but some unknown person who arranged the great wind Serenade (K. 361) as a quintet, and the early Köchel number is misleading. Only the first three movements and the last of this remarkable work were transferred to the string version. The other Quintet which is not original is that in C minor (K. 406), transcribed in 1787 from one of the two fine serenades for wind octet (K. 388), composed in 1781–2. The original form is, of course, preferable, but as performances are bound to be restricted it is good to possess one more work in a series that contains some of Mozart's maturest masterpieces. The C minor Quintet displays some contrapuntal ingenuities such as Haydn often loved to toy with, but which are rare in Mozart: his minuet is in octave canon and at one point in canon at the fourth, while the trio is a specimen of canon *al rovescio,* i.e. with the answer turned upside down. There is not the slightest impression of constraint, which is what makes all the difference between justified and uncalled-for cleverness.

The fifth instrument is in every case a second viola, not the second cello which Schubert chose for his great C major Quintet. Mozart liked to keep his basses in a single line and lucid; it was the dark colour and rich texture the violas imparted to the middle register that fascinated him, and indeed it called up music of a peculiarly profound and impassioned nature from him, as instruments with dark shades of tone (violas, clarinets, basset horns) often did. At times the violas and the cello alone yield him an intricate fabric of a velvety quality:

The Quintet in C major (K. 515), like many of Mozart's works in that key, tends somewhat towards brilliant, concertizing display. Its most original movement, curiously enough, is the minuet, which opens ambiguously in dominant harmony without the clarifying support of the bass and with an oddly-distributed ten-bar phrase.

The G minor Quintet (K. 516) is the most famous. It is, of course, in one of the minor keys that drew some of the greatest music from Mozart, including this work, the great G minor Symphony, the laments of Constanze in *The Elopement* and of Pamina in *The Magic Flute,* not to mention, or rather to defer mentioning until a little later in this chapter, another very significant piece of chamber music. C minor and D minor yielded him perhaps ampler works, but G minor some of the most intimate. The poignantly beautiful slow movement, however, is in E flat major, and the finale, after a slow G minor introduction, clears into G major: a rather too slight movement but worked with admirable lucidity.

The Quintet in D major (K. 593) has a slow introduction at the beginning which is alluded to before the coda of the *allegro*—a rare feature. The slow movement is richly displayed, harmonically rather than contrapuntally. Polyphonic ingenuity is reserved for the finale, which begins with one of those 6–8 themes that look as though they could do nothing but play skittishly, but goes often into the most severe fugal treatment. No, severe is not the word, for it is most enchantingly suave at the same time. There is an example of one of those melting chromatic cadences the ear would like to clamour for over and over again:

It is difficult to choose among the incomparable, but perhaps the E flat major Quintet (K. 614) is the most superb of all. It has probably the highest sum-total of great invention plus great workmanship, and the two are most miraculously balanced. The *andante* movement is the gem, if anything can be singled out as most lovable. It has that touching expression of faithful and confident love which Mozart had made his Belmonte express in *The Elopement* at the time of his engagement. It is in the same key, too, B flat major. The similar expressions we often find turning up in the same keys in Mozart's music sometimes lie years apart.

To complete the chamber music for strings, there are a few works for less than four instruments, among which the Duets for violin and viola (K. 423–4) stand foremost, together with a Divertimento in E flat major for violin, viola and cello (K. 563) of exceptional quality that is not well enough known.

Among the works with pianoforte parts the Quartet in G minor for violin, viola, cello and piano (K. 478) takes the pre-eminent place. It is in fact a great work, worthy to stand next to the later Symphony and the string Quintet in the same key. There is a passionate concentration of thematic work in the first movement as well as an originality of invention and treatment that impresses the hearer at once and never wears off with repetition. The second subject contains two bars of 5–4 time which are none the less plain to the ear because Mozart is too polite a creature of the eighteenth century to draw attention to so subversive a feature. A modern composer would have self-consciously written the passage thus:

(Note how the even bass is kept from interfering with the cross-accentuation.) The slow movement ranks with Mozart's most expressive B-flat-major love music, and the finale, in G major, anticipates the gracious elegance of *Figaro.* It is a rondo that confronts the hearer with the fascinatingly insoluble problem of telling which of its melodies, sprung on his ear with spontaneous nonchalance, is the most delicious.

The other piano Quartet, in E flat major (K. 493), although quite as cunningly laid out and full of enticing opportunities for each instrument, is not so immediately appealing, the composer having relied more on his unfailing accomplishment and his taste in applying stereotyped ideas to his immediate purpose than on irresistible inspiration. There is, however, one incident in the finale so utterly bewitching that it is worth quoting here at length, more especially as it is tucked away in a work that is not often played. It shows Mozart's amazing facility in treating whatever medium he chooses in the most perfect way imaginable, as well as his genius for varying a musical phrase with the lightest of touch, of modulating by way of a harmonic surprise and of going back to the original key in the most natural and graceful way possible. Nothing more perfectly polished and tasteful is imaginable than this:

Of trios with a pianoforte part eight are preserved, though one of them not completed by Mozart himself, but by Maximilian Stadler. Seven of them are for the normal combination of violin, cello and piano and one is the Trio for the unusual medium of clarinet, viola and piano (K. 498). This is a great work, in which the sombre colour of the wind and the string instrument as well as the affection Mozart had for both of them called splendidly knit and emotionally fully charged music from him. If one would like to show that there was a kind of Emily Brontë-like quality of smouldering passion in Mozart, which could betray itself even through so decorous a piece of music as a minuet, one could hardly do better than point to the astonishingly tense minuet in this wonderful work.

The more normal trios—more normal in idiom as well as in medium—cannot be discussed in detail, and need not be, since by this time the characteristics of Mozart's chamber music in which they participate have been fairly extensively discussed. Several of them are masterpieces and very delightful to play, though not nearly as easy as they may sound to the unpractised ear. Perhaps the most adorable is the Trio in E major (K. 542), a key very rarely used by Mozart for some reason or another, but certainly not that of aversion, to judge by this work and other pieces. An example of how Mozart deals with the always difficult problem of the piano-trio texture, with its uncomfortable gap between the two string instruments, may be shown here from the second movement of this Trio. The extract will at the same time demonstrate his unique way of delicately spicing a melody by discreet harmonic inflections:

The cello parts are, for modern ideas, treated a little shabbily in these trios, though not as much so as in Haydn's. But then modern ideas cannot reasonably be applied to music of the past, which is never to be properly appreciated unless it is accepted on its own terms and not in the light of later works, be they better or less good, with which it cannot conceivably have anything whatever to do. For this reason it is futile, for example, to complain that Mozart's trios are less satisfying than Beethoven's because they are less profound, even if one could be quite sure that this is true—and it is very doubtful in the case of the clarinet Trio at any rate. There is no possible comparison between two complete but utterly different masters like Mozart and Beethoven, and although personal preferences are perfectly legitimate, there is no point in dragging them into public discussions. This can only result in such comic absurdities as some recent Franco-Russian theories according to which Mozart was to be upheld because he is an 'objective' composer and Beethoven belittled, if not anathematized, because of his 'subjectivity,' as though any man could ever hope to become a great artist by remaining objectively detached from human experience. There would have been some sense in drawing a distinction according to which Beethoven was made out to be a very consciously subjective composer and

Mozart an unwittingly subjective one, a sort of deliberate classic and willy-nilly romantic; but that is partly a matter of the very different social conditions under which they lived, and I will not risk incurring Sir Donald Tovey's scorn—no doubt amply deserved already—by talking about the French Revolution when I am expected to discuss music.

A dozen or so of chamber works for various instrumental combinations remain, but cannot all be enumerated here. The Quartets for flute and strings (K. 285, 298) and oboe and strings (K. 370), for example, are typical Mozartian works of a lighter kind which it is always safe to produce when a rare occasion calls for them. Of the two wind Serenades for oboes, clarinets, horns and bassoons in pairs, in E flat major (K. 375) and C minor (K. 388), the latter has been referred to as being arranged for a string quintet, and it is to be wished that the former were available in a similar transcription, for both are admirable works, very mature for their period. Another endearing composition of the serenade type in the Quintet in E flat major for oboe, clarinet, horn, bassoon and piano (K. 452), which suffers from neglect for the only reason that keeps the wind octet serenades from the public: the regrettably few opportunities wind players have to appear as chamber performers.

The Quintet in A major for clarinet and strings (K. 581) ranks with the clarinet Concerto, which is in the same key, as one of the finest of Mozart's instrumental works of his all too early late years. Very transparent in texture and apparently light in character, it has a gentle pathos akin to that of the most touching passages in *Don Giovanni,* and the way in which Mozart not only deals with the special problems of the clarinet, but adjusts the whole string quartet fabric to fit them, is nothing short of miraculous. The Quintet has that quality of clairvoyance which so often surprises and gently oppresses us when we are confronted with his best work, the kind of infallibility in doing precisely the right thing at precisely the right moment which must often have made him stand back, not to say stagger back, from his work and ask himself in happy consternation: 'How did I do it?'

CHAPTER XIX

SONATAS AND PIANOFORTE PIECES

THE sonatas for violin and pianoforte (or harpsichord at first) are more properly reviewed with those for keyboard alone than with the chamber music. The eighteenth-century convention was that such works should be essentially keyboard music. Sonatas were written for clavier. The violin could join in if it was available,[1] but the composer was not going to have the popularity of his domestic music threatened by the comparative rarity of players on that instrument. Every household had a harpsichord or clavichord, displaced some time during the second half of the century by the rapidly spreading pianoforte, and sonatas were so devised that they could be played just as well without a second instrument, though their effect was heightened by its participation.

Mozart himself started out by adhering to this fashion without questioning its justification. His early sonatas for violin and clavier dating from 1762 to 1766, only sixteen of which are now regarded as genuine, all show this tendency towards a subordinate violin part very distinctly. They are thus of small interest to the modern player, quite apart from their immaturity as music, which makes them merely historically worthy of study nowadays. They are very properly published in the complete Mozart edition, but as rightly omitted by modern editors from the ordinary collections for home and concert use.

Such collections usually begin with the Sonata in C major (K. 296), written at Mannheim in 1778 and dedicated to Therese Pierron-Serrarius, a girl of fifteen whom Mozart taught the clavier during his visit there. That is perhaps why

[1] Or in England the alternative 'German flute.'

the violin part here is still largely an accompaniment. Pretty well the whole Sonata might be played on the piano alone without loss of many essential melodic features, though certainly with a distinct lessening of those charming effects produced by the collaboration of two antagonistic instruments. The opening of the work will show at once how the violin part is made merely to fill in:

and this is typical of much of Mozart's writing, not only in this composition, but in the later ones for the same two instruments. The old habit persisted, and it is significant that so late a work of his as a piano Sonata in B flat major (K. 570) is better known with an accompanying violin part which did not come from his pen at all. All the same, these participations of the violin, even if they happen to be only a supplementing of the melody a third or a sixth below or a tiny echo phrase, are becoming astonishingly attractive, and when the violin does suddenly blossom out into a melody of its own, the surprise is peculiarly appealing. Mozart's method in this C major Sonata has the touching appeal of adolescence: an anxious clinging to the support of the conventions in which the violin sonata had been brought up, with little shy outbursts of independence.

The six Sonatas (K. 301–6), written for the Electress Palatine, apparently at Mannheim on his return from Paris, begin to show greater freedom in the violin parts, though the delightful element of chamber-musicianly collaboration between the two instruments remains. Note, for instance, how a purely accompanying figure in the sixth of these Sonatas suddenly flowers into a melody that may be merely supplementary, but without which the bloom would be stripped off this passage:

These six works show that surprising maturity in a young man of twenty-two which one notices that his music reflects very strikingly at the time of his falling in love with Aloysia and the death of his mother. There is something of a new, chastened tone about the gentle gravity of the *andante grazioso* rondo of the E flat major Sonata (K. 302), which makes a slow middle movement superfluous. The C major Sonata (K. 303) for the first time has a slow introduction and, more curiously, an *adagio* interruption in the middle of the first *allegro*. The A major (K. 305) boldly presents the first subject turned upside down and in a minor key at the beginning of the working-out section, and there is a set of variations for a second movement. The D major (K. 306) is the only one of these works in three fully developed movements.

The most arresting, however, is the fourth, in E minor (K. 304). Once again we find Mozart surprisingly daring, dramatic and individual on taking to a minor key, as he did so strikingly seldom but scarcely ever without producing what in a less fastidious composer one would be tempted to call a sensation. In the proper sense of the term it certainly is that here. This Sonata is startling in its emotional tension and ripeness. From the very opening, with its hollow unison, we are held spellbound by the tragic force of the music:

The second subject, in the relative major at first, has a kind of sorrowful grace, and the presentation of the first subject in canon, but without any extra harmony, makes a positively grisly climax to the exposition. The working-out heightens the dramatic tension by a new, ingeniously interlaced figure in answer to the main theme, and there is almost a touch of horror when at the recapitulation the subject breaks in surprisingly harmonized:

A coda of almost Beethovenish breadth and importance, quite strange in Mozart at this period, concludes the movement. The second, which is also the last, is slighter, yet far more portentous than its minuet time would seem to indicate. There is an episode in E major of heavenly loveliness, pointing ten years ahead to the major trio of the minuet in the great G minor Symphony, and indeed to Schubert's favourite device for bringing the hearer to the edge of tears, too easily at times, but irresistibly.

Three years later, in 1781, came another set of violin sonatas, five in number, but apparently intended for a half-dozen, for there is an *allegro* of a B flat major Sonata (K. 372) which for some reason remained detached. The second, F major (K. 377), and the fourth, G major-minor (K. 379), have sets of variations as second movements, and the latter is particularly interesting by reason of its large slow introduction in G major, followed by a passionate G minor *allegro.* The former makes use, at the start and elsewhere, of effective repeated triplets for the violin:

The third Sonata of this set, in B flat major (K. 378), has a first movement of concerto-like brilliance. It opens in the old accompanying style, the violin suddenly emerging into prominence with delightful unobtrusiveness, and there is a second subject that must be counted among Mozart's prettiest inventions:

It is introduced by the piano alone and then continued by both instruments in a whole long chain of charming ideas, perfectly strung together in a sort of happy inevitability of sequence. The final *Rondeau* has a showy episode in a different tempo in the manner of the violin concertos. The E flat major Sonata (K. 380) is another piece designed for display, but display of the true Mozartian quality, enhancing the musical value, not smothering it under meaningless ornaments. There is a fine, spacious slow movement in G minor and a well-developed rondo.

The next Sonata is the work in B flat major (K. 454) written for Regina Strinasacchi in 1784, on a scale similar to that of the preceding, and not unlike it in character. The famous soloist is given plenty of opportunities, but even here there is give and take between the players, so that if the work is a concerto, it is a *concerto da camera.* If Mozart really did play the piano part from memory just as he wrote it out afterwards, there can have been no vestige of improvisation about the performance, for as usual everything is inevitable, everything comes at the right moment and stands in the right position. If anything, the working-out is perhaps unduly free of thematic allusions; but then it often is, even in mature works of Mozart's, showing clearly that his sonata movements have their root in the old *da capo* aria of Alessandro Scarlatti and Handel, to mention only two exponents who are well known, one by reputation and the other from practice. Even where the development is intended to be elaborately thematic, as here it is not, Mozart often slyly begins his workings-out as though he were going to wander casually away from the matter in hand, only to spring the sudden surprise of an extraordinarily rich and subtle allusiveness. The *andante* is a long and exquisite dialogue between the two instruments, with stabbing accents of passion here and there. One cannot resist the thought that if the composer and his young Italian performer did not fall in love with each other while they played this movement, it can only have been that they both possessed the imagination which is the perfect artist's substitute for experience. Only the second-rate, both among creators and interpreters, feel that they must have personally touched everything before they attain to the insight they need.

The E flat major Sonata (K. 481) of the following year is a somewhat less important work. At any rate the final variations come near insignificance. Although it could not be played without the violin part, the old habit of the accompanying manner makes itself felt in the first and last movements. The *adagio,* however, is a grand piece of work, full of suppressed temperamental expressions and twice boldly taking the roundabout way of enharmonic modulation, an effect which, like that of the diminished seventh, had not become stale by abuse and certainly was not overworked by Mozart himself.

Grand all through is the Sonata in A major (K. 526) of 1787—just before *Don Giovanni.* The first movement is, rather exceptionally, in 6–8 time. It receives a very close development, with a scrupulously thematic working-out section this time. The violin part is most artfully interlaced with the right-hand piano part and the cadential ends of phrases are extended by harmonic circumlocutions which somehow retain their quality of surprise however often one has heard the music. But expansion here is wonderfully made amends for by concentration elsewhere. In the slow movement a similar balance by compensation is effected, but this time by harmonic means. Mozart goes out of his way to keep his texture bare almost to the point of bleakness here and there:

only to apply heavily chromatic touches elsewhere, with the result that they are never in the least cloying:

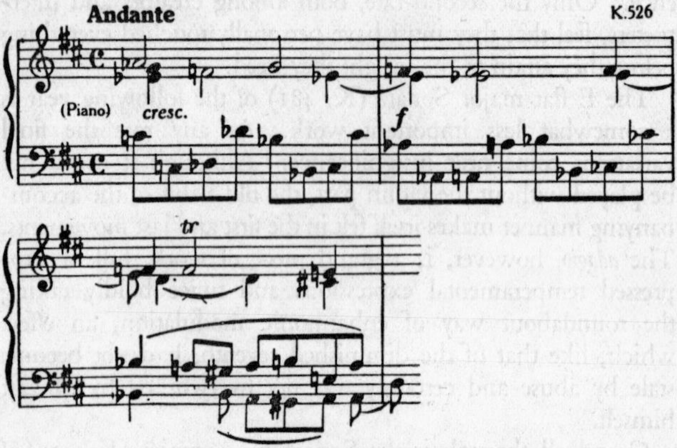

Apart from that, this is one of the most original slow movements he ever wrote. The final *presto* is akin in character to that of the greater of the two piano Concertos in the same key (K. 488), and scarcely less difficult for the keyboard player, the violin part requiring some very neat fitting in. The movement is one of those, not infrequent in Mozart, in which animation makes an impression of stress, not of gaiety. The whole is perfectly organized, spun out at great length without letting the interest drop for an instant, and an extraordinary richness is gained by a minimum of harmonic filling-in. The movement goes by so fast that, as in Domenico Scarlatti's sonatas, the witty dryness of which it somewhat resembles, a greater number of notes would inevitably mean an effect of redundancy.

The F major Sonata (K. 547) is only a curious kind of appendix. Like the little piano Sonata in C major (K. 545), it is supposed to be an easy piece for beginners, though any hopeful pianist or fiddler might be only too glad to begin like this. It is so oddly arranged that one wonders whether the *allegro* in the middle ought not to have come before the *andante cantabile* at the beginning, or indeed whether the whole work is not merely jumbled together at random. At any rate it is suspicious that the *allegro* exists also in an arrangement for piano alone, with the little rondo of K. 545, transposed into F major, as a finale, and that the final variations, with a modestly accompanying violin part, got into Köchel's catalogue as a piano solo with the very early number 54.

Two separate sets of Variations for violin and piano (K. 359, 360) are agreeably entertaining. Of much greater interest is the fragment of a Sonata in A major-minor (K. 402), which even as finished by Maximilian Stadler still remains a torso, for it was not like Mozart to write a prelude in A major for a fugue in A minor and leave it at that. The introduction is a very powerful piece of work, the fugue rather dry and crabbed. It dates from the time (1782) when Constanze urged fugal writing upon Mozart, and it is not the only work of the kind written in the year of their marriage which shows a certain lack of interest.[1] To judge from this that he was not a contrapuntist would be the height of absurdity. At the most it might be said that he was a contrapuntist by nature rather than by taste. To write a fugue for fugue's sake meant nothing to him, but when one was required of him—in a mass, let us say—he could produce it with Bach's own facility and triumphant skill. More than that, he could turn out the most elaborate fugal fabrics where they were not particularly required, as in the G major string Quartet (K. 387), in the 'Jupiter' Symphony, in *The Magic Flute,* and so on. But it is curious that Constanze could not induce him to give himself at least the

[1] Can it be doubted that the unfinished *Overture* in the style of Handel (K. 399) was intended to finish with a fugue?

pleasure of pleasing her by writing fugues unapplied to any other purpose. However, he may have been too busy with other things in 1782. He certainly left two other violin Sonatas, both in C major (K. 403–4), incomplete as well as one for piano in B flat major (K. 400).

Unlike Beethoven's, Mozart's sonatas for piano alone are on the whole less valuable than those for violin and piano. Altogether they occupy nothing like the place in his complete output that his successor's do in his own. This is not surprising. For one thing, Beethoven had a much more finished, much more enticing and exciting instrument at his disposal than Mozart ever knew, although the actual supersession of the harpsichord took place during the earlier master's career, and for another Beethoven realized, as it was too early for Mozart to do completely, that the writing of pianoforte music is bound up chiefly with dynamic problems. Everything you play on that instrument is a series of explosions, greatly varying in force (and, one might perhaps say, in destructiveness), but all alike subject to the fundamental law that governs its tone-production, which is an initial accent followed automatically by an immediate decrease. Mozart was anything but an explosive artist, while Beethoven was nothing else quite so much. Hence Mozart's relative ineffectiveness on the keyboard instrument; hence also the fact that when he writes for it in combination with other instruments, the great fascination is its interplay with them in detail after detail of extraordinary felicity. In his music for pianoforte alone such interplay is either absent or suggested by subterfuge, and you miss to a great extent that subtle influence of the great contrapuntist's art of easy combination that is Mozart's even in his most rigidly harmonic passages. It must also be borne in mind that he wrote almost all his piano sonatas early in his career.

A study of the gradual development of Mozart's keyboard style would be a fascinating adventure for any writer on music, and it is the more vexing to find no room for it here because nothing of the kind has been attempted to any appreciable extent in English musical literature; but it must be enough for the moment to refer those who read either French or German to other works.[1]

Mozart's childhood pieces begin timidly with the habit fostered by the *continuo*: they are essentially tunes accompanied by a single bass line, with harmonic fillings-in at first almost forgotten and then gradually becoming more enterprising. The Variations in G major (K. 24), written at the age of ten, for instance, are mostly in two parts and never in more than three, with a left-hand part uniformly in single notes, and those on *Wilhelmus van Nassouwe* (K. 25) show very little more daring: it is mainly the originality of the Dutch folk-song that makes the little composer look comparatively original himself. The treatment grows much bolder in the Variations on minuets by Fischer and Salieri (K. 179–80), composed at the age of seventeen, for all that here the tunes themselves are very conventional.

In 1774–5 came the first six piano Sonatas of any importance. The very first, in C major (K. 279), shows new departures mixed with that old stand-by, the Alberti bass:

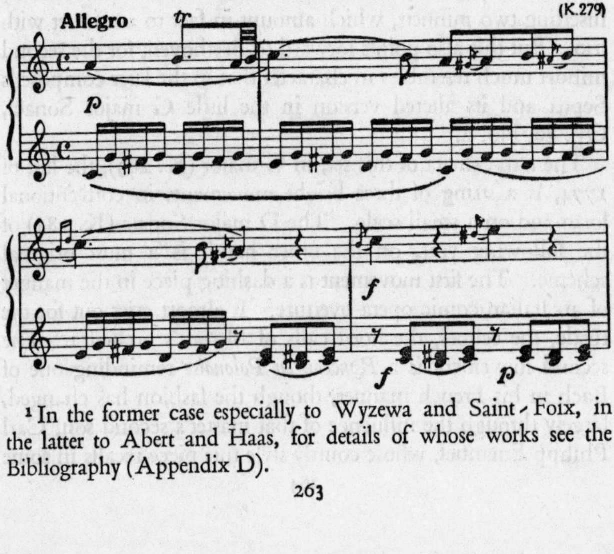

[1] In the former case especially to Wyzewa and Saint-Foix, in the latter to Abert and Haas, for details of whose works see the Bibliography (Appendix D).

The short appoggiaturas are such a feature in this work that one suspects the fascination of a new discovery. The second, in F major (K. 280), has a beautiful slow movement in the tonic minor with a well-judged scheme of modulations and harmonic inflections. The third, in B flat major (K. 281), shines by a highly original first movement in a very moderate tempo but with quick figuration, and it seems clear that it was this which gave Mozart the idea of beginning the next Sonata, in E flat major (K. 282), not merely with a slow introduction, but with an *adagio* first movement in well-developed sonata form rounded off by a coda expressly so named by the composer. A second slow movement being out of the question, Mozart reverts to the old suite form by inserting two minuets, which amount in fact to a minuet with trio. But this also points forward to Beethoven, for the second minuet much resembles in character that in the later composer's Septet and its altered version in the little G major Sonata, Op. 49, No. 2.

The fifth Sonata of this set, in G major (K. 283), the last of 1774, is a string of three bright movements in conventional form and on a small scale. The D major Sonata (K. 284) of the following year, on the other hand, is a most original scheme. The first movement is a dashing piece in the manner of an Italian comic opera overture. It almost cries out for the rustle, the echoes, the horn calls of Mozart's orchestra. The second movement is a *Rondeau en Polonaise* reminding one of Bach in his French manner, though the fashion has changed, largely through the influence of that master's second son, Carl Philipp Emanuel, whose courtly style this piece recalls in some ways. A set of variations concludes the Sonata. The *andante* theme is quite unlike any other tune of Mozart's and so immediately memorable as to lend itself most admirably to its purpose, since there is no point in varying anything the hearer cannot retain in his mind. There are two apparently equal sections, but the second is extended by a lengthened cadence followed by a pause, features which later call for insertions of various witty comments.

The strangeness of this theme is not often matched elsewhere in Mozart, and phrases of unusual lengths are rare in his music, compared, for example, with Haydn's, which abounds in irregular metres. With Mozart phrases of four or eight bars are the rule. Altogether he cannot, in fact, be called one of the world's most distinctive melodists, for the plain truth is that he is often, even in his greatest works, content to use tunes that are part of the common stock of the composers of his time, sometimes very unimportant composers indeed.[1] His greatness lies elsewhere: in his infallible taste for saying exactly the right thing at the right time and at the right length, for making the most sensitive choice even among commonplaces, and above all in his miraculous power to convert perfectly ordinary material into new inventions by an insuperable certainty of treatment. He was incapable of the slightest offence against good taste, not even that of being too priggishly tasteful.[2] His music will be searched in vain for any evidence of a trespass against good musical manners, even where it happens to be most superficial, as, of course, it could be when his heart was not engaged as well as his discernment, and it is this absolute

[1] Dr. Robert Haas has done magnificent work in the way of comparative studies showing the derivation of supposedly Mozartian phrases from minor composers, though it must be said that he sometimes goes to fantastic lengths in attributing significance to mere coincidences.

[2] That, however, was not a typical vice of his time; it was introduced into music more recently, especially by the modern French school.

certainty of judgment which makes him, I repeat, the greatest artist among creative musicians. Others have been much more individual in their inventions, including minor masters like Borodin or Grieg or Chabrier and composers of far less assured taste like Tchaikovsky or Puccini, who have written far more personal and more immediately striking music and found compensation for their lack of the most judicious artistry in a much more easily gained and general popularity.

The C major Sonata (K. 309), written at Mannheim in 1777, is the one with the portrait of Rosa Cannabich for a slow movement. Elsewhere it lays stress on keyboard problems and is not especially distinguished as music. Neither is the D major Sonata (K. 311) of the following year; but the work immediately preceding it, A minor (K. 310), has the arresting quality we have already noticed in the first work in a minor key in other categories of Mozart's catalogue. The opening movement has a concerto-like carriage and a curiously breathless, dramatic precipitancy. Abrupt modulations and (in the working-out) suspensions with bold clashes of semitones assail the ear, and the very opening phrase has an audacious discord in the accompanying harmony:

The spaciously developed slow movement makes a lyrical point of repose without dispelling the dramatic note altogether. It is lavishly marked with directions for sudden dynamic changes which scholars like to attribute to the direct influence of the Mannheim school, whose activities were, however, as good as over by 1778 and had in any case already infected composers even farther off than those of the Austrian school long before. The *presto* finale has a Scarlattian speed and transparency of texture, but a genuinely Mozartian passion, enhanced rather than relieved by a brief major episode.

We have now reached the Paris period, to which belong five sets of Variations on themes whose provenance is not difficult to guess: 'Lison dormait' (K. 264), 'Ah, vous dirai-je, maman' (K. 265), a March from Grétry's *Les Mariages Samnites* (K. 352), 'La Belle Françoise' (K. 353), and 'Je suis Lindor' from Beaumarchais's *Le Barbier de Séville* (K. 354). The best theme is Grétry's, and Mozart's lavish treatment of it shows that he was aware of the fact; but the most engaging variations are those on the childish tune of 'Ah, vous dirai-je,' which is stated with a kind of deceptive ingenuousness that keeps up its pretence of simplicity throughout the set, while in reality some very cunning things are done on the sly. The variation in the minor is written in the most delicate string quartet manner.

Four more piano Sonatas belong to 1778. C major (K. 330), though not otherwise very striking, shines by a slow movement with grave and beautiful minor sections. The next work, in A major (K. 331), is well known as perhaps the most curious of all in the way in which it departs from the normal sonata procedure, though we have seen that it is not unique in this respect. It begins with variations on that lovely theme in Mozart's happiest A major vein. The keyboard writing in some of the variations, especially the second and fourth, is so ingenious as to anticipate later pianistic specialists, particularly Dussek, of whose luminous and at the same time saturated tone-quality one cannot help thinking here. The minor variation, with its rapping octaves, is strangely interesting. The last, which according to Mozart's usual procedure, brings with it a fast *tempo* in a different metre after an extended variation in slow time, already hints at the Turkish rondo that forms the amusing finale and itself points forward to a larger essay in exotic music stylized to be made acceptable to a polite western public: the Turkish music in *Die Entführung*. The most arresting movement, however, is the minuet in the middle, which in spite of its conventional form is like nothing else in Mozart's work, at any rate at this period. It has a frail, wistful quality that makes it as haunting a piece of romantic piano music as anything one can think of in Schumann or Chopin.

Another fine work is the F major Sonata (K. 332) that follows, though it is more traditional and its expression more normal. The first movement has the same kind of dramatic tension, kept in order by perfect formal polish, that distinguishes the trio, 'Susanna, or via sortite!' in the second act of *Figaro*. Its time and rhythmic pulse are the same, too. I cannot forbear quoting a lengthy passage and, once more, writing out a rhythmic refinement as a modern composer would have shown it, though Mozart, of course, keeps to his 3–4 signature throughout:

Could anything be more moving than that sudden clearing into F major after the sullen harmonic and rhythmic turbulence preceding it? The slow movement makes a point—an almost Schubertian point—of a sudden transition from minor to major. The vivacious finale has the sound of a rondo, but is a sonata movement with an abnormally long working-out of two and a half pages or so and a coda surprisingly approached by an interrupted cadence. The fourth Sonata (K. 333) of the 1778 group just discussed has fewer arresting features, but contains a cluster of subversive modernities, harmonic and rhythmic at once, in the slow movement that must have seemed to poor Leopold Mozart quite as alarming a spurning of authority on his son's part as any plan for a runaway marriage. How a composer of to-day would draw attention to its audacities I dare not contemplate and therefore set it down as Mozart wrote it:

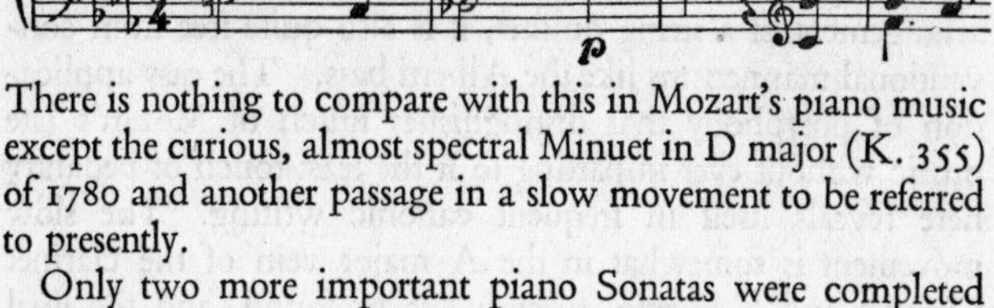

There is nothing to compare with this in Mozart's piano music except the curious, almost spectral Minuet in D major (K. 355) of 1780 and another passage in a slow movement to be referred to presently.

Only two more important piano Sonatas were completed by Mozart after his twenty-second year, for the little easy Sonata in C major (K. 545), turned out for teaching purposes, is not of much account, though charming, nor is the B flat major Sonata (K. 570) for which an accompanying violin part from an unknown hand exists. These two works, however, together with an unfinished one to be mentioned in a moment, throw out more than a hint as to what Mozart might have come to make of the piano sonata, not only had he lived longer, but had he cultivated it more assiduously in his later years.

The C minor Sonata (K. 457) of 1784 is a great piece of work in a sombre vein beginning with an octave unison theme very much like that of Beethoven's first published piano Sonata, but much more portentous. The development of the whole first movement is on a large scale, with a working-out keeping closely to the thematic material, a coda of Beethovenian breadth, and contrapuntal devices applied here and there to enhance the dramatic drive of the music. The big slow movement is essentially a set of variations, with richly developed incidents between the appearances of the theme that make it into a kind of serious rondo. However, the finale is also a rondo, although one that only deepens the tragic tone of the whole work. Its syncopated theme has an unhappy agitation about it, a fleeting episode in a major key reinforces the gloom, declamatory pauses give an impression of some inarticulate dread, and there is a cutting finality about the closing page that freezes the hearer.

The D major Sonata (K. 576) of 1789 is a less expressive work, but a magnificent piece of writing. If it is not particularly pianistic in lay-out, but looks rather like a keyboard arrangement of a string quintet, it is also quite free from conventional mannerisms like the Alberti bass. The easy application of polyphony that distinguishes much of Mozart's late music without ever imparting to it the least touch of pedantry here reveals itself in frequent canonic writing. The slow movement is somewhat in the A major vein of the clarinet Quintet and Concerto, though less profound, and the final *allegretto,* a difficult piece to play well, again shows a preoccupation with contrapuntal writing.

Even more so does the first movement of the splendid Sonata in F major (K. 533), a very remarkable piece of work where technical ingenuity never fails to result in beauty, of a somewhat austere sort, it is true, yet beauty always limpid even when it is attained by means of a scientific trick. The end of the movement is astonishing: there is no coda, but an extension of the recapitulation in which Mozart quite unexpectedly combines with the first subject, in the most natural way in the world, a supplementary theme that had appeared alone at the end of the exposition. The slow movement is curiously compounded of a strange beauty and a severity that becomes positively rigorous soon after the double bar, where an extraordinary passage of sequences rising by sixths, thirds and even sevenths makes one realize with a gasp that the most well-bred of composers sticks at nothing to obtain a special effect he happens to want. The Rondo (K. 494), an earlier work to which Mozart had added the first two movements (K. 533), though agreeable and containing a lovely F minor episode, a remarkable stretto later on and a mysterious ending low down on the keyboard, is not quite on the same level.

A considerable number of miscellaneous pianoforte pieces belong to the later years. Four Fantasies stand out from among them as especially noteworthy, the more so because they may probably be regarded as records of the kind of thing Mozart must have improvised to his audiences. The C major Fantasy (K. 394) is followed by one of those fugues written at the behest of Constanze in 1782. The D minor (K. 397) is the smallest, but contains some fine touches and a gracious D major *allegretto* at the end. The two C minor Fantasies (K. 396, 475) are the fullest of meaning. The earlier, originally written for piano and violin, makes a great feature of arpeggios and crossed hands and has a melting major cadence at the end of each section. The later is the work Mozart published with the C minor Sonata (K. 457), with which indeed it goes very well. But it is in no way a mere prelude; it is a completely rounded-off composition, planned fancifully yet logically, full of apprehensive heartbeats and melodic apparitions of a ghostly beauty.

Of two Rondos, D major (K. 485) and A minor (K. 511), the second is of outstanding importance, in fact one of the most characteristic of the piano works, blending technical skill and poetry into an impression of dreamlike strangeness.

A few sets of Variations still remain to be mentioned. Those on Paisiello's 'Salve tu, Domine' (K. 398) and on an *Allegretto* in B flat major (K. 500) do not amount to much, while those on 'Come un agnello' from Sarti's *Fra due litiganti* (K. 460) are of interest only because this is one of the three popular tunes Mozart used later for the dinner music in *Don Giovanni.* Those on 'Ein Weib ist das herrlichste Ding' (K. 613) are rather more important, and interesting because the tune is a song by Mozart's first Tamino, the tenor and flute player Benedict Schack.

But the best of the later sets of Variations is that on the song 'Unser dummer Pöbel meint' (K. 455) from Gluck's comic opera, *La Rencontre imprévue,* and evidently taken from its German version known as *Die Pilgrimme von Mecca.* Mozart began by adapting the tune to his purpose and, whatever one may say to such an arbitrary procedure, unquestionably improving it. Then he let his fancy roam at will, holding it close to the model, but playing with his material with a sort of kittenish elegance. A variation in the minor is like a little trio for two clarinets and bassoon and the next variation like a string quartet, with the instruments by turns, top or bottom, playing shakes while the others carry on the modifications of the theme with delicious chromatic inflections:

The *Overture* in the style of Handel (K. 399), i.e. a French overture in several movements approximating to the suite form, is only a curiosity. It is neither good Handel nor good Mozart, and in any case it remained unfinished. Two isolated pieces, on the other hand, are exceptionally striking: an *Adagio* in B minor (K. 540), dating from 1788, which is in that pathetic, valedictory manner that makes much of the music of Mozart's last two or three years seem to sound death-haunted, and the little *Gigue* in G major (K. 574), written in Berlin in 1789 under the influence, Abert thinks, of the impressions received from Bach's music at Leipzig. The treatment is freely fugal and the feeling of the short piece not unlike that of the minuet in the G minor Symphony. The convention of turning the jig tune upside down at the beginning of the second part is retained as an extra inducement to a display of cleverness, which, as usual in Mozart, results in pure music of the most natural beauty.

A word must be said about the original compositions for piano duet, which make ideal home music—indeed a kind of keyboard chamber music. There are six Sonatas, four of which are usually found in the published collections. Of these the works in B flat major (K. 358) and D major (K. 381) are pleasant, entertaining music without any particular depth. The late Sonata in C major (K. 521) is a more mature work of the same kind, with a pouncingly brilliant first movement, a finely elaborated *andante* and one of those friendly *allegretto* finales that seem so characteristic of classical music but are in fact rare in it. That in spite of their mildness they should be effective in Mozart's work when they do occur is surely due to their infrequency.

The F major Sonata (K. 497) removes us to another world —the world of the great chamber music, especially of the string quintets. Indeed an arrangement of some sort for a combination of instruments would make a magnificent concert work of this almost uncomfortably great piece of domestic music, though the writing is at times splendidly suited to the keyboard.

It is a tempting idea to transfer the Sonata to the medium for which Schubert wrote his Octet. A performance of it with that work would make an evening's programme enough to draw one anywhere on the wettest of nights. Sir Donald Tovey, to whom we are indebted for a masterly note on this Sonata in the first volume of his *Essays in Musical Analysis*, suggests a string quintet with two cellos.

There is also a set of four-hand Variations (K. 501) on an *andante* theme of the most enchanting shape and expression: light and luminous music of perfect behaviour. Nor must one forget the two arrangements—one possibly the composer's own, the other, or both, by Johann Mederitsch—of his two great pieces in F minor (K. 594, 608) written for that mechanical organ that bored him so much and for which he wrote what are masterpieces in that amazing late style of his which allows him to use hair-raising contrapuntal feats with apparent unconcern to make music of extraordinary emotional significance.

The short and very intricate Fugue in G minor (K. 401) is again one of the polyphonic works Constanze urged him to write after she had been smitten by Bach and Handel at van Swieten's. But he seems hardly to have had his heart in it: like the C minor Fugue for two pianos (K. 426) it is very ingenious, but rather dry. Not so the Sonata in D major for two pianos (K. 448), an elegant and endearing work, beautifully devised for its special medium. Once again one notices that emotional detachment in Mozart when it came to matters of life and even of love: he wrote better music for the ugly and exasperating Miss Aurnhammer than for his dear Constanze.

CHAPTER XX

THE OPERAS

Now that this book is drawing to an end, a subject presents itself which for its adequate treatment demands a whole volume. Fortunately there is one[1] to which English readers who desire a more detailed study of Mozart's works for the stage may be directed with the utmost confidence, indeed with enthusiasm.

It is tempting to deal with the early works, dead though they are to the modern theatre, and to examine those which the composer for one reason or another left unfinished; but as space will hardly be found for a sufficient review of the five works which still hold the stage and will hold it as long as opera continues to live as a form of art, and scarcely enough for the briefer treatment of the four or five which are not too unlikely to be revived as curiosities, there is nothing for it but to pass over those which are merely history to-day as cursorily as possible.

The music for the German sacred play, *Die Schuldigkeit des ersten Gebotes* (K. 35) and for the Latin comedy, *Apollo et Hyacinthus* (K. 38) is still quite baroque in style, with *sinfonie* for overtures and arias tending to adhere to the *da capo* form of Alessandro Scarlatti, which the boy Mozart was more likely to know from Hasse, from Jommelli or from Piccinni, if not merely from the Salzburg master Eberlin, who cultivated it at a time when it had already begun to grow old-fashioned. The treatment of the earlier work, perhaps because of its religious subject, is more akin to that of the Passion music by composers a generation before Mozart than to any operatic precedent: it

[1] By Professor Edward J. Dent (see Bibliography, Appendix D).

is descriptive rather than dramatic.[1] The Latin comedy is both stiffer and duller than the German play, but then there is no reason to suppose that Latin was less of a burden to Mozart than to any other boy of eleven.

The small German operetta of *Bastien und Bastienne* (K. 50), written at the age of twelve, is a very different thing. Unlike its two predecessors, it is astonishingly alive. Clearly it was a toy he loved to play with, not a lesson. The music is on a minute scale throughout: the solo pieces are small songs, not arias; but the pastoral and gently ironical character of the play borrowed from Jean-Jacques Rousseau amd Madame Favart is hit off to a nicety, and there is even some attempt at characterizing the three personages who enact the innocent intrigue, very successful in the case of the pretended magician. The whole piece is delightfully childlike, but never childish. It is charming to sing and play, pretty to watch, and one is never inclined to make allowances for the composer's youth, only to take pleasure in it and be glad on the whole that he wrote *Bastien und Bastienne* just when he did, and not years later.

La finta semplice (K. 51) of the same year is less successful because the task was a much more ambitious one, and less characteristic because for Mozart at that time such a libretto could only mean a setting to conventional Italian and Italianate patterns. It is surprisingly well done for a child who was attempting a new style, but his early *opera buffa* manner is much more brilliantly and variedly exhibited in *La finta giardiniera,* composed six years later.

In between came the works for the Milan and Salzburg stage, beginning in 1770 with the *opera seria* of *Mitridate* (K. 87), yet another essay in a new species. This again, as well as the more mature and independent *Lucio Silla* (K. 135) of 1772, is naturally imitative of earlier models, according to Haas especially of Traetta, Piccinni and Gluck. The later

[1] The second and third parts of the work, by Michael Haydn and Adlgasser, are lost.

work is said by Fausto Torrefranca, less convincingly, to be indebted mainly to Rauzzini, of all people. These works, like the two dramatic *serenate* or festival plays, *Ascanio in Alba* (K. 111) and *Il sogno di Scipione* (K. 126), as well as a similar though rather more pastoral piece of 1775, *Il Rè pastore* (K. 208), the exquisite aria with a solo violin from which, 'L'amerò, sarò costante,' is still favoured by sopranos—all this is, so far as the modern world is concerned, so much sketching for the first *opera seria* of enduring importance, *Idomeneo,* sketching done by a young composer whose extraordinary adaptability would have been a danger to any musician with a less assertive individuality of genius. As it was, this readiness of absorption and pliability merely helped him to accustom himself immediately to new conditions, though it also precluded him from doing so at once with any personal independence.

It was this sketching habit, too, which perhaps led him to abandon the German opera of *Zaide* (K. 344), in which yet another new style, that of the *Singspiel,* was essayed, sometimes with quite novel results. A drinking song with chorus, 'Brüder, lasst uns lustig sein,' for instance, is like nothing that could possibly occur in any of Mozart's Italian operas: it might easily have become popular as one of those Teutonic students' songs which got themselves perpetuated, artistically as distinct from bibulously, in Brahms's *Academic Festival Overture.* But if *Zaide* was left incomplete, it did help Mozart to crystallize a new idiom for his next *Singspiel,* which is also his first opera of unqualified greatness, *Die Entführung.*

After what has been said about the early operas in an admittedly much too casual way, it may now be deemed sufficient for the present purpose if the three works which summarize the efforts of Mozart's apprenticeship in as many different species of opera are a little more fully discussed. These three species are, then, the *opera buffa,* the *opera seria* and the *Singspiel.*

The representative early work of the first kind is *La finta giardiniera* (K. 196), a long piece in three acts dealing with the comic-opera absurdities accepted at the time, incredible imbroglios of a set of characters in which it is quite impossible to take the slightest human interest. Or rather it would be impossible had not the youthful composer succeeded in making those who enact them, if not into real personalities, at least into very appealing puppets. For in some inexplicable way, though he does not replace sawdust by flesh and blood, he is often able to drop the guiding wires and galvanize these figures for a moment into a semblance of a life of their own. The Podestà, an amorous old fop, is well delineated in an aria in which he declares that he will not consent to his niece's marriage. Violante, the heroine, finds some accents that touch the hearer's heart on her behalf. Arminda, a spitfire who might almost be an ancestress of Donna Elvira, has a fine dramatic G minor 'revenge aria.' Ramiro, one of the lovers, is given songs of a charming youthful tenderness. Belfiore, the hero, is somewhat colourless, but has a song in which he enumerates the historical personages from whom he claims descent that is a little masterpiece of comic writing. A more purely musical delight is the Podestà's aria, the words of which refer to the sounds of various instruments, with suitable accompaniments in the orchestra. This was a common diversion in comic opera,[1] but Mozart's treatment shows considerable originality. Another musical sally of this kind occurs in the aria in which Violante's servant, Nardo, woos the chambermaid Serpetta in four different languages and the score reflects national characteristics as the young composer understood them.

Not only character, situation too is well handled up to a point, for a lad of eighteen extremely well. He was to some extent hampered by a libretto which, apart from being unbelievably muddled and extravagant, provided for next to nothing but an incessant string of vocal solo pieces, except for brief opening and closing numbers for the seven characters in the nature of choruses and two fairly extended finales. It was in these that the dramatist in Mozart began to assert himself

[1] It still survived in Bishop's *Clari,* the piece which has 'Home, sweet home' for a *Leitmotiv.*

decisively. Where situations at last take the place of static, reflective musical points of repose, which is all the arias are as a rule, he seizes every opportunity quickly and sometimes shows a surprising amount of ready wit.

The music of *La finta giardiniera* as such very naturally adheres to conventional Italian formulas for the most part and, with its too frequent repetitions of even quavers in the basses and inner parts, it lacks interest of texture. Still, a musical inventiveness that makes many of the songs unforgettably haunting plainly shows the growing master.

With *Idomeneo* (K. 366) mastery may well be said to have been reached. It is the great *opera seria* of a composer not peculiarly fitted for that species. Compared with Gluck and taken as seriously as its style would appear to demand, it seems almost frivolous; but then the comparison is too odiously impertinent, for although Mozart took certain hints from Gluck—for the oracle scene, for instance—there is simply no question of his attempting anything in the nature of the self-conscious reformer's work, here or anywhere else. *Idomeneo* was never meant to be anything but an *opera seria* of the common run, more in the manner of Piccinni, really, than in that of Gluck, and so far as its appeal to the audience went that type of work actually was frivolous. It was an entertainment of a special kind, not a sermon, a morality play or an example of dramatic reform. A libretto, more or less poetical and nobly magniloquent, was supplied, by Metastasio if the composer was lucky, and the musician was expected to pour into it the finest work he was capable of producing. The characters were not too minutely drawn and any situations would do as long as they tied themselves now and again into concerted numbers.

Fine work Mozart certainly did put into *Idomeneo,* and in spite of the influence of Piccinni and of certain conventions (mainly choral) of French grand opera, he was becoming an independent musical personality. His treatment of accompanied recitative shows a very sensitive readiness to apply expressive touches. Ilia's recitative at the first rise of the curtain is already full of them, and the approach to her lovely G minor lament (a worthy counterpart to those of Constanze in *The Elopement* and of Pamina in *The Magic Flute*) is one of those great moments in music which never lose their wondrous surprise. What you expect is something like this:

And then, after this clean cut, the aria. But no: what happens is this:

Andante con moto K.366

Another imperishable thrill of this sort is an interrupted cadence in Electra's recitative in the second act:

a very simple thing, really, *mais qu'il fallait trouver.* The aria that follows distinguishes itself by merging straight into a march: Mozart had the courage to deprive the singer of applause in the interests of his own musico-dramatic intentions. In the eighteenth century that was heroism. Poor Electra—a tragic character altogether—suffers the same fate in the first act, where a chorus is joined on to her agitated aria in D minor, expressive of jealousy. Note how in the end she loses her head: the music suddenly produces an effect of going from common into triple time:

But Mozart does not lose his. It is enough for him that the ear should receive this impression of rhythmic distortion and he does not advertise such occasional expansions of the musical means at the disposal of eighteenth-century composers by any freaks of notation.

He is not always so original in *Idomeneo,* nor is all the music alive. The marches are simply in the manner of those in his cassations, and I have already said that some of the arias are excessively stilted and ornamented. The characters are not quite consistent, either. The suave aria, 'Idol mio,' does not suit Electra any too well, and the sweetly artificial 'Zeffiretti lusinghieri' would seem to be for Dorabella in *Così fan tutte* rather than for Ilia, the Trojan princess. But at its best this is a great and noble score, in which nothing is finer, perhaps, than the superb dramatic quartet in the third act, a number which, with its magnificent fling and incisive harmonic beauty, not to mention its astonishing close, with a single voice trailing away without a conclusive cadence, could never fail to thrill an audience.

In *Die Entführung aus dem Serail* (K. 384) Mozart was at last wholly in his element, not because of any especial liking for the German *Singspiel* or even because he was himself planning an elopement of sorts, but chiefly because by 1782 he was a fully matured master of his craft and had learnt a good deal about life. Not that his engagement to Constanze was entirely without influence,[1] we may be sure. Weber was not far wrong when he suggested that, although Mozart produced greater works later on, he could never recapture that blithe bridal tone that pervades this ever youthful and endearing work. It is impossible for anyone with the least musical sensibility to imagine a happier evening at a theatre than one spent at a good performance of *The Elopement*.

The subject was not by any means new. Stories of ladies carried off to Oriental harems and rescued by their lovers were a favourite subject for plays and operas, including Mozart's own *Zaide*,[2] and Gluck's French comic opera of 1764, *La*

[1] The fact that the heroine bears the name of Mozart's betrothed is, however, without the least significance, for Bretzner's play on which Stephanie based his libretto was already called *Belmont und Constanze*.

[2] Monsigny and Grétry had both produced kindred operas, and that Blonde in Mozart's work calls herself an Englishwoman for no apparent reason is remarkable in view of the fact that there was a

Rencontre imprévue (not unforeseen by us, for we have already encountered it in connection with Mozart in the previous chapter) has a somewhat similar plot. That Mozart was familiar with it we know; but what is worth pointing out is that he was not above taking hints from it. In Rézia's air, 'Ah! qu'il est doux de se revoir,' for instance, Gluck has the following phrase:

and Mozart's hero sings this in his second aria of the first act:[1]

---

play on this subject by Isaac Bickerstaffe entitled *The Sultan, or A Peep into the Harem.* Rossini's *L'Italiana in Algeri* is a later example of the same type of plot.

[1] I shall hereafter give scarcely any musical extracts from the well-known and easily accessible operas, for having once started quoting, I should be too strongly tempted never to stop.

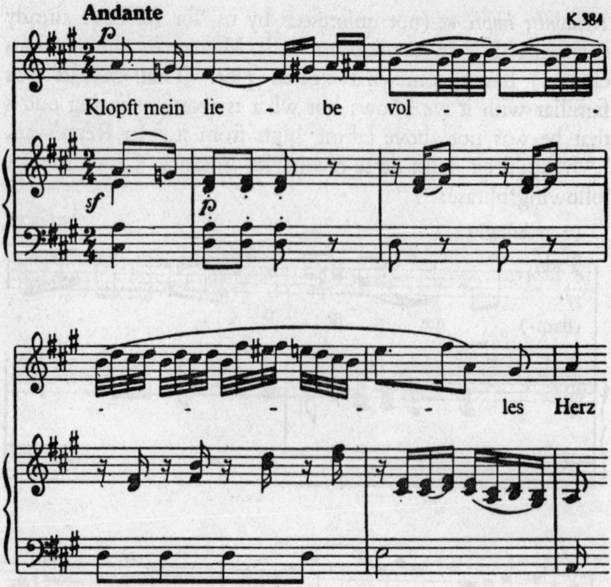

The greater distinction of Mozart is at once evident; but it is true that Gluck's French opera shows many other features resembling the younger master's very curiously. The whole of this air of Rézia might have been bodily transferred to Belmonte, whose phraseology it often anticipates.

The aria I have just quoted from is one of the things about which Mozart wrote to his father with such ingenuous pride in his happy inspiration and in those touches of idealized realism—the beating heart, the trembling and sighing—which he knew would give pleasure to the world but would not condescend to make meretricious. He also enjoyed donning again that amusing Turkish fashion he had already worn in the A major piano Sonata (K. 331) and for which he found plenty of opportunity in the overture, the janissaries' choruses and especially the music for that magnificent figure of fun, the amorous, jealous, cunning and yet gullible Osmin, a character that is to opera what Shakespeare's Falstaff—the greater Falstaff of the historical plays (and incidentally of Elgar's symphonic masterpiece)—is to drama. It is Osmin especially who gives that peculiar and unrepeatable flavour of Viennese *turquerie* to this most delectable of operettas—for that is what *The Elopement* really is, with its spoken dialogue, its lack of a finale to the first act and its conclusion with a mere *vaudeville*. Like Sullivan's pieces, which by the way almost match its musicianly refinements at times, we can call it an opera only by a courteous habit.

This is not to say that it is wanting in great music. Indeed one would not have a note different even where it falls a little short of greatness, for it never ceases to be as delicious as it is apt to its type and subject. Constanze's so-called 'torture aria,' with its brilliant ornamentation fitted to Cavalieri's 'glib gullet,' may possibly deserve that name; at any rate certain singers could easily make one think so. Her other two songs are heaven-sent things for virtuoso sopranos, one in the finest bravura style of the concert arias, the other that poignant plaint in G minor I have been unable to refrain from mentioning before.

Blonde's songs are as spritely as Belmonte's are tender. She is a second high soprano (top E) with a part almost as difficult as Constanze's. Pedrillo is a second tenor of the comic servant type, and his aria in which he boasts of his bravery while he trembles at the stirring of every leaf is an admirable piece of *buffo* art. The device of writing high parts for both pairs of lovers yields the most enchantingly airy vocal texture for the quartet in the second act, which is quite extended enough to make an adequate finale for so light a musical play. Adequate, did I say? It is a structure and a collection of tunes of such fascinating grace that one would like to call back every phrase of it to hug it over and over again. But it just flows on happily and will not wait to be loved. That is the worst of music—and the best: it will not be possessed. However, to such a score as that of *The Elopement* you can at least always go back for another spell of enticement, and you will never fail to find it fresh.

The two abandoned *opere buffe* of 1783, *L'oca del Cairo* (K. 422) and *Lo sposo deluso* (K. 430), well worth examining although left in a state of not much more than sketches, must of necessity be passed over. But three years after them comes a small masterpiece, forgotten only because of its topical, long-drawn and impossibly stupid libretto. It is *Der Schauspieldirektor* (K 486), usually called *The Impresario* in English, the occasional piece that came to interrupt *Figaro.* Curiously enough it is quite unlike that first perfect example of *opera buffa* of Mozart's, and he doubtless gave free rein to his musical cosmopolitanism here because in the festivity for which it was written members of both the German and the Italian opera took part, though only three of the former with some non-singing actors appeared in Mozart's own work.

The festively bustling C major overture, well known in the concert room, is a typical Italian movement, indeed stereotyped to a point that suggests deliberate, tongue-in-the-cheek parody; the two trial arias for the rival prima donnas resemble some of the more mature of Mozart's German songs, and both of them are touchingly beautiful; the trio which dramatically advances the action and at the same time achieves a perfect kind of free sonata form is in the ripest manner of his Italian concerted numbers, and on an exceptionally large scale; whereas for the finale he reverts to the French *vaudeville* after the manner of the concluding number in *The Elopement,* except that the action here allows for greater formal perfection: it is, in fact, a modified rondo (without any initial statement of the theme) with several engaging episodes suited to the characters who sing them and a principal tune acting as a refrain that sends the hearer home contentedly humming. The characters of the two ladies, one a Lydia Languish, the other a Petruchio's Kate, as well as their quarrels and the perplexities of the impresario, are outlined by a Mozart in full command of his dramatic mastery, while musically he is individual and fertile throughout. Parody is ever at arm's length, and during the singing tests well within the composer's grasp.

And then came *Le nozze di Figaro* (K. 492). The perfect *opera buffa,* I have just called it. True, of course; but it is much more than that. Beaumarchais's exposure of a refined but pernicious civilization is here made the pretext for music as sunnily civilized as the world ought to have become if the dreamers of Mozart's age had been right and the French Revolution had not merely replaced one kind of barbarity by another that has not even the merits of elegance and taste. These qualities *Figaro* has to a degree never again attained in music, and it has moreover a profound humanity, a sympathetic penetration into the hearts of men and women—especially women—prompted by the complete artist's understanding of both good and evil, by a kind of sublimated amorality and naïve philosophy based on feelings rather than on principles.

Music dictated by this frame of mind could hardly have been anything but flawless, and the score of *Figaro,* so far as the composer is concerned, really is without a blemish, apart from its pouring forth an incessant stream of the most bewitching and the most perfectly behaved, aristocratic music imaginable. Where there is a fault or so, it is imposed on the music from the outside. The fact that the first and third acts have no finales may pass, for one may regard the work as being conceived in two acts, divided into four scenes, and consider, moreover, that two more such towering structures and incredibly well managed musico-dramatic developments as the two existing finales would have been too much. The serious defect of that set of arias which brings the action of the fourth act to a standstill, and most of which may fortunately be cut without damage to the work, is due partly to the flagging invention of da Ponte and partly to the convention that allowed opera singers to indulge their exhibitionist instincts at some point or other in a comic opera.

Figaro is Italian comic opera in its final stage of perfection. It humanizes and glorifies the traditional figures of the *commedia dell' arte*[1] which are very clearly the ancestry of Beaumarchais's characters. Susanna is not only the daughter of Pergolesi's Serpina and the sister of all the *cameriere* of the Italian musical stage, she is the type of Columbine grown into a lovable individuality, and after having shown many traits of the operatic *servetta* in the course of the first three acts, she assumes a warm and noble womanliness in her aria, 'Deh vieni, non tardar,' in the garden scene, where she sounds quite a new note.

Cherubino points two ways. He is at once the adolescent Don Juan and the descendant of Leandro, who in the Italian improvised comedy is the disciple of Lelio and kindred more or less dissolute fine gentlemen, who gave Beaumarchais his model for the Count. At the same time Cherubino, being given a soprano part, is a late survivor of the male soprano, though by no means the last, for all through the nineteenth century and beyond (e.g. Octavian in Strauss's *Rose Cavalier*) this convention lingered on. Even the English pantomime boy must be counted among the progeny of Farinelli and Senesino and the rest, if the idea is not too fantastic in such a case, even from the artistic point of view.

Figaro himself is a survival of Harlequin, or more exactly a modern compound of Arlecchino and Brighella, two servant types with different traits. Bartolo, of course, is no other than the Bolognese doctor who took his idiosyncrasies from Cassandro or Pantalone; Basilio is partly Tartaglia and partly Brighella; Marcellina has the elements of Columbine which are lacking in Susanna; the Countess—the Rosina of *The Barber of Seville*—is the young lady of the Italian comedy, most commonly called Isabella, who is generally the niece or ward, or both, of Pantaloon.

Now all these figures of the *commedia dell' arte* were mere skeletons, as indeed were the plots of their plays, and the

[1] A detailed study of the descent of the characters in *Figaro* will be found in my extensive article on the subject in *The Musical Quarterly* (New York) of October 1927.

actors were expected to improvise on them as the inspiration of the moment dictated. Something of the same kind is done by Mozart with his music. It is true that Beaumarchais had already made these types into personalities, and that da Ponte had by no means spoiled them. But it is Mozart who made them our personal acquaintances, people to be loved or liked or despised, but all of them to be perfectly understood. For he understood them to the last tremor of the heart, the last twinge of conscience. Each is given infallibly the right music, and each keeps to it even when the parts intermingle in those impeccably elegant concerted pieces, of which the two finales and the sextet in the third act are the major miracles, but not one of which can be imagined capable of improvement in the slightest detail. And it is all immaculately beautiful, most of all, perhaps, the wonderful consolatory music lavished on the unhappy Countess, if a choice must be made. But then it should not, for the opera is as great as a whole as it is captivating in detail.

With all its overwhelming perfection, *Figaro* still shows an almost disconcerting readiness to use the current idiom of the time. Likenesses to Galuppi or Paisiello[1] or Sarti may crop up at any moment, always, of course, ennobled and individualized by the context in which they appear. But the next opera, and the greatest of all, one thinks on the whole, until one is seduced by one of the others into an at least temporary preference, *Don Giovanni* (K. 527), makes a tremendous advance in achieving originality already, so to speak, at the fountainhead of inspiration. It is true that the opening scene resembles that in Gazzaniga's Don Juan opera; it may be true that other features recall that by Righini of 1777; but it is impossible to conceive that any notion as here set down by Mozart could have come from the pen of any other composer, then or later. What is more, not a single number in *Don Giovanni* can be

[1] The introduction of the Fandango into the third act of *Figaro*, too, seems to have been suggested by Paisiello, who has a Seguidilla (so-called) in *Il barbiere di Siviglia*.

imagined to occur in any other opera by Mozart himself. Everything is in character, everything coloured by the particular mood into which this great tragi-comic subject cast him.

Tragi-comic, yes, so much is certain; but nobody knows exactly where comedy ends and tragedy begins in what is formally an opera in D minor with a cheerful coda in D major. It is all inextricably blended, laughter for some and tears for others, and then again both in succession, indeed almost together, for one and the same person. Donna Elvira rampages up and down the stage furiously at her first entry with her E flat major aria, but Don Juan and Leporello laugh behind her back while the orchestra chuckles with kindly understanding of the whole situation. And when in that miraculous trio near the beginning of the second act the same two men plan a cruel jest at Elvira's expense, we feel inclined to weep at the tender loveliness of the music, such music as only Mozart could pour out to comfort a woman whose loving heart is about to break, be she Ilia or Constanze, the Countess Almaviva or Pamina, or indeed that most ill-used of all—foolish, infatuated Elvira, wavering miserably between vengeance and forgiveness.

It may be a too personal impression, but I have come to feel certain that this close sympathy with his women characters was his compensation for his lack of that complete understanding between him and any real woman that was one of the afflictions of his life. He became its supreme poet because he was deprived of it by fate, not through any fault of his, much less of Constanze's. That communion between two beings that needs no words was never his; but he knew an artistic equivalent, and it needed music—his music.

How sharply all the characters in *Don Giovanni* stand out! They do so even—this is Mozart's great dramatic secret—when they sing in concert and weave a piece the shape of which leaves nothing to be desired in a purely musical way. The stony-hearted and domineering Donna Anna; her almost despicably humble wooer Ottavio, who saves himself from our contempt by his tenderness; the minx Zerlina, made more sympathetic than perhaps she deserves by a touch of peasant common sense and simple affection; honest Masetto, too dense to be quite clear about the causes of his jealousy; the Commandant, equally dignified as a man and as a statue: they are all, like Elvira, outlined indelibly by music one can never forget.

Ah, if only one could! If only one might recapture that thrill of first acquaintance! There are times at which one would gladly give up the understanding of a score of which one need never fear to reach the bottom, an understanding that deepens with each new hearing or reading and reveals new secrets, for that first rapture on coming into touch with the *Don Giovanni* music. Not a careless rapture, though; rather a careworn one. This opera oppresses its lover with its beauty and with that sympathy with all aspects of life which is almost unhuman. For Mozart seems to love all his characters impartially, if one may judge from the fact that he lavishes the most wonderful music on all, though vastly different music on each. His Shakespearian indulgence covers Don Juan's vices as well as the weakness of Donna Elvira or the hardness of Donna Anna. Each is for him simply a phase of life to be transmuted into a value of art as good as any other. They or Leporello's garlicky vulgarity and pandering knavery. Before Mozart's overmastering art they are all equal.

The originality even of *Don Giovanni* is not so much in the material as in its application, as it were. At times the simplest formulas will serve, and of course the perfect cadence does admirable service again, though less frequently in the sub-mediant-subdominant-dominant-tonic form which the basses repeat in *Figaro* with a truly Italian comic-opera persistence. An utterly commonplace little figure, for instance:

constantly repeated in the quartet, 'Non ti fidar,' has the most haunting effect, as much so as perfect cadences still have in far more modern works, for some reason it would be irrelevant to examine here. One need only think of the overpowering impression made by Sieglinde's 'Sorrow and solace in one' in the first act of Wagner's *Valkyrie* or of Desdemona's cry of 'Emilia, addio!' in the last of Verdi's *Othello*.

For all such conventional turns of phrase, there is a gripping originality about the whole of *Don Giovanni* that is not to be withstood, for Mozart himself was evidently abandoned resistlessly to the inspiration engendered in him by what is, with Oedipus and Othello and Faust, one of the world's great dramatic subjects. Nowhere else are we so conscious of that 'daemonic' element in him of which a great deal has been made by modern criticism, and too much only because some strong reaction was called for against the maddening notion from which some people are still unable to free themselves, that Mozart's music is pretty. Pretty, forsooth! It is, of course, true that it can suggest the prettiness of a Susanna or a Zerlina, whose music makes it quite impossible for plain or fat sopranos to interpret these parts satisfactorily, just as it can suggest any other imaginable human attribute. But, with all its never-failing euphony, does it for a moment convey the idea that the whole picture-gallery of Mozartian characters, including Osmin, Bartolo, Basilio, Marcellina and Leporello, consists of beauties? Are even his girls like a set of Greuze portraits?

Not only a gift for the supernatural is what is meant by 'daemonic,' though the significance of the word becomes perhaps most obvious in the scenes of the graveyard and the supper at which the stone guest appears, with their ghostly trombones [1] and their wonderful suggestion of grisly situations

[1] Even these were not an innovation of Mozart's. He had already used them in the oracle scene in *Idomeneo,* which is almost an exact copy of a similar one in Gluck's *Alceste.*

that is frankly theatrical without ever becoming merely stagy. What the term implies is that unconscious piling up of layer upon layer of meaning, to be understood only by intuition, that many-sided significance which pervades the whole of this opera and in various degrees a much larger portion of Mozart's work as a whole than the ingenuous listener is ready to suspect—all of it, in fact, that is not either immature or merely entertaining. And even there unguessed-at glimmerings of it are apt to leap at you suddenly out of a minor work you imagine to have seen through long ago.

After *Don Giovanni* we are magically transported into yet another world: that of *Così fan tutte* (K. 588). Well, scarcely a world at all; only a show of marionettes. For nothing could be more ridiculous than to pretend that the preposterous people, the still more preposterous situations of this utterly artificial intrigue, were meant to be believed in, and nothing more absurd than to take da Ponte and Mozart to task for believing in them, which of course they never did. The philistinism of the nineteenth century which professed to take umbrage at this story of two girls who become enamoured of each other's lovers disguised as outlandish adventurers (a disguise which could not take in anybody for a moment) and which led either to the banishment of this fascinating work from the stage or to disastrous attempts at providing it with an expurgated libretto of some kind, was due to the confusion of moral and artistic values that was one of the gross immoralities of that century, with Ruskin presiding as high priest over the orgies held by addicts to aesthetic perversion. The supreme joke is that one cannot possibly help seeing the utter harmlessness of this mildly amusing piece, which contains nothing so seriously unpleasant as the Count's pursuit of Susanna in *Figaro*. Nor is it possible to see how any one could fail to be captivated by its deliberately and delectably artificial music. For once again Mozart achieved the miraculous feat of writing a score which, consistent in style from start to finish, could not by any conceivable chance lend a single one of its numbers to any other work of his. The whole perfume and flavour of the music is new and unique.

Artifice is the keynote of it. What else could it have been? But then again, who else could have made it as unfailingly charming as the master who remains the finest artificer as well as the greatest artist whose services music ever enjoyed? At the same time, of course, he infallibly hits upon the truth of his characters—the truth of their stage existences, which is all there is to them. And he does it by means of parody that has both infinite gusto and endless sympathy in it. Laughing at them, he is never cruel, and takes away the sting of his satire by making game, at the same time, of the musical mannerisms of his time, including his own. The 'leading motive':[1]

is simply a jest at the expense of the eternal cadences of Italian opera, not excepting *Figaro,* which is notoriously crowded with them.

Despina is deliberately kept in the Italian *servetta* tradition; Don Alfonso is a *buffo* bass grown into a Mozartian philosopher, neither moral nor immoral, a cynic with a warmer understanding than any censorious busybody could hope to attain. That understanding never fails Mozart himself. When the two fickle ladies have been sufficiently derided, Fiordiligi with a pompous number in the manner of the Italian 'metaphor

[1] It actually is an early example of the Wagnerian *Leitmotiv,* for it occurs again in the opera to the motto of 'così fan tutte,' and any one who has a mind to indulge in greater ingenuity of analysis than Mozart did in that of composition may find it hidden away in many a bass throughout the work. There are such people, and they will not be deterred by the fact that similar basses occur in all the other Mozart operas as well, to say nothing of dozens of Italian composers of his time.

aria' in which she likens her unflinching fidelity to a rock in a seething sea (note the wonderful low trumpet figure which you may or may not care to take for a symbol of that rock); Dorabella with a grand mock-tragic aria expressing an agitation she does not believe in even herself; then, in the second act, both are given the most tenderly compassionate music. Fiordiligi has another great song of the most exquisite artificial beauty, 'Per pietà, ben mio, perdona,' in E major with elaborate horn parts,[1] with which she is most gently consoled for her distress at finding her proud heart melting to an unsought love. Dorabella's graceful toying with a new affection—not quite so unsought—is commented on with equal sympathy, for the amoralist in Mozart does not for a moment consider that she deserves less of it, and that lavishing of tender beauty on her does not even cease when towards the end, declaring herself vanquished, she falls into a tone Mozart ironically approximates to that of the unscrupulous maid Despina. Irony, too, is the predominant tone in the parts of the lovers, Ferrando and Guglielmo, although each has a character entirely his own and consistently maintained: one grave, the other gay, to put it briefly and all too roughly.

Mozart's return to the *opera seria* with *La clemenza di Tito* (K. 621) had nothing of that exciting new departure which each of the five great operas shows. He was not interested in this commission, nor, one fancies, in Roman history, and Metastasio's frigid libretto made no appeal to him, even in Mazzola's altered version, which he considered an improvement. Technically the work is a masterpiece. His craftsmanship functions as beautifully as ever; the manufacture of concerted numbers is wonderful; but it is a masterpiece in cold marble, not in the living flesh and blood he knew so well how to set in action on the stage. Sometimes the sculpture is of the

[1] Beethoven, though among the first to take exception to the libretto of *Così fan tutte,* clearly took this aria as his model for Leonora's great E major aria (with *obbligato* horns) in the first act of *Fidelio.*

very finest, as in the beautiful duet between Servilia and Annius:

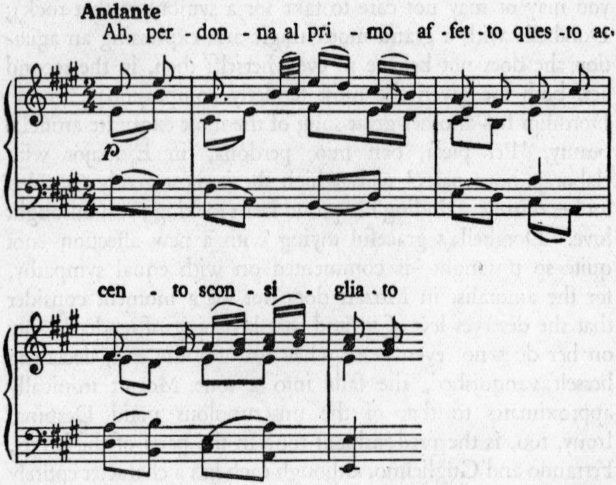
Andante
Ah, per - don - na al pri - mo af - fet - to ques - to ac-
p
cen - to scon - si - glia - to

and when all is said the music is never colder than anything Gluck produced in this vein. The fact remains, however, that it was the vein which suited Gluck's artistic temperament. With perfect emotional equanimity he could always match a classical subject with admirably measured musical equivalents of Racine's alexandrines or Goethe's blank verse at its most austere. Indeed it might be said, without intending any disparagement, that he wrote 'blank music.' And that he was better at this kind of thing than Mozart *La clemenza di Tito* proves abundantly.

What Mozart wanted was not declamation but spontaneous emotional expression, not grandly ordered drama but the variety of life, even if his librettist happened to be clumsy enough to make it a pell-mell variety. That is why he was not in the least disturbed by the hair-raising inconsistencies, the pantomime absurdities of *Die Zauberflöte* (K. 620), to which he was delighted to return as soon as he had shaken off the opera for the coronation in Prague. Here was a great deal of nonsense, but it was good theatre, it was alive, and there was a multiformity of setting, of situation, of character such as he had never before had occasion to handle. In fact, none of his earlier styles would in the least do for *The Magic Flute,* and that no doubt was the chief reason why he welcomed Schikaneder's proposal. A new problem arose: the problem of unifying a scrappy hotch-potch full of enticing details and not devoid of congenial allegory into a consistent work of art. Plays of that kind had been set to music before and were eventually to culminate in the typically Viennese farcical fairy-tales of Raimund and Nestroy, but never before nor since *The Magic Flute* has their native inferiority been ennobled by great music.[1]

The variety of the *Magic Flute* score ought to be bewildering; somehow it is only astonishing in a favourable sense. Its musical ups and downs, from a Bach-like elaboration of a chorale with fugal treatment to songs to be whistled by Vienna's butcher-boys, ought to be annoyingly disconcerting; the truth is that it is incessantly entertaining and, in spite of the naïvety of even the most solemn incidents, truly uplifting. A large orchestra is now used from the beginning, trombones being no longer dragged in merely because supernatural effects ask for them as a matter of convention, and Papageno's chime bells add a new colour.[2] Altogether Mozart is here seen to take delight in orchestral experiments, as in Sarastro's aria with a priests' chorus at the beginning of the second act, which is kept in the dark colours of two basset horns, two bassoons, three trombones, violas divided into two parts and cellos.

[1] The work of a similar kind that comes nearest to it in quality is Weber's *Oberon*; but the libretto of that was not a Viennese spectacular piece, but an English one.

[2] So might the singing of the three genii by boys, an experiment that has, so far as I am aware, never been tried since the original production, at which two boys sang with Schikaneder's daughter.

At suitable moments in the opera the flute, needless to say, has concerto-like solo parts, especially interesting in the march accompanying the ordeal by fire and water, where the flute melody is punctuated by nothing but chords for brass and rhythmic drum figures.

But not only the orchestration matches the scenic variety of this half seriously allegorical, half flippant pantomime. The music itself is much more diversified than that of any opera of Mozart's; yet unlike other works of the kind—Strauss's *Frau ohne Schatten,* for instance, which is a kind of modern *Magic Flute*—the disparity of its styles miraculously results in one single and wholly new style. The flashy Italian arias of the Queen of Night next to Sarastro's solemn utterances in Mozart's 'masonic' manner; the popular ditties of Papageno side by side with the profound humanity of Pamina's tear-compelling G minor lament and the wonderful dramatic truth of her brief mad scene; the noble classical strains expressing Tamino's love and fortitude; the comic melodrama villainy of Monostatos; the lightly touched-in fairy-tale seriousness of the three genii; the high-minded fugal craft displayed in the overture and the fire-and-water scene contrasted with the easy fun of the Viennese suburban theatre in the incidents of the slaves bewitched by Papageno's bells and the latter's light-hearted scene of pretended suicide; the intrigues of the three ladies-in-waiting outlined in two cunningly devised and most beautiful quintets and in their dark conspirators' music with the queen and the blackamoor just before the end; all this and more is by some marvel of genius fashioned into a single gem of many facets—and of inestimable value.

For all that, it is unjustifiable to say that *The Magic Flute* is Mozart's greatest opera, and none the less so because it is one of the commonplaces of German criticism, to which one must ever pay deference for its scholarship and immensely painstaking research, but by which it is not therefore necessary to let oneself be overawed in the matter of aesthetic apprehension. Where Mozart's operas are concerned, at any rate,

German critics, who to begin with can seldom quite reconcile themselves to the vexing fact that Mozart could be as much inspired by the Italian language as by their own, have over and over again fallen into the error of the kind of moral judgment which is capable of leading to so serious a blunder as that of imagining that the music of *Così fan tutte* could possibly be vitiated by its libretto, and it is the same attitude which is responsible for the false notion that because *The Magic Flute* contains elements of greater idealistic aspiration than any other stage work of Mozart's, it necessarily also contains his greatest music. Is it not enough that it should be in its own way as great as the other supreme masterpieces?

To Mozart it was all the same: religious aspiration or amorous pursuits—there was no difference between such extremes for him as an artist. And it was as an artist and nothing else that he approached his opera subjects, though we may be sure that he would not have succeeded so wonderfully had he not understood life from top to bottom as a human being. He could not specialize in any one emotion. His artistic intuition had taught him too much about life as a whole, and it was his mission to pour his knowledge into his work, to be the possession neither of ascetics nor of rakes, but of those in whom the multiform phases of existence had found some sort of balance.

This is his title to lasting glory. It was his tragedy too, no doubt, while he lived, for the conviction grows as one studies him that, occupied as he was with all human experience, he was incapable of devoting himself particularly to one. The happiness that passes all understanding did not come anywhere into his short life, so that it is perhaps a consolation to know how short that life was. But he has had his compensation ever since, for although other great composers have been more admired, more exclusively worshipped and during some phases of musical life more assiduously cultivated, none has ever been so adored as Mozart is by those who apprehend his music. Such apprehension is not easy, and the whole mystery of him is never to be grasped, for his art too passes understanding. That is why to come to something approaching a penetration of the secret of his unsentimental but profoundly affecting art is to make what this book cannot help finishing with—a declaration of love.

APPENDICES

APPENDIX A

CALENDAR

(Figures in brackets denote the age reached by the person mentioned during the year in question.)

Year	*Age*	*Life*	*Contemporary Musicians*
1756		Wolfgang Amadeus Mozart born, January 27, at Salzburg, son of Leopold Mozart (37), court musician to the Archbishop Sigismund von Schrattenbach.	Umlauf born. Albrechtsberger aged 20; Anfossi *c.* 20; Arne 46; Arnold 16; Bach (W. F.) 46; Bach (C. P. E.) 42; Bach (J. C.) 21; Benda (F.) 47; Benda (G.) 34; Boccherini 13; Bonno 46; Bortniansky 5; Boyce 46; Cannabich 25; Cimarosa 7; Clementi 4; Dagincourt 72; Dalayrac 3; Daquin 62; Dibdin 11; Dittersdorf 17; Eberlin 54; Galuppi 50; Gassmann 33; Gazzaniga 13; Geminiani 76; Gluck 42; Gossec 22; Graun 55; Grétry 15; Guglielmi 42; Handel 71; Hasse 57; Haydn 24; Haydn (M.) 19; Holzbauer 45; Jommelli 42; Kirnberger 35; Kozeluch 2; Linley 24; Locatelli 63; Martín y Solar *c.* 2; Martini 50; Monsigny 27; Mysliweček 19; Paisiello 15;

Year	*Age*	*Life*	*Contemporary Musicians*
			Philidor 30; Piccinni 28; Porpora 70; Rameau 73; Richter (F. X.) 47; Sacchini 22; Salieri 6; Sammartini (G. B.) *c.* 55; Sarti 27; Scarlatti (D.) 71; Shield 8; Stadler 8; Stamitz (J. W.) 39; Stamitz (C.) 10; Tartini 64; Telemann 75; Traetta 29; Vio mann 75; Traetta 29; Viotti 3; Vogler 7; Wagenseil 41; Wanhal 17; Winter 1; Zingarelli 4.
1757	1	Leopold (38) receives the title of court composer from the archbishop.	Pleyel born, June 1; Scarlatti (D.) (72) dies; Stamitz (J. W.) (40) dies, March 30.
1758	2		Dagincourt (74) dies; Zelter born, Dec. 11.
1759	3	Begins to find chords on the keyboard instruments and to remember passages heard.	Graun (58) dies, Aug. 8; Handel (74) dies, April 14.
1760	4	Is taught small clavier pieces by his father (41) and plays them correctly.	Cherubini born, Sept. 4; Lesueur born, Feb. 15.
1761	5	Begins to compose small clavier pieces, which his father (42) writes down.	Dussek born, Feb. 9; Schenk born, Nov. 30.
1762	6	Is taken to Munich for three weeks by his father (43) with his sister, Maria Anna (11) to play before the Elector of Bavaria, Jan.–Feb. Leopold takes his children to Vienna, Sept., where they play at court and at many fashionable gatherings. At one of	Eberlin (60) dies, June 21; Haydn (M.) (25) enters the service of the Archbishop of Salzburg as musical director; Kelly born.

Year	*Age*	*Life*	*Contemporary Musicians*
		them M. plays a Concerto by Wagenseil (47), who turns over pages for him. Visit to Pressburg, Dec. 4 Minuets and Allegro for piano (K. 1–5).	
1763	7	Return to Salzburg, Jan. Small pieces for clavier appear in print and he is found to play the violin tolerably without tuition. Extensive concert tour begun, June 9. Leopold (44) is appointed vice musical director by the archbishop. He and his children visit Munich, Augsburg, Ludwigsburg, Schwetzingen, Heidelberg, Mainz, Frankfort, Coblenz, Cologne, Aix-la-Chapelle and Brussels. Arrival in Paris, Nov. 18. Visit to Versailles for a fortnight, Dec. 24. Sonatas for clavier and violin (K. 6–8).	Gyrowetz born, Feb. 19; Mayr born, June 14; Méhul born, June 22; Storace born, Jan. 4.
1764	8	At Versailles the M.'s are invited to attend supper by Louis XV (54), Jan. 1. The children play at numerous concerts. Departure for London, April 10. Arrival, April 22. M. and Maria Anna (13) play at the court of George III (26), April 27 and May 19. M. attracts the atten-	Locatelli (71) dies, April 1; Rameau (81) dies, Sept. 22.

Year	*Age*	*Life*	*Contemporary Musicians*
		tion of J. C. Bach (29), who influences him. First public concert in London, June 5. Symphonies (K. 16 and 19) composed at Chelsea, where Leopold (45) lies ill. Sonatas for piano with violin (or flute) (K. 9–15).	
1765	9	Concerts in London, Feb. 21 and May 13. Symphony (K. 22) composed. Madrigal, 'God is our Refuge' (K. 20), presented to the British Museum. The family leave London, July 24, and spend the rest of the month at Sir Horace Mann's country seat. Departure for Holland via Lille, where illness delays them, and Ghent. Arrival at The Hague, Sept 11. First Maria Anna (14), then M., taken ill.	Attwood born, Nov. 23; Eybler born, Feb. 8; Himmel born, Nov. 20; Steibelt born.
1766	10	Four weeks spent at Amsterdam, where two concerts are given, at which all the instrumental works are by M. Return to The Hague to take part in the festivities at the coming of age of the Prince of Orange, March 11. 6 Sonatas for piano with violin accompaniment (K. 26–31) ordered by and dedicated to the	Süssmayer born; Weigl born, March 28; Wesley (S.) born, Feb. 24.

Year	*Age*	*Life*	*Contemporary Musicians*
		Princess of Nassau-Weilburg. Return to Paris, May. Repeated visits to the court at Versailles. Departure for Dijon and Lyons, July 9. Thence the family go via Ghent to Switzerland. Visits to Geneva, Lausanne, Berne and Zürich, summer. At the last place they stay with Solomon Gessner (36). Going on tour in Germany, they stay twelve days at Donaueschingen, where they play nearly every evening. Arrival in Munich after a prolonged tour, Nov. 8. They dine with the Elector of Bavaria. Return home to Salzburg, end of Nov. The archbishop causes M. to be isolated for a week in order to test his independent powers as a composer.	
1767	11	Composition of the first part of the oratorio, *Die Schuldigkeit des ersten Gebotes* (K. 35), performed March 12. The other parts are by Michael Haydn (30) and the organist Adlgasser. Cantata, *Grabmusik* (K. 42) performed during Lent. Latin comedy, *Apollo et Hyacinthus* (K. 38), performed by the	Porpora (81) dies; Telemann (86) dies, June 25.

Year	Age	Life	Contemporary Musicians
		students of the university, May 13. Piano Concertos adapted from sonatas by other composers (K. 37, 39 – 41), April - July. Symphonies (K. 43, 76). The family's second visit to Vienna, Sept. The death of Princess Maria Josepha from smallpox prevents their giving any concerts. They take refuge at Olmütz, but both M. and Maria Anna (15) catch the disease. They are cared for by the Dean of Olmütz, Count von Podstatsky, and recover after a severe illness.	
1768	12	Return to Vienna after a fortnight at Brünn (Brno), Jan. 10. Maria Theresa (51) sends for them and receives them graciously. Opera, *La finta semplice* (K. 51), commissioned by the Emperor Joseph II (27), finished, spring, but its production is delayed by intrigues and finally abandoned. German operetta, *Bastien und Bastienne* (K. 50), composed for performance in Dr. Mesmer's (35) private theatre. Mass (?lost) written for the opening of the new chapel at the Orphan Asylum,	

Year	*Age*	*Life*	*Contemporary Musicians*
		where M. conducts it, together with the offertory, 'Veni sancte spiritus' (K. 47), Dec. 7. Symphonies (K. 45, 48). *Missa brevis,* G major (K. 49).	
1769	13	Return to Salzburg, Jan. 5. The archbishop orders a performance of *La finta semplice. Missa brevis,* D minor (K. 65), finished, Jan. 14. Mass, C major (K. 66), Oct. Symphonies (K. 73 and 75). Leopold (50) takes M. to Italy, early Dec. They stay at Rovereto and Verona; at the latter place M. creates a sensation by his precocious gifts.	
1770	14	Concert at Mantua, Jan. 16. Arrival in Milan, end of Jan. Meeting with Piccinni (42). Concert at the palace of Count Firmian, at which four arias to words by Metastasio (72) (K. 77–9 and 88) are performed. They were composed as a test of his ability to write dramatic music and result in a commission of an opera for Christmas. First string Quartet, G major (K. 80), written at Lodi on the way to Parma, March 15. There he hears Lucrezia Agujari	Beethoven born, Dec. 16; Tartini (78) dies, Feb. 26.

Year	Age	Life	Contemporary Musicians
		(27). Arrival at Bologna, March 24, where he visits Martini (64) and Farinelli (65). Arrival at Florence, March 30. Concert there with Nardini (48) at the court of the Grand Duke Leopold of Tuscany (23), April 2, and friendship with Thomas Linley (14). Arrival in Rome, Holy Week. He hears Allegri's *Miserere* and writes it down from memory. Symphony (K. 81) composed. Visit to Naples, middle of May. Meeting with Jommelli (56) and Burney (44). Return to Rome, June 25. Receives the Order of the Golden Spur from the Pope, July 8. Return to Bologna, July 20, where he meets Mysliweček (33) and takes lessons from Martini. M. is elected a member of the Philharmonic Society after a severe test, an elaborate contrapuntal setting of a *cantus firmus* (K. 86). Return to Milan, Oct. 18, where he completes the opera. Production of the opera, *Mitridate, Rè di Ponto* (K. 87), in Milan, Dec. 26, with great success. Symphonies (K. 74, 84, 95, 97).	

Year	Age	Life	Contemporary Musicians
1771	15	Receives the title of *Maestro di cappella* from the Accademia Filarmonica of Verona, Jan. 5. *Mitridate* repeated twenty times in Milan. Leopold (52) and M. visit Turin and Venice, where they stay for the carnival. Return to Salzburg via Padua, Vicenza and Verona, March 28. Milan orders another opera for 1773 and Count Firmian commissions, in the name of Maria Theresa (54), a theatrical work for the Archduke Ferdinand's marriage. *Regina Coeli* (K. 108) and Litany (K. 109), May. Symphony (K. 110), July. Leopold and M. leave for Milan, Aug. 13, for the archduke's wedding. Meeting with Hasse (72) there. *Ascanio in Alba* (K. 111), a 'festa teatrale,' produced at the wedding festivities, Oct. 17. It outrivals Hasse's *Ruggiero*. Symphony (K. 112) and Divertimento (K. 113) composed. Return to Salzburg, Dec. 15. Symphonies (K. 96, 114). Oratorio, *La Betulia liberata* (K. 118).	Paer born, June 1.

Year	*Age*	*Life*	*Contemporary Musicians*
1772	16	Hieronymus von Colloredo succeeds Sigismund von Schrattenbach as Archbishop of Salzburg, March. M. is commissioned to write *Il sogno di Scipione* (K. 126), an 'azione teatrale,' for the occasion. Symphony (K. 124), Feb. 21. Litany, 'De venerabili' (K. 125), March. *Regina Coeli* (K. 127) and 3 Symphonies (K. 128–30), May. Divertimento (K. 131), June. 3 Symphonies (K. 132–4), July and Aug. 3 Divertimenti (K. 136–8); 6 string Quartets (K. 155–60). Leopold (53) and M. leave for the third time for Italy, Oct. 24. Arrival in Milan, Nov. 4. Opera, *Lucio Silla* (K. 135), produced there, Dec. 26.	Daquin (78) dies, June 15; Reutter (64) dies, March 12.
1773	17	Motet, *Exsultate* (K. 165), performed in Milan, Jan. Return to Salzburg, March. Symphony (K. 181) and *Concertone* for 2 violins (K. 190), May. Holy Trinity Mass (K. 167), June. Leopold (54) takes M. to Vienna, July 18, in the hope of securing him a post at court. Maria Theresa (56) receives him graciously, but does not appoint him. Serenade, D	Catel born, June 10.

Year	*Age*	*Life*	*Contemporary Musicians*
		major (K. 185), and six string Quartets (K. 168–73) composed in the capital. After various fruitless efforts, they return to Salzburg, early Oct. String Quintet, B flat major (K. 174), and piano Concerto, D major (K. 175), Dec. Symphonies (K. 182–4; two choruses for *Thamos, König in Aegypten* (K. 345); Divertimenti (K. 166, 186–8, 205).	
1774	18	Concerto for bassoon and orchestra (K. 191), June 4. *Missa brevis,* F major (K. 192); *Missa brevis,* D major (K. 194); Symphonies (K. 199 – 202); Serenade (K. 203). M. leaves for Munich with Leopold (55), Dec. 6.	Gassmann (51) dies, Jan. 22; Jommelli (60) dies, Aug. 25; Spontini born, Nov. 14.
1775	19	Opera, *La finta giardiniera* (K. 196), produced in Munich, Jan. 13. Composition of the offertory, 'Misericordias Domini' (K. 222), and 6 clavier Sonatas (K. 279–84). Return to Salzburg, March 7. Opera, *Il Rè pastore* (K. 208), to a libretto by Metastasio (77), performed, April 23. It was hurriedly composed for a visit of the Archduke Maximilian to the archbishop. Violin Concertos	Boieldieu born, Dec. 16; Crotch born, July 5; Sammartini (G. B.) (*c.* 74) dies, Jan. 15.

Year	*Age*	*Life*	*Contemporary Musicians*
		(K. 207, 211, 216, 218, 219).	
1776	20	*Serenata notturna* for two orchestras (K. 239), Jan. Concerto for three pianos (K. 242), Feb. Litany (K. 243) and offertory, 'Venite populi' (K. 260), March. Divertimento, F major (K. 247), June, and D major (K. 251), July. March and Serenade (K. 249, 250) performed at the wedding of Burgomaster Sigmund Haffner's daughter, July 22. Masses (K. 257–9, 262). The archbishop's gradually increasing ill-will discourages composition for his court.	Cavos born; Seyfried born, Aug. 15.
1777	21	Piano Concerto, E flat major (K. 271), Jan. Church music (K. 273, 275–7); Divertimenti (K. 270, 287–9 and 334). Concert aria, 'Ah, lo previdi' (K. 272), Aug. Tired of the archbishop's tyranny and want of appreciation, M. obtains leave for another tour. Leopold (58) not being able to leave as well, M. is accompanied by his mother (57). They leave for Munich, Sept. 23. Failing to obtain an appointment	Wagenseil (62) dies, March 1.

Year	*Age*	*Life*	*Contemporary Musicians*
		in Munich, they leave for Augsburg, Oct. 11, where they visit Leopold's relatives. Public concert at Augsburg, Oct. 22, and departure, Oct. 26. Arrival at Mannheim, Oct. 30. He hears Holzbauer's (66) and Schweitzer's (42) German operas there and finds clarinets in the excellent orchestra of the electoral court. Friendship with Cannabich (46) and his family, also with Holzbauer. Vogler (28) and Winter (22), on the other hand, dislike him.	
1778	22	Having fallen in love with Aloysia Weber (16), M. desires to abandon the projected visit to Paris, Feb. Leopold (59), however, writes and insists on his immediate departure, fearing that he may entangle himself in an imprudent love affair or marriage. M. and his mother (58) leave for Paris, March 14. Arrival there, March 23. The whole musical interest of the capital being absorbed by the feud between the partisans of Gluck (64) and Piccinni (50), M. has small prospects of success. *Sinfonia concertante* for wind	Arne (68) dies, March 5; Hummel born, Nov. 14.

Year	Age	Life	Contemporary Musicians
		quartet and orchestra (K. App. 9) written for the *Concert spirituel,* April. Concerto for flute, harp and orchestra (K. 299) composed for the Duc de Guines and his daughter, April. M. refuses the appointment of court organist at Versailles, which is subordinate and badly paid, May. Production of the ballet, *Les Petits Riens,* composed for Noverre (51), June 11. Symphony, D major (K. 297), produced at the *Concert spirituel.* Death of M.'s mother, July 3. Second performance of the Symphony with a new slow movement, Aug. 15. Sonatas for violin and piano (K. 296, 301–6) composed. Meeting with J. C. Bach (43), Aug. Seeing no prospect of success, M. leaves Paris, Sept. 26. Private concert ar Strasburg, Oct. 17. Return to Mannheim, Nov. 6. The court, and Aloysia, have in the meantime removed to Munich, though some of the musicians have remained behind. There is some chance of M.'s being appointed conductor of the	

Year	*Age*	*Life*	*Contemporary Musicians*
		German opera, but Leopold orders him back to Salzburg, where the archbishop offers him better terms. He arrives in Munich, Dec. 25, where he finds Aloysia attached to the opera but quite detached from himself.	
1779	23	Return to Salzburg, middle of Jan. Mass, C major (K. 317), March 23. Symphonies, G major (K. 318), April, and B flat major (K. 319), July. *Sinfonia concertante* for violin, viola and orchestra (K. 364); Concerto for two pianos (K. 365); Sonatas for organ and orchestra (K. 328, 329); German opera, *Zaide* (K. 344), begun.	Boyce (69) dies, Feb. 7
1780	24	Mass, C major (K. 337), March. Symphony, C major (K. 338), Aug. 29. Incidental music for *Thamos, König in Aegypten* (K. 345) for Schikaneder (29). Two choruses had already been composed at Vienna in 1773. M. is commissioned to compose an opera, *Idomeneo,* to a libretto by Varesco. M. goes to Munich, early Nov., to study the singers and finish the work accordingly.	

Year	Age	Life	Contemporary Musicians
1781	25	Production of *Idomeneo* (K. 366) in Munich, Jan. 29. Quartet for oboe and strings (K. 370). Return to Salzburg and visit to Vienna, March 12, where the archbishop is staying and wishes to display M. He is not allowed to appear independently. Unable to endure servitude any longer, M. resigns his post and is dismissed in the most humiliating manner, May 9. He decides to remain in Vienna, where he lodges in the house of the Weber family and falls in love with Aloysia's (19) sister, Constanze Weber (18). His father (62) insists on his leaving the house. He obeys, but is already engaged to Constanze. German opera, *Die Entführung aus dem Serail* (K. 384), begun, July. Sonatas for violin and piano (K. 376–80), Nov. Contest with Clementi (29) during some musical festivities arranged by Joseph II (40), Dec. 24. Meeting with Haydn (49).	Mysliweček (44) dies, Feb. 4.
1782	26	First concert given by M., March 3. He appears for the first time at the Augarten, May 26. Production	Auber born, Jan. 29; Bach (J. C.) (47) dies, Jan. 1; Field born, July 26.

Year	*Age*	*Life*	*Contemporary Musicians*
		of *Die Entführung* by command of Joseph II (41), after long delays caused by alterations in the libretto and by intrigues, July 16. Symphony, D major ('Haffner,' K. 385), July. Serenade, C minor (K. 388), Aug. M. marries Constanze Weber (19) against Leopold's (63) wish, Aug. 4. The *Entführung* specially performed at the request of Gluck (68), who invites M. to dinner, Aug. The domestic happiness of the M.s already begins to be troubled by financial cares, though M. contrives to make a little money by subscription concerts. M. appears at van Swieten's (49) Sunday morning concerts. The *Entführung,* performed at various German and Austrian theatres as well as in Prague, begins to spread M.'s fame. Piano Concertos (K. 413–15), Dec. String Quartet, G major (K. 387), Dec. 31.	
1783	27	Piano Concertos (K. 413–15) published by subscription, April. Horn Concerto (K. 417), May. String Quartet, D minor (K. 421), written while his son, Raimund Leopold, is	Hasse (84) dies, Dec. 16; Holzbauer (72) dies, April 7; Kirnberger (62) dies, July 27.

Year	*Age*	*Life*	*Contemporary Musicians*
		born, June 17. He dies, Aug. 19. Visit to Salzburg, to introduce Constanze (20) to his father (64) and sister (32), end of July. He takes with him the Mass in C minor (K. 427), begun as a thanksgiving for his marriage to Constanze in 1782. *L'Oca del Cairo* (K. 422) begun, but laid aside, summer. Duets for violin and viola (K. 423–4) composed to help Michael Haydn (46), who is ill, out of a difficulty. Departure from Salzburg, end of Oct. Visit to Count Thun at Linz, where the Symphony in C major (K. 425) is composed, and performed Nov. 4. Return to Vienna, early Nov. Fantasy for piano, C minor (K. 396); horn Quintet (K. 407); horn Concerto (K. 447); string Quartet, E flat major (K. 428); sketches for the opera, *Lo sposo deluso*; Masonic Cantata, 'Dir, Seele des Weltalls' (K. 429); concert arias (K. 416, 418–20, 431–3, 435).	
1784	28	Performance of the violin and piano Sonata, B flat major (K. 454), with	Bach (W. F.) (74) dies, July 1; Martini (78) dies, Oct. 3; Spohr born, April 5.

Year	*Age*	*Life*	*Contemporary Musicians*
		Regina Strinasacchi (20), for whom it was written so hastily that M. is obliged to fill in the sketchy piano part, April 24. Meeting with Sarti (55), who is on his way to St. Petersburg, and with Paisiello (43), who returns to Italy from there. M. plays several times at the musical evenings of Prince Nicholas Esterházy (70), which are conducted by Haydn (52). Son, Carl Thomas, born, Sept. 21. Piano Concerto (K. 456) written for the blind pianist Marie Therese von Paradies (25). String Quartet, B flat major (K. 458), Nov. 9. Piano Concertos (K. 449–51, 453, 459); Quintet for piano and wind (K. 452).	
1785	29	String Quartets, A major (K. 464), Jan. 10, and C major (K. 465), Jan. 14. Piano Concerto, D minor (K. 466), Feb. Leopold (66) stays with M. and Constanze (22), Feb.–April. Haydn (53), who meets him at the performance of one of the Quartets, tells him his son is the greatest composer known to him. M. frequently plays quartets with	Galuppi (79) dies, Jan. 3.

Year	Age	Life	Contemporary Musicians
		Haydn, Dittersdorf (46) and Wanhal (46) at M.'s house or at the lodgings of his new pupil, Stephen Storace (22), who has come to Vienna with his sister, Ann Selina Storace (19). Attwood (20) is another English pupil of M., and Kelly (23), who is engaged at the opera, becomes a friend. Piano Quartet, G minor (K. 478), Aug. Six string Quartets dedicated to Haydn, autumn. Composition of the opera, *Le nozze di Figaro* (K. 492), begun, autumn. The libretto, based on Beaumarchais (53), is by Lorenzo da Ponte (36). Violin and piano Sonata, E flat major (K. 481), Dec. 12. Piano Concerto, E flat major (K. 482), Dec. 16. Piano Concerto, C major (K. 467); Cantata, *Davidde penitente* (K. 469), based on the unfinished C minor Mass (see 1783).	
1786	30	Production of the comedy, *Der Schauspieldirektor* (K. 486), in the orangery at Schönbrunn, Feb. 7. Piano Concertos, A major (K. 488), March 2, and C minor (K. 491), March 24.	Benda (F.) (77) dies, March 7; Bishop born, Nov. 18; Sacchini (52) dies, Oct. 7; Weber born, Dec. 18.

Year	Age	Life	Contemporary Musicians
		Le Nozze di Figaro produced, May 1, after many intrigues, especially on the part of Righini (30) and Salieri (36), that threatened its prospects. It is a triumphant success, but is withdrawn after nine performances. Son, Johann Thomas Leopold, born, Oct. 18; dies, Nov. 15. Piano Quartet, E flat major (K. 493), June 3; piano Trio, G major (K. 496), July 8; clarinet Trio (K. 498), Aug. 5; string Quartet, D major (K. 499), Aug. 19; piano Trio, B flat major (K. 502), Nov. 18; piano Concerto, C major (K. 503), Dec. 4; Symphony, D major ('Prague,' K. 504), Dec. 6.	
1787	31	Visit to Prague, where the Symphony (K. 504) is performed, and an opera commissioned, Jan. On his return to Vienna M. consults da Ponte (38) about a libretto, and the latter suggests *Don Giovanni*, to which M. agrees. String Quintet, C major (K. 515), April 19. Beethoven (17) calls on M., who agrees to give him some lessons, May. String Quintet, G minor (K.	Gluck (73) dies, Nov. 15.

Year	Age	Life	Contemporary Musicians
		516). Death of Leopold Mozart (68) at Salzburg, May 28. Serenade, *Eine kleine Nachtmusik* (K. 525), Aug. 10. Violin and piano Sonata, A major (K. 526), Aug. 24. Visit to Prague with the unfinished *Don Giovanni,* Sept. Constanze (24) accompanies him. Production of *Don Giovanni* (K. 527) in Prague, Oct. 29. Concert aria, 'Bella mia fiamma' K. 528), composed for Josepha Dušek (31) Nov. 3. Return to Vienna, Nov. 12. M. is appointed chamber musician and court composer by Joseph II (46), Dec. 7. Daughter, Theresia, born, Dec. 27.	
1788	32	Piano Concerto, D major K. 537), Feb. 24. First performance of *Don Giovanni* in Vienna, with some additional numbers, May 7. It is at first a failure. Symphony, E flat major (K. 543), June 26. Daughter, Theresia, dies, June 29. Symphony, G minor (K. 550), July 25; C major ('Jupiter,' K. 551), Aug. 10. As court chamber musician M. composes a large quantity of minuets, country dances	Bach (C. P. E.) (74) dies, Dec. 15; Bonno (78) dies, April 15.

Year	*Age*	*Life*	*Contemporary Musicians*
		and waltzes for the masked balls at court. Piano Trios (K. 542, 548, 564); string Trio (K. 563). Baron van Swieten (55) begins to commission M. to amplify the accompaniments to Handel oratorios for his private performances.	
1789	33	Leaves Vienna in the company of Prince Carl Lichnowsky, who has invited him to go to Berlin with him, April 8. At Dresden M. plays at the court of Frederick Augustus of Saxony (39) and receives 100 ducats, April 14. Visit to Leipzig, where he meets Doles (74), with whom he discusses Bach, Doles's predecessor at St. Thomas's, where he plays on Bach's organ, middle of April. Arrival in Berlin, end of April, and presentation to Frederick William II of Prussia (45) at Potsdam. Meeting with the cellist Jean Pierre Duport (40), on a Minuet by whom he writes variations for piano (K. 573). Return to Vienna via Dresden and Prague, May 28. String Quartet, D major (K. 575), dedicated to the King of Prussia, June.	

Year	*Age*	*Life*	*Contemporary Musicians*
		Constanze (26) is ill and has to be sent to Baden, and M. is repeatedly obliged to borrow money. Clarinet Quintet, A major (K. 581), Sept. 29. Joseph II (48) commissions a new comic opera, *Così fan tutte,* on a libretto by da Ponte (40), autumn. Daughter, Anna, born and dies, Nov. 16.	
1790	34	Production of *Così fan tutte* (K. 588), Jan. 26. M. continues to be worried by financial embarrassments. On the death of Joseph II (49) he hopes to be appointed *Capellmeister* by Leopold II (43), who, however ignores him. String Quartets, B flat major (K. 589), May, and F major (K. 590), June, both dedicated to the King of Prussia (46). Constanze (27) has to go to Baden again. Visit to Frankfort, Sept. 23, where Leopold II is crowned. Although M. is excluded from the imperial retinue, he hopes to make some money by giving concerts. He plays the piano Concerto in D major (K. 537, 'Coronation' Concerto, see 1788), Oct. 15. Visits to	Vaccai born, March 15.

Year	*Age*	*Life*	*Contemporary Musicians*
		Mainz and Mannheim. At the latter place he hears a performance of *Figaro,* Oct. 24. Return to Vienna via Munich, where he is invited by the Elector of Bavaria to play at a concert in honour of the King of Naples, Nov. 4. On his return to Vienna, Nov., he finds his position in no way improved. String Quintet, D major (K. 593), Dec. Adagio and Allegro for a mechanical organ (K. 594).	
1791	35	Piano Concerto, B flat major (K. 595), Jan. 5. String Quintet, E flat major (K. 614), April 12. Meeting with Schikaneder (40), who suggests the collaboration in a German fairy opera for the Theater auf der Wieden, spring. Constanze (28), who is pregnant and ill again, goes to Baden, June. 'Ave, verum corpus' (K. 618) composed during a visit there, June 18. Son, Franz Xaver Wolfgang, born, July 26. Composition of the opera, *Die Zauberflöte* (K. 620), practically finished, July. A mysterious stranger visits M. and commissions a Requiem	Czerny born, Feb. 20; Hérold born, Jan. 28; Meyerbeer born, Sept. 5. Albrechtsberger aged 55; Anfossi *c.* 55; Arnold 51; Attwood 26; Auber 9; Beethoven 21; Benda (G.) 69; Bishop 5; Boccherini 48; Boieldieu 16; Catel 18; Cannabich 60; Cavos 15; Cherubini 31; Cimarosa 42; Clementi 39; Crotch 16; Dalayrac 38; Dibdin 46; Dittersdorf 52; Dussek 30; Eybler 26; Field 9; Gazzaniga 48; Gossec 57; Grétry 50; Guglielmi 77; Gyrowetz 28; Haydn 59; Haydn (M.) 54; Hummel 13; Kelly 29; Kozeluch 37; Lesueur 31; Linley 59;

Year	*Age*	*Life*	*Contemporary Musicians*
		for an anonymous patron, July. M. receives a commission to compose Metastasio's old libretto of *La clemenza di Tito* as a festival opera for the coronation of Leopold II (44) as King of Bohemia, to be held in Prague. He defers the Requiem and leaves at once for Prague, Aug. *La clemenza di Tito* (K. 621) produced there, Sept. 6. Return to Vienna, exhausted and broken in health, middle of Sept. Concerto, A major, for clarinet and orchestra, (K. 622), Sept 28. *Die Zauberflöte* produced, with M. as conductor, Sept. 30. M. again sets to work on the Requiem (K. 626) with feverish excitement, which increases the indisposition that made itself felt during the visit to Prague. He has frequent fainting fits, Oct. His condition becomes more and more critical, and partial paralysis sets in, Dec. 4. Unable to finish the Requiem, he discusses it with Süssmayer (25), his favourite pupil. Mozart dies in Vienna, Dec. 5.	Mayr 28; Méhul 28; Monsigny 62; Paer 20; Paisiello 50; Philidor 65; Piccinni 63; Pleyel 34; Salieri 41; Sarti 62; Schenk 30; Seyfried 15; Shield 43; Spohr 7; Spontini 17; Stadler 43; Stamitz (C.) 45; Steibelt 26; Storace 28; Süssmayr 25; Umlauf 35; Vaccai 1; Viotti 38; Vogler 42; Wanhal 52; Weber 5; Weigl 25; Wesley (S.) 25; Winter 36; Zelter 33; Zingarelli 39.

APPENDIX B

CATALOGUE OF WORKS

THIS list has been compiled from Köchel's Catalogue of Mozart's Works as revised by Dr. Alfred Einstein in a new edition published in the course of 1937.[1] (Many of Köchel's dates are conjectural.)

(*a*) VOCAL

Köchel No. — *Dramatic Works*

35. *Die Schuldigkeit des ersten Gebotes.* Sacred play with music (libretto by Jacobus Antonius Wimmer) (1766).
38. *Apollo et Hyacinthus seu Hyacinthi Metamorphosis.* Latin comedy. Intermezzo to Rufinus Widl's *Clementia Croesi* (1767).
50. *Bastien und Bastienne.* German operetta (Weiskern) (1768).
51. *La finta semplice.* Opera buffa (Marco Coltellini, after Goldoni) (1768).
87. *Mitridate, Rè di Ponto.* Opera seria (Vittorio Amadeo Cigna-Santi, after Racine) (1770).
111. *Ascanio in Alba.* Serenata (Giuseppe Parini) (1771).
126. *Il sogno di Scipione.* Serenata (Metastasio) (1772).
135. *Lucio Silla.* Dramma per musica (Giovanni da Gamerra) (1772).
196. *La finta giardiniera.* Opera buffa (? R. Calzabigi) (1774).
208. *Il Rè pastore.* Dramatic festival play (Metastasio) (1775).
344. *Zaide.* German opera (Schachtner) (1780). Unfinished.
345. *Thamos, König in Aegypten.* Incidental music (Gebler) (1780).
366. *Idomeneo, Rè di Creta.* Opera seria (Varesco) (1781).

---

[1] By Breitkopf & Härtel in Leipzig. I am greatly indebted to Dr. Einstein for placing the results of his researches and new discoveries at my disposal beforehand.—E. B.

Köchel No.

384\. *Die Entführung aus dem Serail.* Komisches Singspiel (Stephanie, jun.) (1782).

422\. *L'oca del Cairo.* Opera buffa (Varesco) (1783). Unfinished.

430\. *Lo sposo deluso, ossia La rivalità di tre donne per un solo amante.* Opera buffa (? Lorenzo da Ponte) (1783). Unfinished.

486\. *Der Schauspieldirektor.* Comedy in one act (Stephanie, jun.) (1786).

492\. *Le nozze di Figaro.* Opera buffa (Lorenzo da Ponte) (1786).

527\. *Il dissoluto punito, ossia Il Don Giovanni.* Dramma giocoso (Lorenzo da Ponte) (1787).

588\. *Così fan tutte, ossia La scuola degli amanti.* Opera buffa (Lorenzo da Ponte) (1790).

620\. *Die Zauberflöte.* German opera (Emanuel Schikaneder) (1791).

621\. *La clemenza di Tito.* Opera seria (Caterino Mazzola, after Metastasio) (1791).

Church Music

33\. *Kyrie,* F major. 4 voices and strings (1766).

34\. *Offertorium in Festo S^ti^ Benedicti.* 4 voices, orchestra and organ (1766–7).

44\. Antiphon, 'Cibavit eos.' 4 voices and organ (1770).

47\. 'Veni sancte spiritus.' 4 voices, orchestra and organ (1768).

49\. *Missa brevis,* G major. 4 voices, strings and organ (1768).

65\. *Missa brevis,* D minor. 4 voices, strings and organ (1769).

66\. Mass, C major. 4 voices, orchestra and organ (1769).

72\. *Offertorium pro Festo S^ti^ Joannis Baptistae.* 4 voices, strings and organ (1769).

85\. *Miserere,* A minor. Alto, tenor, bass and organ (1770).

86\. Antiphon, 'Quaerite primum regnum Dei.' 4 voices unaccompanied (1770)

89\. *Kyrie,* G major. 5 sopranos in canon (1770).

90\. *Kyrie,* D minor. 4 voices and organ (1770).

91\. *Kyrie,* D major. 4 voices, strings and organ (1774).

Köchel No.

93.[1] Psalm, 'De profundis,' C minor. 4 voices, strings and organ (1770).

108. *Regina Coeli,* C major. 4 voices, orchestra and organ (1771).

109. *Litaniae de B.M.V.* (*Lauretanae*). 4 voices, strings and organ (1771).

115. *Missa brevis,* C major, 4 voices and organ (1771).

116. *Missa brevis,* F major. 4 voices, strings and organ (1771).

117. *Offertorium pro omni tempore.* 4 voices, orchestra and organ (1769).

125. *Litaniae de venerabili altaris sacramento.* 4 voices, orchestra and organ (1772).

127. *Regina Coeli,* B flat major. 4 voices, orchestra and organ (1772).

139. Mass, C minor-major. 4 voices, orchestra and organ (1772).

141.[2] *Te Deum,* C major. 4 voices, strings and organ (1769).

165. Motet, 'Exsultate, jubilate.' Soprano, orchestra and organ (1773).

167. *Missa in honorem SS^{mae} Trinitatis,* C major. 4 voices, orchestra and organ (1773).

192.[3] *Missa brevis,* F major. 4 voices, strings and organ (1774).

193. *Dixit* and *Magnificat,* C major. 4 voices, orchestra and organ (1774).

194. *Missa brevis,* D major. 4 voices, strings and organ (1774).

195. *Litaniae Lauretanae,* D major. 4 voices, orchestra and organ (1774).

198.[4] Offertory, 'Sub tuum praesidium.' Soprano, tenor, strings and organ (1773).

220. *Missa brevis,* C major. 4 voices, orchestra and organ (1775).

221. *Kyrie,* C major. 4 voices and organ (1771).

---

[1] Köchel's No. 92, *Salve Regina,* F major, 4 solo voices, chorus, orchestra and organ (1770), is doubtful.

[2] No. 142, *Tantum ergo,* B flat major, 4 voices, orchestra and organ (1772), is doubtful.

[3] No. 177, *Offertorium sub exposito venerabili,* 4 voices, orchestra and organ (1773), is by Leopold Mozart.

[4] No. 197, *Tantum ergo,* D major, 4 voices, orchestra and organ (1774), is doubtful.

Köchel No.

222. *Offertorium de tempore,* 'Misericordias Domini.' 4 voices, orchestra and organ (1775).
223. *Osanna,* C major. 4 voices, strings and organ (1773?).
243. *Litaniae de venerabili altaris sacramento,* E flat major. 4 voices, orchestra and organ (1776).
257. Mass, C major. 4 voices, orchestra and organ (1776).
258. *Missa brevis,* C major. 4 voices, orchestra and organ (1776).
259. *Missa brevis,* C major. 4 voices, orchestra and organ (1776).
260. *Offertorium de venerabili sacramento,* 'Venite, populi.' Double choir, strings and organ (1776).
262. *Missa longa,* C major. 4 voices, orchestra and organ (1776).
273. *Graduale ad festum B.M.V.,* F major. 4 voices, strings and organ (1777).
275. *Missa brevis,* B flat major. 4 voices, strings and organ (1777).
276. *Regina Coeli,* C major. 4 voices, orchestra and organ (1779).
277. *Offertorium de B. V. Maria,* F major. 4 voices, strings and organ (1777).
317. Mass, C major. 4 voices, orchestra and organ (1779)
321. *Vesperae de Dominica,* C major. 4 voices, orchestra and organ (1779).
322. *Kyrie,* E flat major. 4 voices, orchestra and organ (1778).
323.[1] *Kyrie,* C major. 4 voices, orchestra and organ (1779).
326. Hymn, 'Justum deduxit Dominus.' 4 voices and organ (1771).
337.[2] *Missa solemnis,* C major. 4 voices, orchestra and organ (1780).
339. *Vesperae solemnes de confessore.* 4 voices, orchestra and organ (1780).
341.[3] *Kyrie,* D minor. 4 voices, orchestra and organ (1781).

---

[1] Nos. 324–5, Hymns, 'Salus infirmorum' and 'Sancta Maria,' 4 voices and organ (1779), are doubtful.

[2] No. 327, Hymn, 'Adoramus te,' 4 voices and organ (1779), is by Quirino Gasparini.

[3] No. 340, *Kyrie,* C major, 4 voices unaccompanied (1780), is spurious.

Köchel No.

343. *Zwei deutsche Kirchenlieder,* 'O Gottes Lamm,' 'Als aus Aegypten Israel.' 1 voice and bass (1780).
427. Mass, C minor. 4 solo voices, chorus, orchestra and organ (1782–3). Unfinished.
618. Motet, 'Ave, verum corpus.' 4 voices, strings and organ (1791).
626. *Requiem,* D minor. 4 solo voices, chorus, orchestra and organ (1791). Completed by Süssmayer.

Solo Arias with Orchestra

21. 'Va, dal furor portata' (Metastasio). Tenor (1765).
23. 'Conservati fedele' (Metastasio). Soprano and strings (1765).
36. Recit., 'Or che il dover'; Aria, 'Tali e cotanti sono.' Tenor (1766).
70. Recit., 'A Berenice'; Aria, 'Sol nascente.' Soprano (1769).
71. 'Ah, più tremar non voglio' (Metastasio). Tenor (1769).
74B. 'Non curo l'affetto' (Metastasio). Soprano (1771).
77. Recit., 'Misero me'; Aria, 'Misero pargoletto' (Metastasio). Soprano (1770).
78. 'Per pietà, bell'idol mio' (Metastasio). Soprano (1770).
79. Recit., 'O temerario Arbace'; Aria, 'Per quel paterno amplesso' (Metastasio) (1770).
82. 'Se ardire, e speranza' (Metastasio). Soprano (1770).
83. 'Se tutti i mali miei' (Metastasio). Soprano (1770).
88. 'Se cento affanni' (Metastasio). Soprano (1770).
119. 'Der Liebe himmlisches Gefühl.' Soprano (1782?).
143. Recit., 'Ergo interest'; Aria, 'Quaere superna.' Soprano, strings and organ (1770).
146. 'Kommet her, ihr frechen Sünder.' Soprano, strings and organ (1779).
209. 'Si mostra la sorte.' Tenor (1775).
210. 'Con ossequio, con rispetto.' Tenor (1775).
217. 'Voi avete un cor fedele.' Soprano (1775).
255. Recit., 'Ombra felice'; Aria, 'Io ti lascio.' Contralto (1776).
256. 'Clarice cara mia sposa.' Tenor (1776).

Köchel No.

272. Recit., 'Ah, lo previdi'; Aria, 'Ah, t'invola agl'occhi miei. Soprano (1777).

294. Recit., 'Alcandro, lo confesso'; Aria, 'Non so donde viene' (Metastasio). Soprano (1778).

295. Recit., 'Se al labbro mio non credi'; Aria, 'Il cor dolente' (Metastasio). Tenor (1778).

316. Recit., 'Popoli di Tessaglia'; Aria, 'Io non chiedo, eterni' (Calzabigi). Soprano (1778).

368. Recit., 'Ma che vi fece'; Aria, 'Sperai vicino al lido' (Metastasio). Soprano (1781).

369. Scena, 'Misera, dove son?'; Aria, 'Ah, non son' io che parlo' (Metastasio). Soprano (1781).

374. Recit., 'A questo seno deh vieni'; Aria, 'Or che il cielo a me ti rende.' Soprano (1781).

383. 'Nehmt meinen Dank, ihr holden Gönner.' Soprano (1782).

416. Scena, 'Mia speranza adorata'; Aria, 'Ah, non sai qual' pena.' Soprano (1783).

418. 'Vorrei spiegarvi, oh Dio,' for Anfossi's *Il curioso indiscreto.* Soprano (1783).

419. 'No, no, che non sei capace,' for the same. Soprano (1783).

420. 'Per pietà, non ricercate,' for the same. Tenor (1783).

431. Recit., 'Misero! o sogno!'; Aria, 'Aura, che intorno spiri.' Tenor (1783).

432. Recit., 'Così dunque tradisci'; Aria, 'Aspri rimorsi atroci' (Metastasio). Bass (1783).

433. 'Männer suchen stets zu naschen.' Bass (1783).

435. 'Müsst ich auch durch tausend Drachen.' Tenor (1783).

486A. Recit., 'Basta, vincesti'; Aria, 'Ah, non lasciarmi' (Metastasio). Soprano (1778–86).

490. Scena, 'Non più, tutto ascoltai'; Rondo, 'Non temer, amato bene' (Varesco). Soprano (1786). Extra number for *Idomeneo,* K. 366.

505. Scena, 'Ch'io mi scordi di te'; Rondo, 'Non temer, amato bene' (Varesco). Soprano with pianoforte obbligato (1786).

512. Recit., 'Alcandro, lo confesso'; Aria, 'Non so, donde viene' (Metastasio). Bass (1787).

Köchel No.

513. 'Mentre ti lascio, o figlia' (Duca Sant' Angioli Morbilli). Bass (1787).
528. Scena, 'Bella mia fiamma'; Aria, 'Resta, oh caro.' Soprano (1787).
538. 'Ah, se in ciel, benigne stelle' (Metastasio). Soprano (1788).
539. *Ein deutsches Kriegslied,* 'Ich möchte wohl der Kaiser sein' (Gleim). Baritone (1788).
541. Arietta, 'Un bacio di mano.' Bass (1788).
569. 'Ohne Zwang, aus eignem Triebe' (1789). (Known only from Mozart's own catalogue.)
577. Rondo, 'Al desio di chi t'adora.' Soprano (1789). Extra number for Susanna in *Le nozze di Figaro.*
578. 'Alma grande e nobil core' (Palomba). Soprano (1789). For Cimarosa's *I due baroni.*
579. 'Un moto di gioia.' Soprano (1789). Extra number for Susanna in *Le nozze di Figaro.*
580. 'Schon lacht der holde Frühling.' Soprano (1789). For Paisiello's *Il barbiere di Siviglia.*
582. 'Chi sa, chi sa, qual sia' (da Ponte). Soprano (1789). For Martín's *Il burbero di buon core.*
583. 'Vado, ma dove?' (da Ponte). Soprano (1789). For Martín's *Il burbero di buon core.*
584. 'Rivolgete a lui lo sguardo' (Lorenzo da Ponte). Bass (1789). Originally for *Così fan tutte.*
612. 'Per questa bella mano.' Bass (1791).
621A. 'Io ti lascio.' Bass (1791).

Songs for Voice and Piano

52. 'Daphne, deine Rosenwangen' (1768).
53. *An die Freude* (Uz) (1767).
147. 'Wie unglücklich bin ich' (1772).
148. 'O heiliges Band' (1772).
149. *Die grossmüthige Gelassenheit* (J. C. Günther) (1772).
150. *Geheime Liebe* (J. C. Günther) (1772).
151. *Die Zufriedenheit im niedrigen Stande* (F. R. von Canitz) (1783).
152. Canzonetta, 'Ridente la calma' (1775?).
178. Aria, 'Ah, spiegarti, oh Dio' (1783).

Köchel
No.

307. Arietta, 'Oiseaux, si tous les ans' (1778).
308. Arietta, 'Dans un bois solitaire' (Houdart de la Motte) (1778).
349. *Die Zufriedenheit* (Johann Martin Miller) (1780).
351.[1] 'Komm, liebe Zither,' with mandoline (1780).
390. *An die Hoffnung* (J. T. Hermes) (1782).
391. *An die Einsamkeit* (J. T. Hermes) (1782).
392. 'Verdankt sei es dem Glanz' (J. T. Hermes) (1782).
468. *Gesellenreise* (Joseph Franz von Ratschky) (1785).
472. *Der Zauberer* (C. F. Weisse) (1785).
473. *Die Zufriedenheit* (C. F. Weisse) (1785).
474. *Die betrogene Welt* (C. F. Weisse) (1785).
476. *Das Veilchen* (Goethe) (1785).
506. *Lied der Freiheit* (Blumauer) (1786).
517. *Die Alte* (Friedrich von Hagedorn) (1787).
518. *Die Verschweigung* (C. F. Weisse) (1787).
519. *Das Lied der Trennung* (Klamer Schmidt) (1787).
520. *Als Luise die Briefe ihres ungetreuen Liebhabers verbrannte* (Gabriele von Baumberg) (1787).
523. *Abendempfindung* (Campe) (1787).
524. *An Chloe* (J. G. Jacobi) (1787).
529. *Des kleinen Friedrichs Geburtstag* (Mildheim's *Liederbuch*) (1787).
530. *Das Traumbild* (Hölty) (1787).
531. *Die kleine Spinnerin* (?; extra verses by D. Jäger) (1787).
552. *Beim Auszug in das Feld* (1788).
596. *Sehnsucht nach dem Frühlinge,* 'Komm, lieber Mai' (C. A. Overbeck) (1791).
597. *Im Frühlings Anfang* (C. C. Sturm) (1791).
598. *Das Kinderspiel* (C. A. Overbeck) (1791).
619. *Eine kleine deutsche Kantate,* 'Die ihr des unermesslichen Weltalls' (F. H. Ziegenhagen) (1791).

---

[1] The well-known *Wiegenlied,* 'Schlafe, mein Prinzchen,' previously No. 350 in Köchel's list, is not by Mozart, but by Bernhard Flies.

Köchel No.

Choral Works with Orchestra [1]

42\. *Grabmusik.* Passion Cantata (1767).
118\. *La Betulia liberata.* Oratorio (Metastasio). Solo voices, chorus and orchestra (1771).
429\. Cantata, 'Dir, Seele des Weltalls.' Male voices and orchestra (1783).
429B. Cantata, 'Dir, Seele des Weltalls.' Soprano solo, mixed chorus and orchestra (1783).
469\. Cantata, *Davidde Penitente.* 3 solo voices, chorus and orchestra (1785). Mainly based on the Mass in C minor, K. 427.
471\. Cantata, *Die Maurerfreude* (Franz Petran). Tenor solo, male chorus and orchestra (1785).
615\. Final chorus, 'Viviamo felici,' for Sarti's *Le Gelosie villane* (1791). (Known only from Mozart's own catalogue.)
623\. *Eine kleine Freimaurer-Kantate* (Schikaneder). Male chorus and orchestra (1791).

Music for Several Voices

(Unaccompanied)

20\. Madrigal (chorus), 'God is our refuge' (1765).
89A. Five Riddle Canons.
228.[2] Double Canon, 'Ach, zu kurz ist unsers Lebens Lauf' (1787).
229\. Canon, 'Sie ist dahin' (Hölty) (1782).
230\. Canon, 'Selig, selig alle' (Hölty) (1782).
231\. Canon, 'Lasst froh uns sein' (1782).
232\. Canon, 'Wer nicht liebt Wein und Weiber' (1787).
233\. Canon, 'Nichts labt mich mehr' (1782).
234\. Canon, 'Essen, trinken' (1782).
347\. Canon, 'Lasst uns ziehn (1782).
348\. Canon, 'V'amo di core teneramente' (1782).

---

[1] Köchel gives the following numbers to Mozart's additional instrumentation of works by Handel: 566. *Acis and Galatea*; 572. *Messiah*; 591. *Alexander's Feast*; 592. *Ode for St. Cecilia's Day.*

[2] Nos. 226–7, Canons, 'O Schwestern traut dem Amor nicht' 1775) and 'O wunderschön ist Gottes Erde' (1775), are spurious.

Köchel No.

507. Canon, 'Heiterkeit und leichtes Blut' (1786).
508. Canon, 'Auf das Wohl aller Freunde' (1786).
508A. Eight Canons (1786).
553. Canon, 'Alleluja' (1788).
554. Canon, 'Ave Maria' (1788).
555. Canon, 'Lacrimoso son io' (1788).
556. Canon, 'G'rechtelt's eng' (1788).
557. Canon, 'Nascoso è il mio sol' (1788).
558. Canon, 'Gehn ma in'n Prada' (1788).
559. Canon, 'Difficile lectu mihi' (1788).
560A. Canon, 'O du eselhafter Martin' (1788).
560B. Canon, 'O du eselhafter Peierl' (1788).
561. Canon, 'Bona Nox, bist a rechta Ox' (1788).
562. Canon, 'Caro bell' idol mio' (1788).

Miscellaneous

346. Trio, 'Luci care, luci belle.' 3 voices and 3 basset horns (1783).
389. Duet, 'Welch ängstliches Beben.' 2 tenors and orchestra (1782). Originally in *Die Entführung aus dem Serail,* K. 384.
393. Solfeggi for voice (1782).
429A. Cantata, 'Dir, Seele des Weltalls.' Soprano solo, male chorus and piano (1783).
434. Trio, 'Del gran regno delle Amazoni.' Tenor, 2 basses and orchestra (1783).
436. Trio, 'Ecco quel fiero istante' (Metastasio). 2 sopranos, bass and 3 basset horns (1783).
437. Trio, 'Mi lagnerò tacendo' (Metastasio). 2 sopranos, bass, 2 clarinets and basset horn (1783).
438. Trio, 'Se lontan, ben mio, tu sei.' 3 voices, 2 clarinets and basset horn (1783).
439. Trio, 'Due pupille amabili.' 2 sopranos, bass and 3 basset horns (1783).
440. Aria, 'In te spero, o sposo' (Metastasio). Soprano and instrumental bass (1783). Fragment.
441. Trio, 'Liebes Mandel, wo is's Bandel.' Soprano, tenor, bass and strings (1783).

Köchel No.

479. Quartet, 'Dite almeno,' for Bianchi's *La villanella rapita* (1785).
480. Trio, 'Mandina amabile,' for Bianchi's *La villanella rapita* (1785).
483. Song, 'Zerfliesset heut', geliebte Brüder' (Augustin Veith, Edler v. Schittlersberg). Tenor solo, chorus and organ (1785).
484. Chorus, 'Ihr unsre neuen Leiter' (Schittlersberg). 3 voices and organ (1785).
489. Duet, 'Spiegarti, oh Dio, non posso.' Soprano, tenor and orchestra (1786). Extra number for *Idomeneo,* K. 366.
532. Trio, 'Grazie agl'inganni tuoi' (Metastasio). Soprano, tenor, bass and orchestra (1787).
549. Canzonetta, 'Più non si trovano' (Metastasio). 2 sopranos, bass and 3 basset horns (1788).
625. Comic Duet, 'Nun, liebes Weibchen.' Soprano, bass and orchestra (1790). For Schikaneder's *Stein der Weisen.* (Doubtful, probably by B. Schack).

App.

5. Comic Quartet, 'Caro mio, Druck und Schluck,' for soprano, 2 tenors, bass and piano (1789).

(*b*) Instrumental

Symphonies

16. (1)[1] E flat major (1764).
19. (4) D major (1764).
22. (5) B flat major (1765).
43. (6) F major (1767).
45. (7) D major (1768).
48. (8) D major (1768).
73. (9) C major (1769).
74. (10) G major (1770).
75. (42) F major (1769).

[1] Numbers in brackets are those of the Breitkopf & Härtel edition. Köchel's Nos. 17 (2) and 98 (48) are spurious; No. 18 (3) is by C. F. Abel, No. 81 (44) may be by Leopold Mozart.

Köchel No.		
76.	(43)	F major (1767).
81.	(44)	D major (1770).
84.	(11)	D major (1770).
95.	(45)	D major (1770).
96.	(46)	C major (1771).
97.	(47)	D major (1770).
102.	(49)	C major (finale only, to the overture of *Il Rè pastore*) (1775).
110.	(12)	G major (1770).
112.	(13)	F major (1771).
114.	(14)	A major (1771).
120.	(50)	D major (finale only, to the overture of *Ascanio in Alba*) (1771).
121.		D major (finale only, to the overture of *La finta giardiniera*) (1771).
124.	(15)	G major (1772).
128.	(16)	C major (1772).
129.	(17)	G major (1772).
130.	(16)	F major (1772).
132.	(19)	E flat major (1772).
133.	(20)	D major (1772).
134.	(21)	A major (1772).
161.		D major (1772). (First two movements identical with the overture to *Il sogno di Scipione*, K. 126.)
162.	(22)	C major (1772).
163.	(51)	D major (finale only, to the overture of *Il sogno di Scipione*) (1772).
181.	(23)	D major (1773).
182.	(24)	B flat major (1773).
183.	(25)	G minor (1773).
184.	(26)	E flat major (1773).
199.	(27)	G major (1774).
200.	(28)	C major (1774).
201.	(29)	A major (1774).
202.	(30)	D major (1774).
297.	(31)	D major ('Paris') (1778).
318.	(31)	G major (? overture to *Zaide*) (1779).
319.	(33)	B flat major (1779).

Köchel No.		
338.	(34)	C major (1780).
385.	(35)	D major ('Haffner') (1782).
425.	(36)	C major ('Linz') (1783).
444.	(37)	G major (1783). (Only the Introduction; the rest by Michael Haydn.)
504.	(38)	D major ('Prague') (1786).
543.	(39)	E flat major (1788).
550.	(40)	G minor (1788).
551.	(41)	C major ('Jupiter') (1788).
App.		
214.		B flat major (1768).
216.		B flat major (1771).
221.		G major (1768).

Various Orchestral Works

32.[1] *Galimathias musicum* (1766).
61G. 2 Minuets (1769).
61H. 6 Minuets (1769).
62. March for a Cassation, D major (1769).
63. Cassation, G major (1769).
64. Minuet, D major (1769).
65A. 7 Minuets (1769).
99. Cassation, B flat major (1769).
100. Serenade, D major (1769).
101. Serenade (*Contredanse*), F major (1776?).
103. 19 Minuets (1769).
104. 6 Minuets (1769).
105. 6 Minuets (1769).
106. Overture and 3 Country Dances (1790).
113. Divertimento, E flat major (1771).
122. Minuet, E flat major (1770).
123. Country Dance, B flat major (1770).
131. Divertimento, D major (1772).
136. Divertimento, D major (1772).
137. Divertimento, B flat major (1772).

[1] Köchel's No. 25A, Minuet and Trio, C major, is probably by Beethoven.

Köchel No.

138. Divertimento, F major (1772).
164. 6 Minuets (1772).
166. Divertimento, E flat major (1773).
176. 6 Minuets (1773).
185. Serenade, D major (1773).
186. Divertimento, B flat major (1773).
187. Divertimento, C major (1773).
188. Divertimento, C major (1773).
189. March, D major (1773).
203. Serenade, D major (1774).
204. Serenade, D major (1775).
205. Divertimento, D major (1773).
206. March (1774). (Afterwards used in *Idomeneo,* K. 366.)
213. Divertimento, F major (1775).
214. March, C major (1775).
215. March, D major (1775).
237. March, D major (1774).
239. *Serenata notturna,* D major, for 2 orchestras (1776).
240. Divertimento, B flat major (1776).
247. Divertimento, F major (1776).
248. March, F major (1776).
249. March, D major (1776).
250. Serenade, D major ('Haffner') (1776).
251. Divertimento, D major (1776).
252. Divertimento, E flat major (1776).
253. Divertimento, F major (1776).
267. 4 Country Dances (1776).
270. Divertimento, B flat major (1777).
286. *Notturno,* D major, for 4 orchestras (1777).
287. Divertimento, B flat major (1777).
288. Divertimento, F major (1777).
289. Divertimento, E flat major (1777).
290. March, D major (1773).
300.[1] Gavotte, B flat major (1778).

---

[1] No. 291, Fugue, D major (1777), is by Michael Haydn; finished by Simon Sechter.

Köchel No.

320. Serenade, D major (1779).
334. Divertimento, D major (1779).
335. 2 Marches (1779).
361. Serenade, B flat major (1780).
362. March (1780). (Afterwards used in *Idomeneo,* K. 366.)
363. 3 Minuets (1780).
367. Ballet Music to *Idomeneo* (1781).
375. Serenade, E flat major, for wind instruments (1781).
388. Serenade, C minor, for wind instruments (1782).
408. 2 Marches (1782).
409. Minuet for a Symphony, C major (1782).
445. March, D major (1779).
446. Music for a Pantomime, for strings (1783). Incomplete.
461. 5 Minuets (1784).
462. 6 Country Dances (1784).
463. 2 Minuets and 2 Country Dances (1784).
477. *Maurerische Trauermusik* (Masonic Funeral Music) (1785).
509. 6 German Dances (*Teutsche*) (1787).
522.[1] *Ein musikalischer Spass* (1787).
525. *Eine kleine Nachtmusik,* for strings (1787).
534. Country Dance (*Das Donnerwetter*) (1788).
535. Country Dance (*La Bataille*) (1788).
535A. 3 Country Dances (1788).
536. 6 German Dances (1788).
544. *Ein kleiner Marsch,* D major (1788).
565. 2 Country Dances (1788).
567. 6 German Dances (1788).
568. 12 Minuets (1788).
571. 6 German Dances (1789).
585. 12 Minuets (1789).
586. 12 German Dances (1789).
587. Country Dance (*Der Sieg vom Helden Koburg*) (1789).
599. 6 Minuets (1791).
600. 6 German Dances (1791).
601. 4 Minuets (1791).

---

[1] K. 510, 9 Country Dances or Quadrilles (1787), is spurious.

Köchel No.

602. 4 German Dances (1791).
603. 2 Country Dances (1791).
604. 2 Minuets (1791).
605. 3 German Dances (1791).
606. *Sechs ländlerische Tänze* (1791).
607. Country Dance, E flat major (1791).
609. 5 Country Dances (1791).
610. Country Dances, G major (1791).
611. German Dance, C major (1791).

App.

10. Ballet Music for the Pantomime, *Les Petits Riens* (1778).
226. Divertimento, E flat major (1775).
227. Divertimento, B flat major (1775).

Köchel No. — *Concertos for Pianoforte and Orchestra*

37. F major (1767). (Arrangement of sonata-movements by Raupach and Honauer.)
39. B flat major (1767). (Arrangement of sonata-movements by Raupach and Schobert.)
40. D major (1767). (Arrangement of sonata-movements by Honauer, Eckhardt and ? P. E. Bach.)
41. G major (1767). (Arrangement of sonata-movements by Honauer and Raupach.)
107. 3 Sonatas by J. C. Bach arranged as Concertos with string orchestra (1765).
175. D major (1773).
238. B flat major (1776).
242. F major, for 3 pianos (1776).
246. C major (1776).
271. E flat major (1777).
365. E flat major, for 2 pianos (1779).
382. Concert Rondo, D major, ? to K. 175 (1782).
386. Concert Rondo, A major, ? discarded from K. 414 (1782).
413. F major (1782).

Köchel No.

414. A major (1782).
415. C major (1782).
449. E flat major (1784).
450. B flat major (1784).
451. D major (1784).
453. G major (1784).
456. B flat major (1784).
459. F major (1784).
466. D minor (1785).
467. C major (1785).
482. E flat major (1785).
488. A major (1786).
491. C minor (1786).
503. C major (1786).
537. D major ('Coronation') (1788).
595. B flat major (1791).
624. Cadenzas to his Concertos (1773–91).

Concertos for Violin and Orchestra [1]

190. *Concertone,* C major, for 2 violins (1773).
207. B flat major (1775).
211. D major (1775).
216. G major (1775).
218. D major (1775).
219. A major (1775).
261. Adagio, to K. 219 (1776).
268. E flat major (? authentic) (? 1780–81).
269. *Rondo concertant,* B flat major, to K. 207 (1776).
271A. D major (1777).
373. Rondo, C major (1781).
470. Andante for a Concerto, A major (1785).

---

[1] The Concerto in D major (originally in E major) recently edited by Marius Casadesus and supposed to have been written at Versailles for the Princess Adélaïde of France in 1766 has not yet been conclusively proved to be authentic.

Köchel No. — *Various Concertos*

191. B flat major, for bassoon (1774).
293. F major, for oboe (1783). Fragment.
299. C major, for flute and harp (1778).
313. G major, for flute (1778).
314. D major, for flute (1778).
315. Andante, C major, for flute (1778).
364. *Sinfonia concertante,* E flat major, for violin and viola (1779).
371. Concert Rondo, E flat major, for horn (1781).
412. D major, for horn (1782).
417. E flat major, for horn (1783).
447. E flat major, for horn (1783).
495. E flat major, for horn (1786).
514. Rondo, D major, for horn (identical with that of the Concerto, K. 412).
622. A major, for clarinet (1791).

App.

9. *Sinfonia concertante,* E flat major, for flute, oboe, horn and bassoon (1778).

Köchel No. — *Sonatas for Organ and Orchestra*

263. C major, with violins, trumpets and bass (1776).
278. C major, with orchestra (1777).
329. C major, with orchestra (1779).

Sonatas for Organ and Strings

67. E flat major (1767).
68. B flat major (1767).
69. D major (1767).
144. D major (1772).
145. F major (1772).
212. B flat major (1775).
224. F major (1776).
225. A major (1776).
241. G major (1776).

Köchel No.

244. F major (1776).
245. D major (1776).
274. G major (1777).
328. C major (1779).
336. C major (1780).

String Quintets

174.[1] B flat major (1773).
406. C minor (1787). (Arrangement of the Serenade for wind instruments, K. 388.)
515. C major (1787).
516. G minor (1787).
593. D major (1790).
614. E flat major (1791).

String Quartets

80. G major (1770).
155. D major (1772).
156. G major (1772).
157. C major (1772).
158. F major (1772).
159. B flat major (1772).
160. E flat major (1772).
168. F major (1773).
169. A major (1773).
170. C major (1773).
171. E flat major (1773).
172. B flat major (1773).
173. D minor (1773).
387. G major (Haydn set No. 1) (1782).
405. 5 Fugues from Bach's *Well-tempered Clavier* (1782).
421. D minor (Haydn set No. 2) (1783).
428. E flat major (Haydn set No. 3) (1783).
458. B flat major (Haydn set No. 4) (1784).
464. A major (Haydn set No. 5) (1785).
465. C major (Haydn set No. 6) (1785).

[1] The string quintet arrangement of the Serenade, K. 361, listed by Köchel as No. 46, was not made by Mozart.

Köchel No.

499. D major (1786).
546. Adagio and Fugue, C minor (1788). (Fugue identical with K. 426 for two pianos.)
575. D major (King of Prussia set No. 1) (1789).
589. B flat major (King of Prussia set No. 2) (1790).
590. F major (King of Prussia set No. 3) (1790).

String Trios and Duets

266. Trio, B flat major, for 2 violins and bass (1776).
405A. Introductions to Fugues of J. S. Bach and others (1782).
423. Duet, G major, for violin and viola (1783).
424. Duet, B flat major, for violin and viola (1783).
563. Divertimento, E flat major, for violin, viola and violoncello (1788).

Piano Quartets

478. G minor (1785).
493. E flat major (1786).

Piano Trios

254. B flat major (1776).
442. D minor-major (1783). Completed by Stadler.
496. G major (1786).
498. E flat major, for clarinet, viola and piano (1786).
502. B flat major (1786).
542. E major (1788).
548. C major (1788).
564. G major (1788).

Various Chamber Music

64. Minuet, D major, for 2 violins, 2 horns and bass (1769).
65A. 7 Minuets with Trio, for 2 violins and bass (1769).
285. Quartet, D major, for flute and strings (1777).
292. Sonata, B flat major, for bassoon and violoncello (1775).
298. Quartet, A major, for flute and strings (1778).
370. Quartet, F major, for oboe and strings (1781).

Köchel No.

407. Quintet, E flat major, for violin, 2 violas, horn and violoncello (1783).
410. Adagio in Canon, F major, for 2 basset horns and bassoon (1782).
411. Adagio, F major, for 2 clarinets and 3 basset horns (1782).
452. Quintet, E flat major, for piano, oboe, clarinet, horn and bassoon (1784).
487. 12 Duets for 2 horns (1786).
581. Quintet, A major, for clarinet and strings (1789).
617. Adagio and Rondo, C minor-major, for harmonica, flute, oboe, viola and violoncello (1791).

App.

171. Quartet, C major, for flute and strings (1778).
229. 5 Divertimenti for 2 clarinets and bassoon (1783).

Violin and Pianoforte [1]

Köchel No.

6. Sonata, C major (1762–4).
7. Sonata, D major (1763–4).
8. Sonata, B flat major (1763–4).
9. Sonata, G major (1764).
10. Sonata, B flat major (1764).
11. Sonata, G major (1764).
12. Sonata, A major (1764).
13. Sonata, F major (1764).
14. Sonata, C major (1764).
15. Sonata, B flat major (1764).
26. Sonata, E flat major (1766).
27. Sonata, G major (1766).
28. Sonata, C major (1766).
29. Sonata, D major (1766).
30. Sonata, F major (1766).
31. Sonata, B flat major (1766).

[1] Köchel's Nos. 55–60 are spurious. K. 61 is a sonata by H. F. Raupach.

Köchel No.

46D. Sonata, C major (1768).
46E. Sonata, F major (1768).
296. Sonata, C major (1778).
301. Sonata, G major (1778).
302. Sonata, E flat major (1778).
303. Sonata, C major (1778).
304. Sonata, E minor (1778).
305. Sonata, A major (1778).
306. Sonata, D major (1778).
359. 12 Variations on 'La Bergère Célimène' (1781).
360. 6 Variations on 'Hélas, j'ai perdu mon amant' (1780).
372. Allegro of a Sonata, B flat major (1781).
376. Sonata, F major (1781).
377. Sonata, F major (1781).
378. Sonata, B flat major (1779).
379. Sonata, G major-minor (1781).
380. Sonata, E flat major (1781).
402. Sonata, A major-minor (1782). Finished by Stadler.
403. Sonata, C major (1782). Unfinished.
404. Sonata, C major (1782). Unfinished.
454. Sonata, B flat major (1784).
481. Sonata, E flat major (1785).
526. Sonata, A major (1787).
547. Sonata, F major (1788).
570. (See under *Pianoforte Solo.*)

Pianoforte Solo

1. Minuet and Trio, G major (1761–2).
2. Minuet, F major (1762).
3. Allegro, B flat major (1762).
4. Minuet, F major (1762).
5. Minuet, F major (1762).
9A. Allegro, C major (1763).
9B. Andante, B flat major (1763).
24. 8 Variations on 'Laat ons juichen' (air by C. E. Graaf), G major (1766).
25. 7 Variations on 'Wilhelmus van Nassouwe' (1766).

Köchel
No.

94. Minuet, D major (1770).
153. Fugue, E flat major (1782?). Completed by Simon Sechter.
154.[1] Fugue, G minor (1782?). Unfinished.
179. 12 Variations on a Minuet by Fischer (1773).
180. 6 Variations on 'Mio caro Adone,' from Salieri's *La fiera di Venezia* (1773).
236. Andantino, E flat major (1790).
264. 9 Variations on 'Lison dormait,' from Dezède's *Julie* (1778).
265. 12 Variations on 'Ah, vous dirai-je, maman' (1778).
279. Sonata, C major (1774).
280. Sonata, F major (1774).
281. Sonata, B flat major (1774).
282. Sonata, E flat major (1774).
283. Sonata, G major (1774).
284. Sonata, D major (1774).
309. Sonata, C major (1777).
310. Sonata, A minor (1778).
311. Sonata, D major (1778).
312. Allegro of a Sonata, G minor (1774).
315A. 8 Minuets and Trios (1779).
330. Sonata, C major (1778).
331. Sonata, A major (1778).
332. Sonata, F major (1778).
333. Sonata, B flat major (1778).
352. 8 Variations on a March in Grétry's *Mariages Samnites* (1778).
353. 12 Variations on 'La belle Françoise' (1778).
354. 12 Variations on 'Je suis Lindor' in Beaumarchais's *Le Barbier de Séville* (1778).
355. Minuet, D major (1790).
394. Fantasy and Fugue, C major (1782).
395. Little Fantasy, C major (1778).
396. Fantasy, C minor (1782). Originally for piano and violin.
397. Fantasy, D minor (1782).
398. 6 Variations on Paisiello's 'Salve tu, Domine' (1783).
399. Overture in the style of Handel (1782). Unfinished.

---

[1] No. 154A, 2 small Fugues, G major and D major (1772), are spurious.

Köchel
No.

400. First movement of a Sonata, B flat major (1782).
453A. *Kleiner Trauermarsch,* C minor (1784).
455. 10 Variations on 'Unser dummer Pöbel meint,' from Gluck's *Pilgrimme von Mecca* (1784).
457. Sonata, C minor (1784).
460. 8 Variations on 'Come un agnello,' from Sarti's *Fra due litiganti* (1784).
475. Fantasy, C minor (1785).
485. Rondo, D major (1786).
494. Rondo, F major (1786). (Generally used as finale for K. 533.)
500. 12 Variations on an Allegretto, B flat major (1786).
511.[1] Rondo, A minor (1787).
533. Allegro and Andante (Sonata, F major, with Rondo, K. 494) (1788).
540. Adagio, B minor (1788).
545. Sonata (Sonatina), C major (1788).
570. Sonata, B flat major (1789). (Better known as a violin Sonata, but the accompanying violin part is not by Mozart.)
573. 9 Variations on a Minuet by Duport (1789).
574. *Eine kleine Gigue,* G minor (1789).
576. Sonata, D major (1789).
613. 6 Variations on B. Schack's 'Ein Weib ist das herrlichste Ding' (1791).

App.

109B. 42 Pieces (1764).
135 & 138A. Sonata, F major (1788). (The finale, 6 Variations on an Allegretto, previously K. 54, is identical with the theme used in the violin Sonata, K. 547.)
136. Allegro and Minuet of a Sonata, B flat major (1786).

Pianoforte, 4 Hands

19D. Sonata, C major (1765). Unpublished.
357. Sonata, G major (1786).
358. Sonata, B flat major (1774).

---

[1] Köchel's No. 511A, Rondo in B flat major, is probably by Beethoven.

Köchel No.

381. Sonata, D major (1772).
401. Fugue, G minor (1782).
497. Sonata, F major (1786).
501. Andante and Variations, G major (1786).
521. Sonata, C major (1787).
594. Adagio and Allegro, F minor (1790). (Originally for a mechanical organ.)
608. Fantasy, F minor (1791). (Originally for a mechanical organ.)

Two Pianofortes

426. Fugue, C minor (1783).
448. Sonata, D major (1781).

Miscellaneous

89. Canon in four unspecified parts, A major (1770).
356. Adagio, C major, for harmonica (1791).
443. Fugue, D major, in three unspecified parts (1783).
594. Adagio and Allegro, F minor, for a mechanical organ (1790).
608. Fantasy, F minor, for a mechanical organ (1791).
616. Andante, F major, for a mechanical organ (1791).

APPENDIX C

PERSONALIA

Abel, Carl Friedrich (1725–87), German *viola da gamba* player and composer, educated under Bach in Leipzig and associated with Hasse (q.v.) at Dresden. Went to London in 1759 and settled there, giving concerts and composing.

Adamberger, Valentin (1743–1804), Bavarian tenor singer, studied and sang in Italy, appeared in London in 1777 and went to Vienna, becoming a member of the German opera in 1780 and of the imperial chapel in 1789.

Adlgasser, Anton Cajetan (1728–77), Bavarian organist and composer, pupil of Eberlin (q.v.) at Salzburg, later organist at the cathedral.

Agujari, Lucrezia (1743–83), Italian soprano singer, who made her first appearance at Florence in 1764.

Alberti, Domenico (*c.* 1710–40), Italian composer, singer and harpsichord player. The keyboard device known as the 'Alberti bass' is so called from his frequent use of it.

Allegri, Gregorio (1582–1652), Italian priest and composer, pupil of the Nanini brothers in Rome, where he sang tenor in the papal chapel from 1629.

André, Johann (1741–99), German music publisher and composer, produced his first comic opera in 1760 and set Goethe's *Erwin und Elmire* in 1764. Began a music printing office in 1774.

Anfossi, Pasquale (1727–97), Italian opera composer, pupil of Piccinni (q.v.) at Naples, where he produced his first comic opera in 1758. Later produced operas in Paris, London, Prague and Berlin. In 1792 he became *maestro di cappella* to the Lateran in Rome.

Attwood, Thomas (1765–1838), English organist and composer, boy chorister of the Chapel Royal in London, studied in Naples and under Mozart in Vienna. Appointed organist of St. Paul's Cathedral in 1796.

Bach, Johann (John) Christian (1735–82), youngest son of Johann Sebastian Bach, spent his earlier years in Italy and settled in London as clavier player and composer in 1762.

Appendix C—Personalia

Bachmann, Sixtus (1754–1818), German organist and composer.

Bassi, Luigi (1766–1825), Italian baritone singer, appeared in soprano parts at the age of thirteen and went to Prague in 1784, where he made a great reputation.

Beecké, Ignaz von (1733–1803), German pianist and officer in a Württemberg regiment, where he was adjutant and *Capellmeister* to Prince Oettingen-Wallerstein.

Benda, Georg (Jiři Antonin) (1722–95), Bohemian composer, clavier and oboe player, entered the royal band in Berlin in 1742 and became *Capellmeister* to the Duke of Gotha in 1748, whence he went to Italy for a time.

Bernasconi, Antonia (born *c.* 1745), German soprano singer, made her first appearance in Vienna in 1764, singing the title-part in the production of Gluck's *Alceste.*

Bianchi, Francesco (*c.* 1752–1810), Italian opera composer, became cembalist in Paris under Piccinni (q.v.) in 1775 and produced his first operas there.

Boccherini, Luigi (1743–1805), Italian composer and violoncellist, settled in Madrid after 1769 and for a time in Berlin.

Bonno, Giuseppe (1710–88), Austrian composer of Italian extraction. Master of the Imperial Chapel in Vienna.

Boyce, William (1710–79), English organist, composer and editor, chorister at St. Paul's Cathedral in London under Maurice Greene, pupil of Pepusch, organist of various London churches and of the Chapel Royal from 1758.

Caldara, Antonio (*c.* 1670–1736), Italian composer, pupil of Legrenzi in Venice, worked in Rome and Madrid and settled in Vienna about 1715 as vice-*Capellmeister* under Fux (q.v.).

Campra, André (1660–1744), French operatic composer of Italian extraction, held various provincial organist's appointments and settled in Paris in 1694.

Cannabich, Christian (1731–98), German composer, violinist and conductor at Mannheim, where he was a member of the school of early symphonists, and later in Munich.

Cavalieri, Catharina (1761–1801), Austrian singer, pupil of Salieri in Vienna, where she appeared at the Italian opera at the age of fourteen and was transferred to the German opera a year later.

Cimarosa, Domenico (1749–1801), Italian opera composer, studied at Naples and produced his first opera there in 1772. Travelled much later and went to the court of Catherine II of Russia in 1787.

Dezède, N. (1744–*c.* 1792), French composer of light operas, the first of which was produced in Paris in 1772.

Dittersdorf, Carl Ditters von (1739–99), Austrian composer and violinist, friend of Haydn and Mozart. Prolific composer in various branches of music.

Doles, Johann Friedrich (1715–97), German composer, pupil of Bach in Leipzig from 1739. Cantor at St. Thomas's School there from 1756 in succession to Harrer.

Duni, Egidio Romoaldo (1709–75), Italian composer of French comic operas, studied at Naples, produced his first opera in Rome in 1735, travelled much and settled in Paris in 1757.

Duport, Jean Pierre (1741–1818), French violoncellist, made his first appearance at the *Concert spirituel* in Paris in 1761, went to the Prussian court in 1773.

Dušek, Franz (František Xaver) (1731–99), Bohemian pianist, teacher of his instrument and composer, pupil of Wagenseil (q.v.) in Vienna and, in Prague, master of many famous pupils.

Dušek, Josepha (née Hambacher, 1756), Bohemian soprano singer, wife of the preceding, travelled in Austria and Germany.

Eberlin, Johann Ernst (1702–62), Bavarian organist and church composer. Became a subordinate organist at the cathedral of Salzburg in 1725, chief organist in 1729 and court organist in 1754.

Eckhardt, Johann Gottfried (*c.* 1735–1809), German composer and pianist, settled in Paris from 1758.

Eybler, Joseph von (1765–1846), Austrian composer, pupil of Albrechtsberger and, after holding various appointments in Vienna, chief *Capellmeister* to the Austrian court in 1824.

Farinelli (*Carlo Broschi*) (1705–82), Italian male soprano singer, pupil of Porpora, made his first appearance as a boy, later had a great success in England, then became attached to the Spanish court and retired to Bologna at an advanced age.

Ferrarese del Bene, Adriana (*Francesca Gabrielli*) (born *c.* 1758), pupil of the Ospedaletto in Venice, appeared in London in 1784 and in Vienna in 1789.

Filtz, Anton (*c.* 1725–60), violoncellist and composer of the Mannheim school.

Fischer, Johann Christian (1733–1800), German oboist and composer, long settled in London, son-in-law of Gainsborough.

Fischer, Ludwig (1745–1825), German bass singer who appeared successively in Munich, Vienna (1779–83), Paris, Italy and Berlin.

Fux, Johann Joseph (1660–1741), Austrian composer and theorist, author of the treatise on counterpoint, *Gradus ad Parnassum.*

Galuppi, Baldassare (1706–85), Venetian composer of operas and instrumental music, produced his first opera in Venice in 1722. *Maestro di cappella* at St. Mark's in 1762.

Gassmann, Florian Leopold (1723–74), Bohemian composer settled in Vienna, appointed musical director to the court in 1772.

Gazzaniga, Giuseppe (1743–1819), Italian opera composer, pupil of Porpora and Piccinni (q.v.), produced his first opera in Vienna in 1770.

Gossec, François Joseph (1734–1829), Belgian composer, boy chorister at Antwerp Cathedral, settled in Paris in 1751, produced many operas and church music, cultivated instrumental music.

Graf (or *Graff*), *Friedrich Hartmann* (1727–95), German flute player and composer, became *Capellmeister* at Augsburg in 1772.

Grétry, André Ernest Modeste (1741–1813), Belgian composer of comic operas, began to compose at Liége at the age of seventeen, went to Rome in 1759, studied there and settled in Paris in 1767.

Guglielmi, Pietro (1727–1804), Italian composer of a great variety of music, studied under Durante at Naples and produced his first opera in 1755.

Hasse, Johann Adolph (1699–1783), German composer of Italian operas, singer at Keiser's opera in Hamburg in his early days, travelled much, appointed *Capellmeister* at Dresden in 1731.

Haydn, Michael (1737–1806), Austrian composer and organist, brother of Joseph Haydn. Boy chorister at St. Stephen's in Vienna, appointed musical director to the Bishop of Grosswardein in 1757 and in 1762 became conductor to the Archbishop of Salzburg, where he was afterwards organist. Married the singer Maria Magdalena Lipp in 1768.

Holzbauer, Ignaz (1711–83), Austrian composer, member of the Mannheim school of early symphonists.

Honauer, Leonzi. German composer of instrumental music, settled in Paris from about 1760.

Iommelli, Niccolò (1714–74), Italian composer, pupil of Feo, Mancini and Leo in Naples, produced his first opera in 1737, became famous all over Italy and in Vienna, appointed *Capellmeister* to the Duke of Württemberg at Stuttgart in 1753. Returned to Italy fifteen years later.

Kelly, Michael (1762–1826), Irish tenor singer and composer, friend of Haydn and Mozart in Vienna.

Lampugnani, Giovanni Battista (born *c.* 1706), Italian opera composer who worked in London as well as in Italy.

Le Gros (or *Legros*), *Jean* (1730–93), French tenor singer, impresario and minor composer, made his first appearance at the Paris Opéra in 1764, became director of the *Concert spirituel* in 1777.

Leutgeb (or *Leitgeb*), *Ignaz* (died 1811), Austrian horn player, at first at Salzburg, later in Vienna, where he kept a cheesemonger's shop.

Linley, Thomas (1756–78), English violinist and composer, son of Thomas Linley of Bath, Sheridan's father-in-law. Studied under Boyce (q.v.) and then under Nardini (q.v.) in Florence. Later became leader and soloist at Bath and subsequently in London.

Locatelli, Pietro (1693–1764), Italian violinist and composer, pupil of Corelli in Rome, travelled much and finally settled down in Amsterdam.

Majo, Gian Francesco di (*c.* 1740–71), Italian composer, pupil of Martini (q.v.) at Bologna, produced his first opera at Naples in 1759, had a great but brief success in Italy and Vienna.

Manzuoli, Giovanni (born *c.* 1725), Italian male soprano singer, made an early success in Italy, went to Madrid in 1753 and to London in 1764.

Martín y Solar, Vincente (*c.* 1754–1810), Spanish opera composer, boy chorister at Valencia and organist at Alicante, went to Italy and produced his first Italian opera at Florence in 1781. His first opera produced in Vienna, in 1786, was *Il Burbero di buon core.*

Martini, Giovanni Battista (1706–84), Italian contrapuntist, teacher, composer and priest at Bologna, where he was *maestro di cappella* at the church of San Francesco and established a reputation as the greatest theorist and teacher of the science of music in Europe.

Monn, Georg Matthias (1717–50), Austrian composer, organist at the Karlskirche in Vienna and instrumental composer of the transitional Viennese school.

Monsigny, Pierre Alexandre (1729–1817), French composer, mainly of comic operas, produced his first piece in Paris in 1759.

Mysliweček, Josef (1737–81), Bohemian composer, mainly of Italian operas, with which he had a great success in Italy, Munich, Vienna and elsewhere.

Nardini, Pietro (1722–93), Italian violinist and composer, pupil of Tartini. Appointed musical director to the Duke of Tuscany at Florence in 1770.

Paisiello (or *Paesiello*), *Giovanni* (1741–1816), Italian opera composer, student at the Conservatorio di San Onofrio at Naples, had a great success all over Italy, went to the court of Catherine II of Russia, 1776–84, then made his reputation in Vienna and London, and returned to Naples.

Paradies, Marie Therese von (1759–1824), Viennese pianist, organist, singer and composer, blind from childhood, extended her success to Paris and London.

Pergolesi, Giovanni Battista (1710–36), Italian composer, student at the Conservatorio dei Poveri in Naples, produced a sacred drama with a comic intermezzo in 1731 and several comic operas as well as church and instrumental music during his short career.

Philidor, François André Danican (1726–95), French composer and chess player, did not begin to compose seriously until 1754 and produced his first comic opera in Paris in 1759.

Piccinni, Niccola (1728–1800), Italian composer, pupil of Leo and Durante in Naples, produced his first opera there in 1754. Went to Paris in 1776, where he unwillingly became the rival of Gluck.

Predieri, Luc' Antonio (1688–*c.* 1780), Italian composer, *maestro di cappella* of the cathedral at Bologna, went to the court chapel in Vienna in 1739 and became chief *Capellmeister* in 1746, but returned to Italy in 1751.

Punto. See *Stich.*

Raaff, Anton (1714–97), German tenor singer, studied and sang in Italy, returned to Germany in 1742, but continued to travel, entered the service of the Elector Palatine at Mannheim in 1770.

Raupach, Hermann Friedrich (born *c.* 1726), German composer, conductor of the imperial opera at St. Petersburg about 1756, later settled in Paris.

Rauzzini, Venanzio (1747–1810), Italian singer, teacher and composer, long settled at Bath.

Reutter, Johann Adam Carl Georg von (1708–72), composer in Vienna, chapel master of the cathedral of St. Stephen from 1738.

Richter, Franz Xaver (1709–98), German bass singer and composer, member of the Mannheim school.

Righini, Vincenzo (1756–1812), Italian composer, pupil of Martini (q.v.), went to Prague as opera singer in 1776 and produced three operas there, held appointments at various German courts.

Sacchini, Antonio Maria (1734–86), Italian opera composer, student at the Conservatorio di San Onofrio in Naples, where he learnt the violin and singing, produced his first important opera in Rome in 1762. Visited Germany, London and Paris.

Salieri, Antonio (1750–1825), Italian composer who settled in Vienna in 1766, studied under Gassmann (q.v.), produced his first opera there in 1770 and succeeded Bonno as court *Capellmeister* in 1788.

Sammartini, Giovanni Battista (*c.* 1701–75), Italian composer, mainly of instrumental music, in Milan. Master of Gluck.

Sarti, Giuseppe (1729–1802), Italian opera composer, for some time attached to the courts of Copenhagen and St. Petersburg.

Schack, Benedict (1758–1826), Bohemian tenor singer, flute player and minor composer attached to Schikaneder's theatre in Vienna.

Schikaneder, Emanuel (1748–1812), German actor, singer, playwright and theatrical manager settled in Vienna.

Schobert, Johann (*c.* 1720–67), German clavier player and composer, educated at Strasburg, later organist at Versailles and settled in Paris from 1760, where he began to publish instrumental music.

Stadler, Maximilian (1748–1833), Austrian priest and composer, successively abbot of Lilienfeld and Kremsmünster, a good theorist and musical historian.

Steffani, Agostino (1654–1728), Italian composer and diplomat, spent much of his time in diplomatic service at German courts, but was a remarkable composer as well as a scholar and priest.

Stich, Johann Wenzel (Punto) (1755–1803), Bohemian horn player and composer for his instrument, travelled much under the name of Punto, settled in Paris for a time.

Storace, Ann Selina (Nancy) (1766–1817), English soprano singer of Italian extraction, pupil of Rauzzini (q.v.), made her first appearance in 1777, later went to Italy and was engaged for the Italian opera in Vienna in 1784.

Storace, Stephen (1763–96), English composer of Italian descent, brother of the preceding, studied harpsichord, violin and composition at the Conservatorio di San Onofrio in Naples, became a pupil of Mozart in Vienna, where he produced his first Italian opera in 1785. Returned to England with his sister in 1787.

Strinasacchi, Regina (1764–*c.* 1823), Italian violinist and guitar player, educated in Venice and Paris. Began to travel in 1780 and visited Vienna in 1784.

Süssmayr, Franz Xaver (1766–1803), Austrian composer, pupil of Salieri and Mozart in Vienna, produced his first opera in 1792.

Telemann, Georg Philipp (1681–1767), German composer, studied at Leipzig University, was appointed organist of the New Church in 1704 and founded a *Collegium Musicum.* Held various posts at Sorau, Eisenach and Frankfort, cantor of the Johanneum in Hamburg until his death.

Tenducci, Giusto Ferdinando (born *c.* 1736), Italian male soprano singer, made his first appearance about 1756 and went to London in 1758.

Toeschi, Carlo Giuseppe (*c.* 1723–88), Italian violinist and composer attached to the Mannheim school.

Traetta, Tommaso Michele Francesco (1727–79), Italian opera composer, pupil of Durante at Naples, where he produced his first opera in 1751.

Umlauf, Ignaz (1756–96), composer and conductor in Vienna, especially of light dramatic pieces, produced his first Italian opera in 1772 and his first German *Singspiel* in 1778, when he became conductor of the German opera.

Valesi, Johann Evangelist (real name *Wallishauser*) (1735–1811), Bavarian singer, chamber singer to the Elector of Bavaria from 1756, afterwards studied in Italy and sang there with success.

Vogler, Georg Joseph (1749–1814), German composer, teacher and theorist, pupil of Martini (q.v.) at Bologna and of Mysliweček (q.v.), court chaplain to the Elector Palatine at Mannheim from 1775.

Wagenseil, Georg Christoph (1715–77), Austrian composer, pupil of Fux (q.v.), music master to Maria Theresa and her daughters, composer of serious, chiefly instrumental music and the leading figure of the Viennese transitional symphonic school.

Wanhal (or *Vanhall*), *Johann Baptist* (1739–1813), Bohemian composer, pupil of Dittersdorf, settled in Vienna in 1760, though he visited Italy for study later.

Weber, Aloysia (1760–1839), German soprano singer, second daughter of Fridolin Weber (q.v.), first appeared at the electoral court of Mannheim and Munich and was engaged for Vienna in 1780, where she married the actor Josef Lange.

Weber, Fridolin (1733–79), German singer and violinist, member of the electoral chapel at Mannheim, married Maria Cäcilie Stamm in 1756.

Weber, Josefa (1758–1820), German soprano singer, eldest daughter of Fridolin Weber (q.v.), does not appear to have sung in public until after 1780 in Vienna, where she appeared at Schikaneder's (q.v.) theatre from about 1789, in which year she married the violinist Franz Hofer.

Weigl, Joseph (1740–1820), Austrian violoncellist in the Esterházy band under Haydn, member of the imperial opera orchestra in Vienna from 1769.

Weigl, Joseph (1766–1846), Austrian composer, son of the preceding, pupil of Albrechtsberger and Salieri (q.v.). Wrote his first opera in 1782.

Wendling, Dorothea, née Spourni (1737–1811), German soprano singer at the courts of Mannheim and Munich, wife of Johann Baptist Wendling (q.v.).

Wendling, Elisabeth, née Sarselli (1746–86), German soprano singer attached to the Mannheim and Munich courts, married to the violinist and singer Carl Wendling, brother of J. B. Wendling (q.v.).

Wendling, Johann Baptist (*c.* 1720–97), German flute player attached to the court of Mannheim from 1754.

Winter, Peter von (1755–1825), German composer in Mannheim and Munich, composer of operas produced all over musical Europe.

APPENDIX D

BIBLIOGRAPHY

Abert, Hermann, 'W. A. Mozart.' Revised and enlarged edition of Jahn's biography. 2 vols. (Leipzig, 1923.)

Barrington, Daines, 'Account of a Very Remarkable Young Musician.' Philosophical Transactions of the Royal Society, vol. lx. (London, 1770.)

Bellaigue, Camille, 'Mozart.' (Paris, 1927.)

Blom, Eric, 'Stepchildren of Music' ('Bastien and Bastienne'). (London, 1925.)

—— 'The Limitations of Music: a Study in Aesthetics.' (London, 1928.)

Blümml, E. K., 'Aus Mozarts Freundes- und Familienkreis.' (Vienna, Prague and Leipzig, 1923.)

Boschot, Adolphe, 'La Lumière de Mozart.' (Paris, 1928.)

—— 'Mozart.' (Paris, 1935.)

Breakspeare, Eustace J., 'Mozart.' (London, 1902.)

Cohen, Hermann, 'Die dramatische Idee in Mozarts Operntexten.' (Berlin, 1915.)

Curzon, Henri de, 'Mozart.' (Paris, 1914.)

Dent, Edward J., 'Mozart's Operas: a Critical Study.' (London, 1913.)

Dickinson, A. E. F., 'A Study of Mozart's Last Three Symphonies.' ('Musical Pilgrim' Series) (Oxford & London, 1927).

Dunhill, Thomas, 'Mozart's String Quartets.' (Musical Pilgrim' Series) (Oxford & London, 1927).

Farmer, Henry George, and Smith, Herbert, 'New Mozartiana: the Mozart Relics at the University of Glasgow.' (Glasgow, 1935.)

Fowler, W. Warde, 'Stray Notes on Mozart.' (London, 1910.)

Groag-Belmonte, Carola, 'Die Frauen im Leben Mozarts.' (Vienna & Leipzig, 1923.)

Haas, Robert, 'Wolfgang Amadeus Mozart.' (Potsdam, 1933.)

Hadow, W. H., 'The Viennese Period,' 'Oxford History of Music,' vol. v. (Oxford & London, 1931.)
Hevesy, André de, 'Mozart.' (Paris, 1936.)
Holmes, Edward, 'The Life of Mozart.' (London, 1845.)
Hussey, Dyneley, 'Wolfgang Amade Mozart.' (London, 1928.)

Jahn, Otto, 'The Life of Mozart.' Translated by Pauline D. Townsend. 3 vols. (London, 1891.)

Keller, Otto, 'Wolfgang Amadeus Mozart: Bibliographie und Ikonographie.' (Berlin & Leipzig, 1927.)
Kelly, Michael, 'Reminiscences.' 2 vols. (London, 1826.)
Köchel, Ludwig von, 'Chronologisch-thematisches Verzeichnis sämtlicher Tonwerke Wolfgang Amade Mozarts.' (1862–1905.) New revised edition by Alfred Einstein. (Leipzig, 1937.)
Kreitmeier, Josef, 'Mozart. Eine Charakterzeichnung des grossen Meisters.' (Düsseldorf, 1919.)

Lach, Robert, 'W. A. Mozart als Theoretiker.' (Vienna, 1918.)
Leitzmann, Albert, 'Mozarts Persönlichkeit.' (Leipzig, 1914.)
Lert, Ernst Josef Maria, 'Mozart auf dem Theater.' (Berlin, 1918.)

Marks, F. H., 'The Sonata: its Form and Meaning as Exemplified in the Pianoforte Sonatas of Mozart.' (London.)
Mersmann, Hans, 'Mozart.' (Berlin, 1925.)
Mörike, Eduard, 'Mozart on the Way to Prague.' A novel. Translated by Walter and Catherine Alison Phillips. (Oxford, 1934.)
Mozart, Constanze, 'Briefe—Aufzeichnungen—Dokumente, 1782–1842.' Edited by Arthur Schurig. (Dresden, 1922.)
Mozart, Leopold, 'Briefe an seine Tochter.' Edited by Otto Erich Deutsch and Bernhard Paumgartner. (Salzburg, 1936.)
Mozart, W. A., Letters. Selected and edited by Hans Mersmann. Translated by M. M. Bozman. (London, 1928.)
Mozart Family, 'Briefe.' Edited by Ludwig Schiedermair. 4 vols., with a fifth vol. containing Iconography. (Munich & Leipzig, 1914.)

Nagel, Willibald, 'Gluck und Mozart.' (Langensalza, 1908.)
—— 'Goethe und Mozart.' (Langensalza, 1904.)
Newman, Ernest, 'A Musical Critic's Holiday.' (London, 1925.)
Niemetschek, Franz, 'W. A. Mozarts Leben.' (Prague, 1798; new edition, 1905.)

Nissen, Georg Nikolaus von,[1] 'Biographie W. A. Mozarts.' (Leipzig, 1828.)

Nottebohm, Gustav, 'Mozartiana.' (Leipzig, 1880.)

Oldman, C. B., Article on Mozart in Grove's 'Dictionary of Music and Musicians,' 3rd edition. (London, 1927.)

—— 'Mozart and Modern Research,' in 'Proceedings of the Musical Association.' (London, 1932.)

Oulibishev, Alexander, 'Mozart.' (In French, Moscow, 1843; in German, Stuttgart, 1847 & 1859.)

Parry, C. Hubert H., 'Studies of Great Composers. (London, 1900.)

Paumgartner, Bernhard, 'Mozart.' (Berlin, 1927.)

Pitrou, Robert, 'La Vie de Mozart.' (Paris, 1936.)

Pohl, C. F., 'Haydn und Mozart in London.' (Vienna, 1867.)

Ponte, Lorenzo da, 'Memoirs.' Translated by L. A. Sheppard. (London, 1929.)

Prod'homme, J.-G., 'Mozart, raconté par ceux qui l'ont vu.' (Paris, 1928.)

Rouché, Jacques, 'La Mise-en-scène de *Don Juan*.' (Paris, 1936.)

Schiedermair, Ludwig, 'Mozart, sein Leben und seine Werke.' (Munich, 1922.)

Schurig, Arthur, 'Mozart, sein Leben und seine Werke.' (Leipzig, 1913.)

—— 'Wolfgang Amade Mozart.' (Leipzig, 1923.)

Sitwell, Sacheverell, 'Mozart.' (London, 1932.)

Talbot, J. E., 'Mozart' ('Great Lives' Series). (London, 1934.)

Tenschert, Roland, 'Mozart.' (Leipzig, 1930.)

—— 'Mozart. Ein Künstlerleben in Bildern und Dokumenten.' (Amsterdam, 1931.)

Tobin, J. R., 'Mozart and the Sonata Form.' (London.)

Turner, W. J., 'Wolfgang Mozart,' in 'The Heritage of Music,' edited by Hubert J. Foss. (Oxford & London, 1927.)

Wyzewa, T. de, and Saint-Foix, G. de, 'W.-A. Mozart: sa vie musicale et son œuvre de l'enfance à la pleine maturité (1756–1777).' Essai de biographie critique. 2 vols. (Paris, 1912.)

[1] The second husband of Constanze Mozart.

APPENDIX E

AN OPERATICK SQUABBLE

or

THE IMPRESSARIO PERPLEXT

An Operetta in One Act

by

W. A. MOZART

Translated and Freely Adapted by ERIC BLOM [1]

Dramatis Personae

MR. BUSKIN, manager of the Opera.
MRS. HEARTFELT } opera singers.
MISS SILVERTONE }

SCENE: The manager's room at the opera house. A table with a litter of papers, quill pen, inkpot and sand-box. Three or four chairs. The walls covered with playbills, costume sketches, etc.

PERIOD: Late eighteenth century.

Mr. Buskin discovered at the table with a newly opened letter in each hand, in a state of gleeful anticipation.

Buskin. Well, well, here I am, flushed with anticipation to see the two most delectable singers in Vienna apply to me for the part of Casilda. Who would have thought of such a stroke of fortune? Dear ladies! [*A letter in each hand, he looks as though he would like to kiss them.*] What a pleasure 'twill be to welcome you here!—I wonder which will come first. May Heaven only grant they will not arrive together, for 'tis ever my maxim to keep females of the singing persuasion apart, the more so when they have a name. And *what* names these are, to be sure! Mrs.

---

[1] Copyright and right of performance reserved by the Author, to whom application should be made c/o the Publishers.

Heartfelt! Miss Silvertone! Egad, 'twill never do to let *them* come together; but if I can but secure one of them, the new opera will be the rage of Vienna. But which of the two charmers will do for Casilda? Now I come to think on 't, the part is like a meeting of prima donnas in itself. There never was such contradiction in a character. Fire and water, cat and dog, oil and vinegar are not more opposed than that new part of ours. But soft, I hear someone upon the stairs. Might that be one of the ladies?

[*He busies himself impressively with his papers. There is a gentle knock at the door, which he deliberately ignores. After a pause a louder knock.*

Buskin. Enter!

Enter Mrs. Heartfelt, theatrically melancholy. Buskin takes no notice, but becomes excessively busy with his papers. A gentle cough from Mrs Heartfelt at last induces him to turn.

Buskin. As I live, Mrs. Heartfelt, I do declare! Your servant, madam, and how do you?

Heartfelt. [*Sorrowfully.*] Indifferent well, I thank you, sir. Mr. Ruskin, I believe.

Buskin. Buskin, madam, Buskin. You confound me with some stranger. But I am vastly beholden to you for keeping to your letter. Be seated, I pray, and let me tell you that I have a part for you, if you but care to take it, that will make your pretty mouth water.

Heartfelt. [*Unimpressed.*] A principal part, I trust.

Buskin. *The* principal part, madam, to be sure. I would not ask you to take a seconda donna.

Heartfelt. That would cost you too dear, sir, not a doubt on 't, if I accepted of it, which I need not say I should not. But I do not even care to take a part with a second prima donna next to me. [*Quickly.*] Not that I should fear her rivalry. I consider that I *have* no rival. Howsomever, I should not wish to ruin the chances of an inferior singer in a part equal to mine.

Buskin. Rest assured, dear madam, there is no other chief part next to Casilda. A servetta or so, and a duenna for an alto, nothing more. But will you not give me a song? A little sample of your superb art, I beg of you.

Heartfelt. Willingly, though my reputation, sir, should be enough, I flatter myself.

Buskin. To be sure, to be sure. But do not deny me the pleasure.

Heartfelt. [*Majestically.*] Say no more. I will sing. [*Rises.*

Air

Heartfelt. Farewell, mine own beloved,
I hear the hour of parting.
Alas! my heart is smarting,
How can I live alone?
My spirit shall hover
With thee, O my lover,
Oh, hear my moan.
And thou?
May be, for ever
Thou wilt forget thine own.
Yet stay!
Alas! what do I say?
Canst thou, beloved, faithless be?
Ah me!

Must I for ever fear defection,
Art thou as false as thou art fair?
Will all my fond and true affection
Be but as water and as air?

Buskin. Passing sweet, I protest, and exquisitely melancholy. How well this will become Casilda in the first act, where she is torn from her lover, torn by doubt, torn . . . in short, a young female in shreds of sorrow, in tatters of woe, in very ribands of despair.

Heartfelt You have found your Casilda, dear sir, never a doubt on 't. I dote upon dejection, and they do say my voice is the very carrier-pigeon of the spleen.

Buskin. Excellent good. But stay: there is another side to Casilda, for she hath a double-edged temper, I do assure you. Why, she is a spitfire if ever there was——

[*He is interrupted by Miss Silvertone, who bursts in at the door, speaking angrily and volubly to someone outside.*

Silvertone. I tell you I'll have none of it. To be refused entrance because of some drab of a rival! I insist upon seeing the Signor

Impressario this instant. [*Turns and finds herself in the presence of Buskin and Heartfelt. Ignoring the latter, she pounces on Buskin.*] Signor Impressario, what is the meaning of this? I protest, 'tis monstrous! Do you think I will tolerate being kept in the ante-room while you entertain a lady who, if I mistake not, pretends to rival me in every theatre and at every academy in Vienna, with what success she should judge for herself, if she but *had* any judgment?

Heartfelt. [*Superbly.*] Madam, I disdain to answer.

Silvertone. [*Snappily.*] No answer is called for, madam, since I did not adventure to address you.

Buskin. Ladies, ladies, I beg of you! Dear Miss Silvertone, I adjure you, controul yourself. 'Tis by the purest hazard that Mrs. Heartfelt arrived here first. I give no preference——

Heartfelt. [*Outraged.*] Sir! No preference to *me*? And why not, may I enquire?

Buskin. Dear madam, dear ladies, believe me, I place you both upon an equality. Calm yourselves. You are both of you divine singers, and if I may so far risk myself, both exceeding presentable [1] persons into the bargain. Indeed I know not which looks the more charmingly. To chuse between you will be as perplexing as the opportunity is pleasurable. Permit me to say that I wish for nothing better than to have you both upon my stage together. Unhappily my next opera contains but one part worthy of such surpassing talent, and I have no choice but to content myself with one of you. But which? Dear Miss Silvertone, I have already heard Mrs. Heartfelt; now will *you* favour me with a song?

Silvertone. [*Somewhat mollified, but defiant.*] I am ready enough.

[*During her song Mrs. Heartfelt, who has taken a chair and picked up a book, affects the most unconcerned detachment, except at the florid passage towards the end, where she becomes critically interested.*

Rondo

Silvertone. Dearest shephered, with what rapture
Dost thou my affection woo;
Yet consider that my capture
May be thy disaster too.

---

[1] Pronounce with accent on first syllable.

Then alas! for all thy doting
  Thy reward will be but pain.
Is it worth a heart's devoting?
  Shepherd, better think again.

All the same, I love thee dearly
  And desire thy hand and heart.
Though we see the dangers clearly,
  None will serve to make us part.

Buskin. Ah, exquisite, dear madam! What spirit, what fire, what vivaciousness! You are my very Casilda—that is to say, my Casilda of the second act, where she leads her ancient wooer, and her lover too, who has returned in disguise, so mischievous a dance as no actress alive could achieve better than you. And what a voice, what grace, what accomplishment! Egad, I have a mind——

Heartfelt. [*Rising with dignity.*] I perceive, sir, that your taste cannot rise to the elevation of *my* talent, and indeed I think that your stage will not hold me. By your leave, I withdraw.

Buskin. [*Agitated.*] A moment, madam, I conjure you. Give me time to think. For I confess that you too will do excellent well. Indeed, t' other half of Casilda, the doleful and dumpish half, is not within a league of Miss Silvertone's lightsome temper, and you are the very paragon for it. [*Silvertone is now indignant, Heartfelt triumphant.*] Only curb your enmity a moment, ladies, I implore you, and let me consider of a remedy. Let us consult together in all amity and, pray, tell me what you yourselves say to my vexatious perplexity? [*Turning appealingly from one to the other.*] Mrs. Heartfelt? Miss Silvertone?

Trio

Silvertone. I am the foremost singer here!
Heartfelt. That may be so, and yet, I fear——
Silvertone. Admit that this is undisputed.
Heartfelt. To me 't has never yet been mooted.
Buskin. Well, let this hatred be uprooted.
Silvertone. No other singer can approach me,
That is what ev'rybody says.

Heartfelt. I must confess that I have never
Yet heard the like in all my days.

Buskin. Pray, ladies, pray, I 'll not be able
To hear a word in all this Babel.
Each has her own peculiar ways.

Heartfelt. } I 'm prima donna!
Silvertone. } My praises ev'rybody sings.

Buskin. There, let us try your voices once again:
A squabble no advantage brings.
[*He motions Heartfelt to display her gifts again.*

Heartfelt. Adagio, adagio.
[*Same gesture from Buskin to Silvertone.*

Silvertone. Allegro, allegrissimo.

Buskin. Pian, piano, pianissimo, pianississimo.
[*Making an appeal, which touches them.*
No artist should, another teasing,
Debase his art by envious spite.

Heartfelt. } Well then, no more of this displeasing,
Silvertone. } I quite agree to do what 's right.
Well then, no more of all this teasing,
(I 'm prima donna, they sing my praises),
I quite agree to do what 's right.
(No other singer can approach me,
That is settled!)

Both [*Breaking out again.*
I am the oremost singer here,
I 'm prima donna!
I! I! I!
Adagio!
Allegro, allegrissimo!

Buskin. Piano, pianissimo,
Calando, mancando, diminuendo, decrescendo!
Piano, piano, pianissimo!
[*They all sit down exhausted*

Buskin. I have it, ladies, I have it. I can let neither of you go, that is plain [*W th half-ironical gallantry*], and were it only for what is, though I say it, my tender heart. I am charmed with you both, by turns and simultaneously, I swear it, and so that you may both sing in the new opera, also by turns and simultaneously, I will myself rehandle the part of Casilda in such fashion that she shall grow into two persons out of one. The incompatible parts of her twofold temper shall split her in half altogether, and she shall become a *pair* of heroines, one all water, the other all fire, and need I say to whom of you these said respective parts shall be assigned?

Silvertone. You need not, sir. A capital plan, I declare! I'll set your house on fire nightly, with a will.

Heartfelt. Indeed, sir, you have solved the matter to admiration. It only remains now to draw up a contract.

Buskin. 'Tis done, dear lady. I have the formularies pat to hand. We need but to insert the recompence agreed upon. [*Slyly.*] I propose that, since you are each to be but half a character, you shall divide a single singer's pay.

[*The ladies rise together indignantly.*

Heartfelt. } Sir, I wish you a very good morning.
Silvertone. } Signor Impressario, you have said enough.

[*They turn to go.*

Buskin. Stay, ladies, I beseech you. [*Desperately.*] I was but jesting. Indeed and indeed, 'twould break my heart to part with you thus. I will agree to pay you each a hundred ducats nightly.

Heartfelt. That's better, I agree.

Silvertone. I am sensible of your generosity, sir. I'll set my hand to *that.*

Buskin. Very well. [*Taking a contract form out of a drawer.*] We have but to insert the sum. [*Does so.*] Let me see . . . one . . . hundred . . . ducats . . . and the name . . . Mrs. Heartfelt . . . so; and one . . . hundred . . . ducats . . . Miss Silvertone . . . so. [*With a sigh of regret mingled with relief.*] And that is done. Ladies, I will now beg you to sign. [*He is about to hand the pen to Heartfelt, when he suddenly withdraws it.*] But hold. How will you agree upon the stage? For I can have no disruption and variance within my theatre. I will thus set a codicil to this contract that shall ensure me harmony.

[*Pompously, and with great coughings and splutterings, he prepares to write, creating an atmosphere of some mystic ritual.*

Silvertone. [*Impertinently.*] The legal mind's at work: 'pon my troth, 'tis like a wizard's hocus-pocus.

Heartfelt. Peace, madam, I am imprest.

Buskin. [*Reading slowly word for word while he writes.*] Artists . . . it is true, . . . must ever hold . . . in high esteem . . . their fame; . . . but that . . . each . . . alone is . . . clever is . . . a thought . . . that . . . must . . . for ever . . . be redounding . . . to the . . . shame of . . . an artist with . . . a . . . name.

Heartfelt. [*Theatrically.*] In truth, sir, you have quite frightened me.

Silvertone. [*Unperturbed.*] Now all 's done, I 'll set my hand to this, and keep to it, too. But stay, Mr. Buskin, what is to become of your opera? You say Casilda has a lover. How can he love two Casildas all at once? For 'twill never do, if there is to be peace between us——

Heartfelt. And that will be hard to maintain, in all conscience.

Silvertone. 'Twill never do, I say, for one of us to be jilted. Nor can the hero be in love with both of us at once.

Buskin. [*Puzzled.*] Dear Miss Silvertone, there you have me. [*A sly look comes into his face.*] Or rather, you have me not. Why should not the hero be in love with you both? [*Expanding suddenly and rising.*] Why, *I* am in love with you both. Indeed, how should he help it, or I either?

Heartfelt. [*Flattered and upholding her dignity with difficulty.*] Fie, sir, none of your roguery!

Silvertone. [*Frankly delighted.*] Signor Impressario, I 'll warrant 'tis not the first time you have engaged a prima donna—not to say two—in her affections as much as by her talent.

Heartfelt. But your plot, sir, the plot of your opera?

Buskin. Well, well, 'tis worth straining a little to employ you both, and what is more, to teach you, dear ladies, to sink all jealousy and superiority to serve the operatick art. Each of you has qualities the other lacks, and both kinds are needful. So do, I pray you, acknowledge them mutually and work together in amity to one good end.

Silvertone. Sir, you are right, and what I say is this:

Finale

[*During each lady's solo, the other signs the contract. The refrain is sung from the document the first time, but gradually memorized, until at the last recurrence all know it by heart.*

Silvertone. Ev'ry artist must endeavour
To gain honour, to win fame,

Ev'ry one must endeavour
  To enforce his claim.
For without ambition never
  Would great art remain the same.

All. Artists, it is true, must ever
  Hold in high esteem their fame;
But that each alone is clever
Is a thought that must for ever
  Be redounding to the shame
  Of an artist with a name.

Heartfelt. Let us work with true submission
  Each into the other's hand,
For the great musician's mission
  Is to follow well the band.
When another has a solo,
  Do not envy him his chance,
For your own is soon to follow,
  And then you will lead the dance.

All. Artists, it is true, etc. etc.

Silvertone. Ne'er another's talent grudging,
  Let us prize the art alone.
Let the audience then be judging
  Who the highest praise has won.

All. Artists, it is true, etc. etc.

Buskin. I 'm divided between two wenches
In admiration and in love.
Yet, I declare,
Far too distressing for me the wrench is
To dismiss and reject such treasures from above.
Therefore let me engage the pair,
And if perchance there is a flare,
I 'll ask them with the utmost tact

[*Pointing to the contract.*

To sing according to this pact:

All. Artists, it is true, etc. etc.

CURTAIN

INDEX

(Numbers in brackets are those in Köchel's catalogue)

Made at the Temple Press Letchworth in Great Britain

R·L·K